SAILING PROMISE

AROUND THE WORLD
ON A CATAMARAN

Alayne Main

Base Camp Books

Please visit Alayne Main's web site for information on this book:
http://www.mnsi.net/~main

Cover Design by David Wharton at PanGraphica.
Printed by Webcom in Toronto, Canada.

Grateful acknowledgment to the following for permission to reprint previously published material:

Excerpt from "The Little Gidding" from FOUR QUARTETS, copyright 1943 by T. S. Eliot and renewed 1971 by Esme Valerie Eliot, reprinted by permission of Harcourt Brace & Company.

Excerpt from "The Little Gidding" from FOUR QUARTETS, by T. S. Eliot, reprinted by permission of Faber and Faber.

Canadian Cataloguing in Publication Data

Main, Alayne, 1964-
    Sailing promise : around the world on a catamaran

ISBN 0-9684544-0-2

1. Main, Alayne, 1964- . 2. Main, Alec. 3. Voyages around the world.
4. Catamarans. I. Title.

G440.M34A3 1999   910.4'1'0922   C98-932952-6

For Alec

CONTENTS

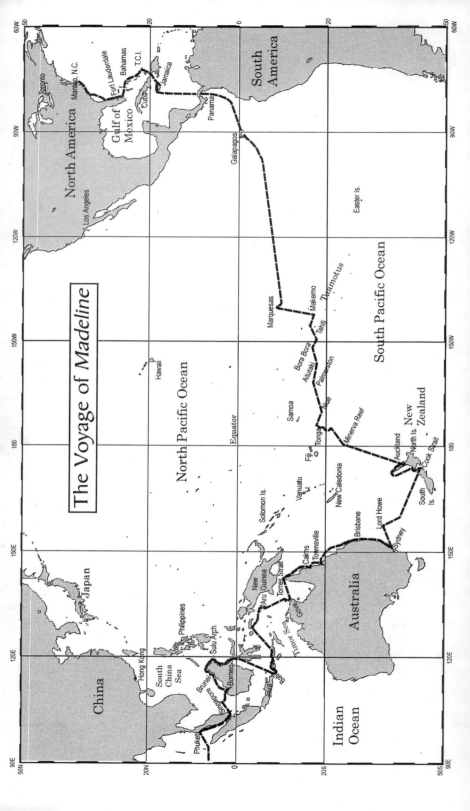

The Voyage of *Madeline*

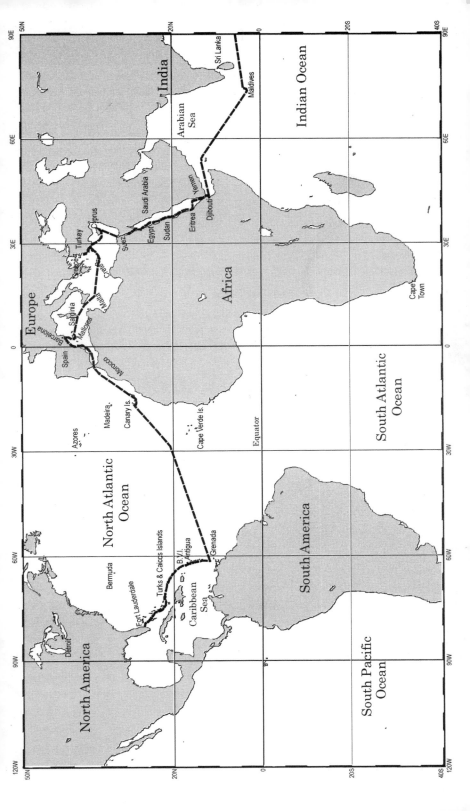

We shall not cease from exploration
And the end of all our exploring
Will be to arrive where we started
And know the place for the first time.

T. S. Eliot
from "Little Gidding"
Four Quartets

PROLOGUE

WE QUIT OUR JOBS, bought a catamaran, outfitted and set off around the world, all within five months. I wouldn't recommend this approach for everyone, but three and a half years later we returned as circumnavigators – and still married.

This story shares the full experience of my husband and I sailing around the world, from my perspective. For me, the voyage was a journey of discovery in more ways than one. It was a physical journey: exploring the vast oceans, distant lands, people and wildlife sharing our planet, and the forces of nature that control it. This was what I expected when I agreed to such an adventurous trip.

More important were the things I didn't anticipate. I didn't expect to be so afraid and I hadn't predicted an emotional journey into my relationship. But as my husband and I struggled to face the challenges together, I had no choice.

Ultimately I was forced to undertake a personal journey into my soul – to question who I was – so that I could understand what drove me to continue sailing. This was the toughest part of the entire voyage, but I believe it has given me a perspective and a confidence to last a lifetime.

Lastly, almost unbeknownst to me at the time, I went on a philosophical journey that challenged my traditional perspective of the world.

One of the greatest rewards of traveling is the chance to be an observer; to note the physical and cultural differences and similarities to life back home. I couldn't help but compare the geological history of the sharp volcanic peaks to the eroded sand atolls, or notice the present-day influence of ancient seafarers who sailed the same waters. I marveled in the subtle changes, such as the evolving shape of locally-baked bread as we sailed from country to country.

Yet as the physical scenery changed in front of my eyes, so did I. This interested me even more – the emotional experience. When I'd read similar adventures before we left, I was constantly left asking the same questions: Did you ever argue with your husband? Weren't you ever scared? What did you feel when you returned home? What was it *really* like?

This is what I've tried to capture. With the help of my journal, I have recounted the experience as it happened. The result is a multidimensional journey where the observer, the traveler, is changing along with the landscape. I'll take you through the troughs and crests of the vast oceans, as well as the dark, jungle-clogged valleys and the sunlit peaks of my emotional journey.

This is an adventure in every sense. A story that I believe both men and women, sailors or not, will enjoy and benefit from.

BOOK ONE

PARADISE

ABOVE THE ANCHORAGE a massive tooth of granite thrust up into the sky, dripping in verdant jungle growth like algae on a crocodile's eyes. A turban of clouds perpetually swathed the peak as the trade winds were parted. The clouds, which had traveled across the vast and featureless Pacific Ocean, shed their load and the jungle rose skyward in prayer for the bountiful rain.

The moss-covered stones gathered the mist, forming tumbling rivers and spontaneous waterfalls that crashed and rushed through the huge lush leaves of taro, papaya, mango, lime, hibiscus and the earthy smell of rotting vegetation. At the base of the pinnacle small areas were cleared, making way for a newly paved road, a soccer field and modest homes. Around the corner, the coconut palms swayed above sand beaches in a small bay.

The anchorage was filled with yachts anchored bow and stern because of the limited room. They ranged from small tired craft to gleaming half-a-million-dollar yachts. Common to every boat was a slightly weathered look that only comes from long-distance sailing. They had accomplished what most only dream. They had crossed 3,000 ocean miles to reach the Marquesas Islands, the start of Polynesia, the start of the South Pacific islands that had lured sailors, writers, painters, opportunists, missionaries and dreamers for hundreds of years and continued to do so.

Although just a snapshot of the cruising sailors that would arrive this season, this group of boats was forming a new floating community. They were sharing stories of the last passage, comparing boats and making plans to meet at the next anchorages.

Everyone was bonded by the sail they had just made, but also because they were romantics. They had left their homes to pursue a dream, ignored what friends and family said, weighed the risks, took the precautions, cut the dock lines and had succeeded.

I was aboard our small 33-foot catamaran. My husband, Alec, and I had sailed from the east coast of the United States, through the Panama Canal and had arrived a few days earlier to become a part of this captivating scene. It was the end of May 1993. We now had six months to sail through the South Pacific until hurricane season began, during which we would cover the same distance as we had in the last month. This was our reward.

On the outside, life was going according to plan. On the inside, our dream was in danger of dying. During the passage I had been overwhelmed by fear. We'd had our fights and our discussions. We both thought that once the passage to the Marquesas, 23 days at sea, was over, my anxieties would fade. But now I seemed afraid of everything. In every situation I saw black; I saw disaster.

I hadn't had this problem before we left, but when I looked back on the year, I could see that I was not emotionally prepared. I had never properly psyched myself up, not just for the last passage, but for the entire trip.

A common question before we left was, "Aren't you scared?" I would rather calmly reply that if I was going to die, I would rather be out at sea than in a car on my way to work. But the truth was, at that time, I didn't know exactly what to be afraid of. I knew some of the fears, and I had pat answers for them. If we were holed, our catamaran was unsinkable. If the catamaran flipped, we could live in it upside down with all our supplies.

I had married a risk taker; something I admired in Alec. I was attracted to risk too, but that was in safe, comfortable Southern Ontario where life was governed by the certainties and security of family, friends, university and a career; all of which allowed me to be confident, spontaneous and outgoing.

Now I dreaded the thought of misfortune, of one or both of us being seriously injured or dying.

Alec wanted me to enjoy the thrill of the risks we were taking. But I couldn't. He was disappointed in me and I felt alone, singled out as the bad guy.

Why couldn't he love me as I loved him? I wanted to be loved for who I was now, but Alec loved the old Alayne. He wanted her back. He wanted this new dark side of me to go away.

STORM WARNINGS

EIGHT MONTHS EARLIER, late on a sunny autumn afternoon, we had parked the rental car at the town docks in Manteo, North Carolina. After two long days of driving, we were both excited. "Let's go have a look at her," Alec said as he hopped out of the car.

"We can take these boxes later," I said, nodding in agreement.

I made sure the car was locked, as it held all our belongings for the next three years of our lives. The current owner had given us keys to the boat so that we could sleep the night on board. Alec swung me off my feet kissing me, and laughing we walked hand in hand down the boardwalk to where the boats were tied.

There she was! A 33-foot offshore catamaran made by a reputable English builder, Prout. Being wide for her length, she had an odd, boxy, but streamlined shape. She was solidly built and had the ability, or so we had been told, to take us around the world.

"Doesn't she look great?" Alec asked enthusiastically. We both walked around her in admiration.

"I can't believe we're actually doing this," I said. "She looks perfect."

We unloaded the car of what remained of our worldly possessions. A month earlier we'd had a garage sale and sold most of our household items, many of them wedding gifts that were just two years old.

I tried to take it all in: the smell of the ocean, the brisk fall breeze, the sound of the boat moving with the waves and tugging at her dock lines. Everything was so new and magical. This was the little boat that we hoped would fulfill our dream.

With the last of our boxes aboard, Alec began inspecting the boat. He was opening lockers, looking in the bilges, rummaging around. I sat in the cockpit and looked up at the stars.

"Hello."

The voice came from the boat next door. I peered through the rigging. What fun, I thought.

A tanned middle-aged man stood in his cockpit. "Are you the new owners?" he asked.

"Not yet," I said. "We sign the papers tomorrow." I told him of our plan to sail around the world.

"That's our dream too. We've been living aboard for three years now, and hope to leave in the next year or two. But my wife's mother isn't doing well, and it's difficult to leave." A woman poked her head out of their companionway. Her clothes had the soft wrinkled look of someone who lived on a small boat. We had more introductions and continued to chat, sharing plans and dreams. I was feeling elated. We'll be meeting such interesting people, I thought, and it had started already.

Alec came outside. He briefly said hello, and then said, "Can I see you inside, Alayne?"

I excused myself from my new friends and joined him. "What is it?" I asked.

"What are you doing out there?" he demanded.

"Just being friendly."

"Well, now isn't the time, Alayne. We have one last night to decide if this is the right boat for us. Once and for all. It's our last chance to take a good close look at her."

This hadn't even occurred to me. We had seen the boat once, two months ago, and she looked fine then, as she did now. I was unsure of what to look for, and I didn't think my opinion would be valued. This was Alec's job. He had done the research, the investigating. He had flown to Acapulco to see her sister ship, and was more able to compare which boat was right for us.

Alec had always wanted to sail around the world. When he was eight, he'd written a class assignment entitled, "Occupations". Most kids probably wrote that they were going to become doctors or firemen. Alec wrote: *"When I grow up I am going to be a diver, because I want to try to talk to a dolfin* (sic)*... I would study the sea. And make books about the ocean. I would go all over the world and I would make maps of how deep the ocean is... And! That is my occupation!"*

7

But it wasn't until his teens that Alec first committed to the dream. He was a national caliber swimmer and was at a sports psychology seminar in a session focusing on the power of the mind. The aim was to convince the swimmers that they could achieve anything they set their minds to. The coach went on, "You can do anything. For example, you could even... sail around the world!" Alec turned to his teammate, and whispered, "That's it! I'm going to sail around the world."

A few years later, I met Alec while competing for our university's Varsity Swim Team. He was an engineering freshman and I was a third-year science student. Since I had skipped two grades, we were actually the same age. I remember one late-night conversation at a party when Alec shared with me that he wanted to sail around the world. I was immediately attracted. I thought, "This guy is different. He's a dreamer." I liked that, without realizing he was also an achiever.

Although I saw the dream as Alec's, and somewhat far-fetched, I encouraged him, and even joined him in his research. We volunteered as crew for boats racing on Lake Huron. Feeling the need for some formal training, we signed up one summer for a course on basic keelboat sailing. Together we raced as crew during weeknights in Toronto, but it was Alec who devoured the sailing books and magazines, researching boat designs and equipment needs.

Now, at last, we were buying our own boat! Alec was a romantic, and I thought he'd be enjoying the moment with me – he was actually following his dream through. But for him, there was nothing romantic about the night. He was tense, stressed by the huge decision before us. Not only would it be the biggest purchase we'd ever made, but he had to choose the right boat; a safe boat that could carry us through storms and currents, and across oceans on trade winds. He had to outfit her, maintain her, and then fix anything that would break along the way. All this weighed heavily on him.

He wanted my agreement and participation, but I was acting as though I was just along for the ride. Our expectations had clashed, but we compromised – I helped him complete the inspection before nightcaps in the cockpit.

Our first night aboard though, and already we'd had a disagreement.

Originally the boat was named *Jellicle*, after one of T.S. Eliot's cats, but it had been changed to *Diva* by the second owner. Since the superstition surrounding the changing of a boat's name had already been broken, we decided to change it again.

I reminded Alec of his Dieffenbachia plant he had named Guenevere. "How about a name like that?"

"I like Madeline," he responded. I did too, so I wrote it down on the ownership registration form.

I unlooped the last of the dock lines and Alec reversed smoothly out of the slip. An early winter storm had held us up in North Carolina for a week, and we were thrilled to get started on the trip south. The bare essentials had been purchased, with the plan to fully outfit the boat once we arrived in Fort Lauderdale, Florida. Winter was fast approaching and we wanted to get somewhere warm to do our work.

Alec explained that we had two options. We could loop north and join the Intracoastal Waterway, or we could take the shorter route and cross the shallow Pamlico Sound before joining the waterway. Since we now owned a catamaran, it made sense to take advantage of our shallow draft, so we both agreed on the more direct route.

There was a winding, marked channel that led out to Pamlico Sound. After about an hour of motoring, we came across a huge multilayer tourist boat, with people fishing over the side.

"Alec, don't you think it's strange that they're fishing in the channel and not out in open water?"

We passed two fishing trawlers, rafted up together on the side of the channel. Then I noticed that in front of us there was a huge barge with machinery on it. Alec commented, "That's a dredging machine. We should be okay if we just stay behind it."

What we should have known was that the Pamlico Sound area was full of sandbanks that shifted with severe storms, sometimes filling channels. We remained in the middle of the channel, red markers on port and green on starboard. All of a sudden, there was a "THUD".

The boat shuddered. "THUD, THUD, THUD!"

"Put it in reverse!" Alec shouted from the cabin top.

I did, but to no avail. Alec jumped down into the cockpit and floored it in reverse. Behind us was churning mud and sand, but we didn't move. Two hours into our circumnavigation and we were stuck aground!

The wind suddenly picked up and choppy waves lifted the boat, dropping her down with more awful thumps, while pushing us further onto the bank.

"What do we do now?" I asked. Alec checked the tide tables, hoping the tide would rise and lift us off. No such luck – the tidal range was three inches. Not enough to make a difference, since the wind was blowing us up onto even higher ground. We had never operated our VHF radio, but I thought out loud, "Maybe we should call somebody."

"Not yet." Alec was not willing to admit defeat. "Look! It's the United States Coast Guard. They've come to rescue us!" We waved as they zipped past, and about 300 feet further, they too went aground! Their engines roared furiously as they revved in forward, then reverse, then forward again, like a car stuck in snow. Clearly we had to rescue ourselves.

Alec took our small anchor and, using the dinghy, dropped it in what we hoped was deeper water. We tied the line to our windlass on the bow, and slowly, by hand, rotated the links in the gypsy with a lever, pulling the line in tight. The anchor was set, and it was just a question of which would give first – the anchor, the line or the boat. It was a painfully slow process – the line came in only fractions of an inch with each turn. Alec soon lost his patience.

"It's not going to work," he said. We both sat there, depressed, feeling helpless. Alec paced the large foredeck, periodically cursing. Huffing and grunting with the lever, I continued to work at the bow. I thought, why not? It was something I could do, and just sitting around was not helping things. Another Coast Guard dinghy approached and our hopes momentarily soared. They roared by, not to help us, but to rescue their comrades.

Alec joined me again, and took a few turns. I took a few more and then felt something give. Could it be working? I turned and turned, and the line came more easily.

"Way to go Alayne! You did it."

Alec pulled in the anchor while I quickly started the engine, and we motored ourselves off, heading back the way we came.

We felt very proud that we'd solved this one on our own. Brute strength and perseverance would become our battle cry when problems occurred in the future.

Our pride faded as we passed our starting point a few hours later. We carried on north laughing at ourselves, before joining the Intracoastal Waterway and eventually turning south.

The first day of our circumnavigation did not take us far in distance, but we had taken a big step up what we were soon to discover was a steep learning curve.

We had made some informal arrangements before we bought the boat. Alec would be captain. This seemed obvious, although in all fairness, the position was offered to me. I declined, not wanting the responsibility. Since I was more extroverted and liked to talk, I assigned myself as communications officer, in addition to other appointments such as medical officer and admiral.

The Intracoastal Waterway is a protected strip of water just inland from the coast. Formed by natural waterways, rivers and canals dug and dredged by the U.S. Army Engineer Corps, the ICW stretches most of the eastern seaboard, permitting small vessels to avoid ocean sailing. Traveling down the waterway required the opening of bridges to allow our mast through. There were all sorts of bridges – drawbridges, swing bridges and pontoon bridges.

Approaching our first bridge, I balked and debated who should call on the radio to request an opening from the bridge operator. What if I didn't request an opening correctly? What if I couldn't answer the questions? I would hate to defer to Alec on the air, when other boats were potentially listening. I crumbled, and made Alec call.

I was surprised at my lack of confidence in such a simple task, but I didn't like trying something new, unless I was fairly sure I would get it right the first time. It seemed we were having to try new things all day long, everyday. I often deferred to Alec using my favorite excuse, "I've never done that before." It was new to Alec too, but he was more willing to risk failure. Challenges ranged from docking the boat against a current to making dinner for the two of us.

Many years earlier, when we first started going out together, I invited Alec over for a home-cooked meal. I'm not sure why, because I rarely cooked. It seemed the proper next step in some ancient stereotypical dating ritual where I was supposed to prove my femininity and my love for him by cooking like his mother. The first meal was a complete flop, but I stubbornly repeated my burnt-pork-chop routine twice before accepting defeat. We fell madly in love despite my lack of culinary skills, but the task of planning and preparing our meals for this trip remained a daunting one. Now our budget forced us to eat in, and this meant having to make three meals a day, seven days a week.

Our plan for heading south was an ambitious one; we rose everyday with the sun and started ticking off the miles. The kettle went on and we ate breakfast under way. One person had to steer at all times since the course constantly changed as we wound our way amongst deserted marshes, down straight canals, past golf courses and small towns, often in the company of local fishermen, regular boat traffic and fellow yachtsmen also making the trek south.

One evening we anchored amidst a sea of tall golden rushes blowing dreamily in the breeze. Alec opened a bottle of wine and romantically led me to the cabin top. With his strong arms around me, we watched the shrimp trawlers ghost along, seemingly on top of the marsh as they weaved their way through the delta.

"Think of all the beautiful nights like this, that lie ahead of us," he said, raising his glass.

"This is great," I said, snuggling closer to him as the last rays of sun disappeared.

"To us, and to exciting times," he toasted.

I was pleased to be coping with the challenges so far. However, through Georgia, the Intracoastal Waterway became tortuous, and it made sense to cover several days of mileage by sailing overnight in the ocean.

It would be our first night alone at sea.

TRULY A SAILBOAT

JUST BEFORE HILTON HEAD ISLAND a channel led out to the Atlantic Ocean. Instead of following the waterway, I turned the wheel over and followed the buoys out to sea. Swirling winds bounced off the rounded, woody islands on each side of the channel, and further out, the ocean looked ruffled by waves. I watched the green shores pass astern with a new longing.

To my relief, the wind faded away, and as the sun sunk below the horizon, the burnt orange rays reflected off a calm sea. When darkness took over, the sky became so black that the horizon was barely discernible beneath it. I could only guess where it was by following the stars down to where they stopped.

I chose the first watch, feeling too on edge to sleep. My duty was to look out for ships, and I watched intently, scanning continuously. My eyes began to play tricks, creating a zigzag, light and dark effect. As a perfectionist, I took my responsibility seriously. I tried blinking, just hoping that I wasn't going to miss the lights of an oncoming vessel. But what would they look like? I had no idea.

Then I saw a red light!

I immediately went inside to wake up Alec. He had insisted I wake him if there was anything that concerned me. He came outside, groggy and squinty-eyed, saying, "Where, Alayne? Where is this ship?"

"It's there!" I said, pointing. "Can't you see it?"

"Oh. There. Well, that light is so tiny that if it is a ship, it's very far away. We'll just sit here and watch it for a while."

So we sat. And we watched.

The little red light slowly got a little bigger, a little brighter, until it rose above the horizon and into the stars. "Congratulations, Alayne. Your first ship was an airplane!" he roared with laughter.

That's okay, I thought. Now I knew what an airplane looked like, and I wouldn't get it confused with a ship again.

A half-hour or so went by, and I saw another red light. It rapidly grew in size, and I couldn't deal with the anticipation. I called Alec again. He came out all chipper this time, probably because he hadn't completely fallen asleep from the last time.

"Wow!" was his response, and I smugly felt that my concern was warranted. "That certainly is a big red light. What the heck is it?" He watched and I bit my tongue, waiting. Before I broke the silence, we saw the glow lighten and transform into a sliver of waxing moon rising above the horizon. His query was answered.

"Okay, so you had me for a minute there," he admitted.

"I just don't have the patience to be at sea," I said shaking my head.

Alec assured me, "You'll get used to it. Nothing happens quickly on a sailboat." But there was still a crucial time when decisions had to be made. I seemed unable to discern when things were okay and when they were not. An uncomfortable feeling of insecurity and incompetence seemed to take root inside me.

Fort Lauderdale is the self-proclaimed "Yachting Capital of the World", and in early November we docked *Madeline* at Hendrick's Isle. This put us within reach of six marine stores and in the heart of the live-aboard sailing scene. The boat outfitting would become our full-time job and a 24-hour-a-day preoccupation.

We discovered that most people spend years preparing for a trip like ours, but with both of us working all out on the project, we figured that we could leave within three months.

Our plan was to transit the Panama Canal in the spring. Alec had a long list of equipment to be bought and projects to be completed before we could set off. He had prioritized the jobs depending on necessity, with safety being considered first and luxuries, such as a refrigerator and new wood floors in the hulls, coming second.

On the first day, he wanted to start with a simple job on the foredeck. During breakfast, he briefed me on our first job together. Suddenly it started to rain. He looked at me, shocked, and then said, "I can't believe this! I didn't figure rain delays into our schedule!"

We changed our plans that day and went shopping for parts for some of the interior jobs on the list. While I could see that Alec was

scrambling up the learning curve, I felt like I was just standing at the bottom of a mountain, already far behind him.

I asked how I could contribute. I wanted to help independently and take partial responsibility for preparing the boat. I didn't want to end up somewhere remote and find myself blaming Alec for things he did or didn't do. We went through the list and other than preparing our medical kit, a very important job in itself, there were few significant jobs I could take over.

Alec needed my help, even if it just meant holding a screwdriver or cleaning up. It seemed I was only wiping his brow and fetching beer. It was all towards our ultimate goal, but in the meantime, I was going out of my mind. I hated looking for things to do, trying to be useful and I resented it when meal preparation fell to me.

I had just left a rewarding career as a physician. I had been in charge of the entire emergency room in a busy downtown Toronto hospital. Eighteen months after Alec had first told me about his dream, I finished my Honors Degree and was accepted into medical school. After graduation I had interned in Toronto where Alec was hard at work and often traveling out of town.

I enjoyed the challenges of the Emergency Room, dealing with patients and discussing cases with my colleagues. My energy and self-esteem were bolstered by the people around me and my environment. I also worked at several clinics and family practices, sometimes logging 100-hour weeks. While Alec did most of the research for the trip, I was content contributing financially.

Now I realized I hadn't done my homework. I hadn't taken the time to visualize what would happen once my medical work stopped. I was accustomed to feeling confident in my undertakings, but with the boat, I felt lost.

Alec encouraged me, but I constantly felt subordinate and no longer the expert. In medicine, my skills at memorizing had served me well, but did little to help me understand the forces of wind on a sail. I started from scratch, and learning was a struggle.

Alec, on the other hand, was a problem solver. After obtaining his degree in electrical engineering he had worked in manufacturing, designing and implementing control systems, and then later as a high-priced management consultant with Andersen Consulting.

On the boat, he enjoyed taking things apart and figuring out how they worked. He wasn't afraid of breaking things or doing something wrong, because he trusted his ability to work out a solution to any problem. "If I break it, it was going to break anyway," he would say, claiming a corollary of Murphy's Law. He was calm and logical, and leaned towards being an introvert. From the outset, he was in his element.

Undeterred by my predicament, I remained disciplined and goal-oriented. I had made a promise and I wasn't going to give in easily. Even though it was an unexpectedly difficult time, I was sure the frustration wouldn't last long and the fun would soon begin.

In less than three months we had completed the major work on *Madeline*. She had been reviewed, renewed, and had several systems newly installed or completely updated. With most things taken care of, we were ready for a week-long Christmas "shakedown", a trial run to the Bahamas and back. It was time to put *Madeline* and ourselves to the test.

We turned *Madeline* into the channel that leads to the Florida Straits and the infamous Gulf Stream. The evening's forecast was for a light wind, but as we entered the channel, large swells rolled in. We debated turning back, but refused to be defeated on our first trip. The engine throbbed and spray blew over the bows. Once offshore, the wind and waves lessened, but our struggle continued, motoring against the wind.

We carefully monitored our progress across the Gulf Stream. I was determined to equally share the responsibilities, but found navigating down at the chart table nauseating. Alec insisted I could do other things but I stubbornly refused, and paid the price. Within minutes I was hanging over the rail in the darkness, feeding the fish.

The hours passed slowly as *Madeline* lurched and pounded. We were growing weary, but were fueled by our adrenaline.

We sighted the Bahamas early the next morning. *Madeline* was coated in salt. As we approached Bimini the spectacular baby blue water redeemed the misery of the night. Alec stood on the bow looking at the clear aquamarine beneath us. We could see coral on the bottom and stingrays undulating over the submarine sand. We both kept doubting the depth, fearing we would hit something, but I called out the readings on the depth sounder, "thirty feet... twenty-eight feet... thirty-two feet..."

"This is it! This is what it's all about," Alec merrily yelled. "Unbelievable."

The anchor splashed down and was quickly buried in the sand. We stood on the bow in each other's arms, happy in our accomplishment.

It had been worth it.

On New Year's Eve we returned successfully to Fort Lauderdale from our trial cruise to the Bahamas. After two more weeks of provisioning and last-minute tasks, we felt our preparations were complete. On the night of January 18th, we departed Fort Lauderdale for what we thought was the last time.

We planned our passage through the Bahamas, a southeasterly route against the prevailing trade winds, with our destination being the Turks and Caicos Islands at the bottom of the Bahama island chain. Alec's parents had arranged a holiday there for the last two weeks in February. We all felt that we would have plenty of time to meet them and take them aboard for a cruise.

In calm winds we motored across the Gulf Stream to Bimini, where we checked in with Bahamian customs and immigration. Our next trip was across the Great Bahama Bank to the Berry Islands about 80 miles to the east.

We picked up anchor before dawn a few days later. It was a quiet morning and it was just us and miles of light blue water as we set across The Great Bahama Bank. The depth was only ten to twelve feet and although we were out of sight of land I could clearly see the bottom rushing past.

Out of nowhere I spotted a boat. A collision course I thought, but, no, they were coming to our boat. Three black guys in a small Boston Whaler approached and turned their boat around to motor alongside us. The boat was bare. The men were well dressed; two teenagers in the bow and one adult in the stern, obviously in charge with his hand at the controls. I was stunned, but continued our pace, motoring at five knots. I waved and the two guys in the bow shyly waved back. The small boat came closer.

"Where's Great Isaac?" the man in the stern asked with a thick Bahamian twang.

The name sounded familiar, but when I turned to tell Alec, I saw him inside the salon with the emergency signal kit open, loading the flare gun! Remaining calm, I turned back to the three guys.

"So, where are you from? Where do you live?" I asked, ignoring the pounding of my heart.

I couldn't hear over the noise of their outboard motor. I made out the word "Andros", a large island to the south.

"Pardon?" I smiled, struggling to maintain my composure. I turned to Alec again, "Alec, they want to go to Great Isaac. Please get out the map. I'm sure I saw it in the *Yachtsman's Guide*." Alec was still wrestling with the flare gun. He put it down, now loaded, and came out into the cockpit.

"Great Isaac?" he shouted. "It's over there." He gestured to the north and without a word they spun the boat around and headed away from *Madeline*. They went north, but not exactly in the direction that Alec had indicated.

We were both taken aback. What were three Bahamians doing out here? Why did they need directions to a rocky, unpopulated islet in the north? Were they checking us out for some other reason?

16

Later in the afternoon we were passed by a fast cabin cruiser. They could make it across the bank in one day, but we stuck to our plan to anchor on the banks for the night. This is a common tactic of sailboats in this area, preferring an uncomfortable night anchored to dodging coral reefs in the dark. As we sipped our rum and coke in the cockpit, I marveled at what awaited us in this cruising life.

"It's amazing how vulnerable we are," I commented.

"I'm going to leave the flare gun loaded in the signal kit," Alec responded.

A few days after crossing the bank, the weather turned sour. We chose to dock in the marina at Chubb Cay, an island that was demolished by Hurricane Andrew six months earlier. They still had some docks and slips, and we weathered the strong winds and rainstorms with fifteen other boats.

Misery loves company, and on the first night, we met Juana and Steve. They were our age and owned a seasonal bar in the panhandle of Florida. They also owned a catamaran named *Island Time* and were spending their second winter in the Bahamas. As the wind roared overhead we discussed catamarans, drank rum and got silly. When they discovered our plans to sail around the world, they insisted we meet Liz and Dan on *Daq' Attack*.

We had seen Dan zip past our boat a few days earlier. He was standing up in a dinghy that was powered by an eight-horsepower motor. His blonde hair was blowing back off his suntanned face and his eyes were hidden behind stylish sunglasses.

"Check out this guy driving his dinghy," Alec had called to me.

Liz and Dan were also starting a circumnavigation, but were not planning on transiting the Panama Canal until the next year. They had a large monohull and the next day as the gale raged on they invited us over for cocktails. They'd already spent one year in the Caribbean preparing the boat and themselves for the cruising life. It turned out that Dan stood up in his dinghy because it leaked so badly that he got wet if he sat down! Dan had collected coconuts that had fallen in the wind. He poured out some of the water and topped them up with rum.

"You just picked these coconuts off the ground?" I asked, wondering if that was allowed.

Alec and I had finally joined the much-vaunted cruising community. After months of hard work, everything was falling into place. We were constantly learning, meeting interesting people, and having a blast together.

That evening the wind began to taper off and the forecast indicated that we could head in our separate directions. *Madeline* was off to

Nassau early in the morning, and the others were heading back to Florida. Steve told us to wake him and he would help us cast off.

When the sky faintly lightened the next morning, we prepared to go. The wind was good for the trip to Nassau and it would help blow us off the dock. I thought about waking Juana and Steve. Then I saw a light go on in *Island Time*.

"Let's just get going," Alec said. He always hated taking help from anyone.

Alec loosened the lines while I stayed at the helm. He stood on the dock at the bow and he let the line free. The bow slowly swung with the wind away from the dock, just as we wanted.

I got excited, as I tended to in these situations. All I could envision was drifting away, leaving Alec behind, and then having to dock again by myself, with Juana and Steve watching.

I called out to Alec, "Hurry up and get on the boat!"

Alec was still onshore, now holding the stern line and I knew *Madeline* wasn't going anywhere until he let go. Responding to my panic, Alec untied the line and hopped on board, but it was probably too soon and too hasty. I turned and noticed the line was not entirely in the boat; a portion seemed to be dangling over the stern. I reached to grab it.

"Stay at the helm, Alayne," he reminded me. I guessed he was going to grab the line. He went to the bow to make sure we would clear the other boats as I tried to motor us around. *Madeline* was only halfway into the 90-degree turn. We had acted too quickly and should have let the wind pivot the boat. Just to be sure, I put the engine into reverse.

BANG!

"The prop has popped up!" I screamed to Alec.

Alec looked back with a scowl. "Impossible. I'll do it."

Our propeller was on a pivoting leg called an outdrive. It was like the outboard prop on some motorboats. It rose up so that under sail, the prop was out of the water, reducing drag. When we motored in reverse, the outdrive had to be locked down or it would "pop" up.

"It was locked when we came in here," Alec said as he hopped into the cockpit. "We haven't touched it, so it should still be locked." We continued to drift away from our dock.

Steve came out of *Island Time* and waved. A few other groggy cruisers poked their heads out. Alec tried the engine, but to no avail.

We were quickly closing with three boats on another pier.

Suddenly people materialized and there were fenders, hands and bodies pushing *Madeline* as she smashed into the sterns of the other boats. I cringed at the awful crunching sound, but luckily the boat we hit hardest was steel. With our forward motion now halted, we tossed our lines to the helpers and were once again tied up and secure.

Everyone breathed a sigh of relief.

One of our new neighbors staggered out of his boat awakened by the commotion and banging. "What's going on?" he asked as he scratched his ruffled hair.

"Everything's fine," someone said. "No one's hurt, no damage, just a few scratches."

"It looks like there's a line in your propeller," another cruiser hollered from the opposite dock.

We couldn't see our stern because our dinghy, lying on the back transom, was blocking our view. Alec grabbed some tools and jumped overboard. I could hear him free our dock line and inspect the outdrive as he splashed in the cold morning water.

"Oh, my god." I heard him say quietly. "We're fucked." He climbed aboard with a ghastly look on his face.

"We snapped the outdrive in half. We're now truly a sailboat."

TRIUMPH

ALEC HAD ASKED ME TO MARRY HIM, on two conditions. One, that we wouldn't have children for five years, and secondly that I would agree to sail around the world with him. I had no problem delaying parenthood as I was only 25 years old and just starting my career as a doctor. I had already begun to share the sailing dream, and although I didn't know all that this promise would entail, I readily accepted.

I was surprised we could set sail so soon, as most people do this sort of thing when they are retired. As we investigated further, we found that the reasons for waiting are not just financial, but are related to the difficulties of leaving the commitments of land life. We knew these obstacles would multiply each year we delayed. We punched some numbers into a spreadsheet program on the computer and came up with a conservative plan that indicated we could leave in seven years. By changing some numbers, lowering our estimated outfitting and cruising budgets, and increasing our savings, we got it down to only three years. To do the trip while we were still young and the world was still healthy made sense.

The night before the wedding, Alec revealed our surprise honeymoon: a bareboat charter, our first ever, in the British Virgin Islands. I was a little apprehensive, but the yacht charter operator tried to alleviate my worries, "This is the Disneyland of sailing. If you can't do this, then you can't do anything." They had the right to put a skipper on board, and we checked out the boat and inventory with this dreadful possibility hanging over our honeymoon. They decided that we were qualified enough, but we almost lost all credibility trying to leave the dock. It took all my strength to pull the buried anchor up from the mud bottom and in doing so, I fell backward with the filthy, rusted chain landing in my lap. My lovely white sailing outfit was ruined, but Alec just turned the boat away without looking behind, hoping they couldn't tell we'd never done this before!

The ten days aboard were glorious. Quickly the holiday was over; a blur of exciting sailing, great snorkeling and romantic evenings. "Still married?" the charter guy asked when we returned the boat.

"I still feel I haven't spent enough time with you," I told Alec. "The sailing was so much fun, and I could have done it longer."

Alec looked at me skeptically and then smiled. "Looks like I've married the right girl to sail with me around the world." He gave me a big hug and a kiss.

After the honeymoon, we jumped into our careers, continued to live like students, and hoped that in two years we could store away enough acorns to break free. We stopped talking about it with our friends and families; we didn't want to make any announcements until we were absolutely positive we could do it, and didn't want our work places to hear about our plans to quit. Also, we didn't want to be influenced by any outside negativity. What we were planning went against many of society's expectations.

Through all this planning lurked the worry that we might not be fully prepared for such a huge undertaking. Alec felt confident that he had read enough, but what we were planning also went against what many sailing people would advise. To embark on an adventure of this magnitude with such little experience was foolhardy to some.

We thought out many options. We could do it with crew. Or, do it as crew, on someone else's boat. Or, spend a year in the Caribbean to see if we liked it, and to gain experience. Or, we could buy a boat in Canada and spend a summer afloat in Toronto to adjust to living in close quarters with each other. After many discussions, we both agreed that we were willing to take on the challenge of doing the circumnavigation with just the two of us, and that was really the only way we would want it. Once we had enough money to finance it, we would quit work, buy our own boat and go for it. We decided on a high-risk, all-or-nothing approach.

Our fellow cruisers at Chubb Cay Marina were waiting for the verdict. Alec explained that the outdrive casting was broken and we couldn't use our motor. Numerous people offered tools and assistance.

Steve came over and asked what we would do. He volunteered to tow us out the winding narrow entrance to the marina, but he was leaving for Florida shortly. We thanked him for the offer, but feeling devastated, we told him we needed some time to think.

We had two options: sail the 35 miles to Nassau, not knowing what to expect in the way of facilities or cost of repair, or sail back to Florida. We estimated at least two weeks in Florida for repairs, because the parts for the outdrive would have to be sent from England. We would have to tell Alec's parents that there wasn't much hope of making it to the Turks and Caicos Islands on schedule. To return would be such a disappointment, but on the other hand three boats were heading that way, including *Island Time* and *Daq' Attack*. We decided on Florida.

With the assistance of Dan and his leaky dinghy, we got away from the dock and *Island Time* towed us out of the marina. While under sail, we kept radio contact with *Island Time* who were enthusiastically planning a Super Bowl party back in Florida, and wanted us to come. It was hard to share their enthusiasm.

The sky was solid blue and there was a gentle breeze from the north. We were having a beautiful sail, but my thoughts were elsewhere. *"Three months of outfitting, a shakedown cruise to the Bahamas, years of planning and we survived two weeks!"* I wrote in my journal. *"We're moping around feeling sad, angry, stupid, disappointed and sorry for ourselves. Why didn't we wake Juana and Steve? Why did I tell Alec to hurry? Why didn't I get that line that was dangling in the water? We have blamed each other, then ourselves and eventually decided it was a team blunder. We have left our predictable lives behind us and joined the world of the unknown... We are going back to Florida. I can't believe it! But I know we'll head out again. We still have each other and our shared commitment to our dream. One of these days we'll begin this cruising life... But what of our big plans – through Panama in April? We're going to sail around the world! Everyone at the marina must be laughing at us and our grandiose plans. To sail around the world. It sounds like a joke now."*

Madeline sailed towards the cut between Gun Cay and Cat Cay to the south. Both islands were flat and dry, with only scrub covering their surface. The turquoise of the Great Bahama Bank gradually changed into the lapis lazuli of the deeper water and then the dark, troubled blue of the Gulf Stream in the distance. The tide was flowing onto the bank so the current between the islands was against us. Without our engine, we made painfully slow progress with all our sails up in the light wind.

I watched closely as the sharp wave-chipped rocks at the edge of the shoreline seemed to take forever to fall astern. Beneath us I could see fish flitting between the coral heads that we silently floated over. Alec was, as usual, full of composure, but my heart was in my throat.

Just when I didn't think I could take it any more, we inched around Gun Cay, getting a view of *Island Time* anchored in the small bay. Steve got on the radio and offered to tow us in, but Alec told him we were going to sail right over to the beach and drop anchor. Nothing like having an audience while anchoring for the first time under sail, I thought.

When we got close, everyone was jumping up and down and waving, happy to see that we made it there safely. We dropped our hook and launched the dinghy off the transom. Putting on our fins and masks, we jumped in the water and quickly checked the anchor to ensure it was buried safely in the sand below.

Towing the dinghy, we swam towards the coral ledges. Steve was right behind us. Within an hour the guys had speared ten lobsters and Juana had them basted with butter and garlic, wrapped in foil and

cooking on the barbecue grill. For a few moments we forgot how depressed we were about going back to Florida.

Island Time and *Daq' Attack* would sail with us across the Gulf Stream and Steve would tow us into Port Everglades. But what then?

Alec and I had the proviso that if one of us didn't like cruising, or if something dreadful were to happen with the boat, then we would accept our losses and write it off to an adventure. I had a one-year sabbatical from the hospital, and Alec was granted a one-and-a-half-year leave of absence, so our jobs were waiting for us.

At this point, neither of us could imagine quitting; we had just started. Still, we had a big decision to make. Should we slow down and peruse the Caribbean, taking away the pressure of getting to Panama by April? We could go to Panama the following year, after gaining more experience and becoming more comfortable sailing the boat. Or, should we make up for lost time and head straight for the Turks and Caicos, and get back on schedule?

The parts arrived on my 29th birthday. Two weeks had passed, but we had made good use of our time in the dirty boat yard. We'd already exceeded our budget outfitting the boat, knowing we wouldn't be spending money where there were no stores. However, now that we were back in consumer land, the outdrive had been only the first item on our rapidly growing to-do list.

We'd been listening to the weather forecasts, and the wind was good for our departure now, but we felt a birthday celebration was due. Alec and I put our anxieties aside and had a rip-roaring night with *Daq' Attack*, dancing at nightclubs and frolicking on the beach of Fort

23

Lauderdale's strip. They urged us to stay in the Caribbean and cross the Pacific with them the next year, but we couldn't give up so easily.

The next morning we were up at sunrise, popping aspirin and drinking orange juice. I rechecked the weather forecast and bought fresh food while Alec assembled the outdrive. By late afternoon *Madeline* was back in the water and the outdrive passed our tests.

At daybreak we motored *Madeline* out of Fort Lauderdale's port and into the Gulf Stream once again. We sailed through the Northwest Providence Channel, through the Bahamas and out into the Atlantic Ocean. As we turned the corner and began heading south for the Turks and Caicos Islands, the wind clocked as predicted. A winter storm system was passing giving us the perfect wind direction. The sailing was comfortable, all downwind and without any difficulty, except for dodging the never-ending parade of cruise ships heading the same way.

During the next two days, the wind slowly turned against us, so we headed into San Salvador, the island believed to be the first landfall of Christopher Columbus 500 years ago. As we brought in the sail for the last beat into San Salvador's shelter, the halyard broke on the genoa.

We had some difficulty getting the sail down, but succeeded, and turned on the motor for the last mile to the anchorage. The water was shallow, calm and the beautiful pale blue of the Bahamas.

We had traveled over 300 miles, our longest passage. I felt good about our decision to push onward.

We continued on to Mayaguana, but the next night the wind turned completely against us and we tacked *Madeline* back and forth making terrible progress. By the next afternoon we gave up, took down our sails and began motoring next to the reef that runs along the north side of the island of Providenciales, or Provo in Turks and Caicos lingo.

The low rising land looked all the same and the waves formed a continuous crashing line along the reef. The islands were undeveloped, but tourism was growing. A British dependency and a tax haven, they were establishing themselves in offshore banking. We were looking for a small break called Sellar's Cut that would take us into Turtle Cove, where Alec's parents had a hotel booked.

Madeline was bouncing around in the tumultuous seas when I noticed a sport-fishing trawler approaching us. I changed direction to get out of his way, but he changed direction towards us. "Alec," I yelled, "this crazy fishing boat's trying to hit us!"

"No he isn't. Why would someone want to do that? And look. You can see someone in the fly bridge at the wheel. They're looking at us."

"Go call them on the radio then."

Alec dutifully headed below to the radio, when it suddenly crackled to life, "*Madeline, Madeline*. This is *Yosemite*."

"*Yosemite!*" we rejoiced together.

Sid was a powerboater we'd met in the Bahamas before the accident. He had steered *Yosemite* close because he wondered what a small boat was doing out in such awful conditions. Then he had recognized us. Alec got the co-ordinates of Sellar's Cut for the Global Positioning System, known as GPS, and directions into Turtle Cove, enabling us to enter the cut and anchor without calling the pilot.

Even with local knowledge, the cut was difficult to negotiate. On both sides of us waves broke on the jagged reef. We followed the smooth path of water between the surf, and wound our way through the shallow coral to the protected cove.

We rowed over to the hotel and surprised Alec's parents.

We passed carefully through Sellar's Cut again with Joan and Jim aboard as we headed out to cruise the neighboring Caicos Cays for a few days. We were fortunate how supportive Alec's parents were from the beginning, and they shared in our enthusiasm for more adventures with *Madeline*. The day we came back through Sellar's Cut provided just that.

The wind and waves were violent and the sky was gray and overcast. We couldn't make out the six-foot marker at the entrance, as the monstrous seas easily obscured it. Trusting our GPS, we knew where the entrance should be, and we went for it. Huge Hawaii Five-O breakers crashed on either side and even though I gripped the wheel white-knuckled, I found it impressive.

As we entered the cut I could hear a roar of water behind us. I turned around and could see only frothy white. I quickly looked forward to Alec and he was frantically signaling for me to pick up the speed. I pushed the throttle down hard, but it was too late.

The big breaker caught up with us, sweeping us into the cut and pummeling us hard. The wave flowed into the cockpit, drenching me and pouring through the companionway. The floors inside were flooded. *Madeline* rocked, rolled and shuddered as if she had hit bottom. The depth sounder went out.

"Alec! I think we've hit!" I yelled. "Is everyone okay?" The thought of more damage to *Madeline* made me sick to my stomach. My second thought was for Joan and Jim's safety. Joan was near me and was holding tightly onto a rail. Jim was forward and he yelled back to me, "What's the speed?" The excitement in his voice revealed the thrill he felt.

Alec yelled back, "Carry on – full revs!"

On later inspection, the hulls were fine. "The depth sounder goes out if there is a lot of turbulence," Alec convinced me. "We didn't hit."

It was a mistake to enter the cut in those conditions, but the fact that the boat was unharmed made me believe someone was looking out for us.

The momentum was with us again. We had our longest passage ever ahead of us, from the Turks and Caicos to Jamaica, but we were back on schedule. Joan caught a flight back to Toronto, because as much as she enjoyed the cruising, she wasn't interested in a passage. Jim couldn't wait.

THE STORM OF THE CENTURY

THE WIND FILLED IN and we caught our first fish as *Madeline* hummed along. It was a nice-sized dolphin fish, also known as dorado or mahi mahi, that would feed us for three days. The next day was tough sailing due to choppy seas and high winds, but Jim loved it all. That night, we found ourselves among shipping traffic in the Windward Passage, between Haiti and Cuba.

I was just changing watch with Jim when we saw a ship in front of us dramatically change course to pass on the opposite side. These situations got my adrenaline flowing even if wasn't needed. We quickly woke Alec from his sleep. He got on the radio, but spent most of the time sorting out if he was talking to the right ship.

The ship was rapidly closing with us when it identified itself on the radio as a U.S. Navy warship. "Our course is ten degrees with a speed of 21 knots. The sailing vessel is traveling on a course of 223 degrees magnetic with a speed of five knots. I have changed course and will pass clear to starboard."

It was all happening quickly, and I dashed out to the cockpit as it passed. Bristling guns and turrets on the huge ship were silhouetted in the moonlight. Alec joked that they probably knew more than just our course and speed.

I imagined the first mate saying, "Aye, aye, Captain. There are two males, one female and they all had pan-fried dolphin fish for dinner!"

We watched it go off into the night; they turned off the running lights and the silhouette blended into the darkness. I knew this was an exception. The freighters we were most likely to encounter would have only one or two people watching, if any. We had to be careful and keep a good lookout.

The following morning a U.S. Coast Guard helicopter circled our mast five times. They waved and we waved. Around noon we got a radio call from a Coast Guard cutter requesting permission to board.

Since we were a Canadian vessel, and they had no jurisdiction over these waters, we were under no obligation to cooperate. We'd heard what a hassle a Coast Guard boarding could be, but it was a calm sunny day and we were motoring. Why not?

A 220-foot cutter quickly appeared over the horizon and followed behind us while it launched a boat. We maintained our speed and course and really weren't inconvenienced by the visit.

They sent a bunch of rookies, some visibly nervous. They wore hard hats, coveralls, bulletproof vests, guns, life jackets and well-polished boots. Four came aboard and six stayed in the large inflatable boat beside us. Alec was in command during the boarding and set the ground rules up front. He would lead the search and would terminate the boarding should he wish.

Apparently the Coast Guard was in the Windward Passage because a Haitian exodus was anticipated with U.S. president Bill Clinton's inauguration. They asked to look in our bilges to make sure no Haitians were stowed away. We laughingly opened the covers – our bilges were each the size of a lunch box!

We arrived at Port Antonio on the northeast side of Jamaica and were pleasantly surprised to find a beautiful sleepy town. For five hours Jim and I were prisoners on *Madeline*, while Alec cleared us through customs, immigration and quarantine. We were greeted by a succession of visitors dockside. These young black men all had a given name, but preferred to be addressed by their nicknames. First there was "Lion", then "Chow", "Jaggy", and "Buggy Up". Each of them welcomed us to Jamaica in turn, and then offered their services, such as taxi, tour guide, boat repairs, money exchange; you name it. Each guy was our "man". We finally bought a stalk of 100 green bananas for a dollar from a kid in a sinking canoe! I wanted to try a Jamaican recipe of curried chicken and green bananas. I was slowly adapting to our new life and even enjoyed planning some meals!

In Port Antonio we met David Clark, a 68-year-old American, who was trying to set a Guinness record by being the oldest person to solo circumnavigate. He had left Florida at the same time as we originally had, and now we'd caught up with him. He played the clarinet to help pay for his food, as he was on a very tight budget, hoping to come into big money through his planned up-and-coming fame.

Jim suggested that we go for dinner to the restaurant where David was playing. His music was quite good, but I couldn't imagine living hand-to-mouth. He was a crotchety old man with a lot of get-up-and-go, but not much finesse. His boat was a mess, his equipment seemed to be always breaking, and his wife had given up on his sailing thing long ago; she'd made it to New Zealand with him the first time around.

All in all, it still was a pleasure meeting him and he was the first person on the same seasonal schedule. Not exactly what I'd envisioned as a fellow cruiser, but we had to give him some credit.

"Dolphins!"

I scrambled out of the cabin and dashed forward. There was a school of about 30 dancing and playing in our bow wave! Alec got right out and lay across the starboard bow. *Madeline* was whistling along at six knots and he dangled his arms in the water, stroking the dolphins as they surfaced beneath him. The late afternoon sun bathed us in orange light as we laughed and talked to the dolphins in high squeaky voices. It was moments like this that made our life unique and I was glad I wasn't back home working.

After one night of sailing we would be in Montego Bay. Our sailing with Jim had gone well and he was flying home the following day. The three of us worked well as a team, enjoying each other as well as the thrill of this adventure. Everything was so new, and we'd met the challenge of the passage without difficulty.

But the number of obstacles to this point had been eye opening: the destruction of our outdrive, our clear lack of experience, plus a regular string of equipment failures. Although we had beaten them all and my relationship with Alec was still strong, it was evident that our roles had changed and we were each reacting differently to our new life. I was trying to keep a positive outlook, but the challenges were wearing me thin, something I was only willing to hint at in a letter home to my

parents from Jamaica.

"Alec and I are doing really well – this life agrees with us. We're getting nice and brown, and we're both letting our hair grow as long as it will, however we've both managed to keep up with shaving! Each day we work more and more as a team, as we become more and more familiar with our boat and each other's strengths and weaknesses while aboard. We have discovered that my qualities of being hyper and emotional are nicely balanced with the captain's calm and logical approach to things. He continues to impress me with his control of the ship in all aspects, especially since neither of us had any real experience before we set out. I tend to get anxious in situations when I feel not in control or unsure of what is happening. Luckily for us, Alec shines in these circumstances, applying what he knows and using common sense. We have agreed that I am the pessimistic idealist and that he is the optimistic cynic. Our life together is quite different now, spending everyday together. I like it like this – the more time we spend together, the better it gets!... So far, the challenges of the trip are still outweighing the pleasures, but the pleasures are quickly catching up! Especially the last two weeks. We have renewed confidence in ourselves and our abilities, and look forward to the unknown ahead. This is quickly becoming the adventure of a lifetime."

When Alec had started investigating boats, he immediately realized the advantages of a catamaran. Most sailors think of quick passages in a light, speedy catamaran, but that's far from reality with most multihulls out cruising. Cruising catamarans tended to be heavily built and when all the equipment and provisions were added, most catamarans sailed at the same speed as traditional monohulls. Even though you could push the boat faster, most cruising couples preferred a comfortable passage

Reaching with a heeled monohull in 25-knot winds

30

to a fast one.

Madeline was comfortable, and in hindsight, this was probably the most important feature for me. Sailing against the wind, the boat hardly heeled, and there was no pendulum-like rolling when sailing downwind. We could put down our drinks, except in the worst weather at sea, without spilling. At anchor, where we spent 75 percent of our nights, *Madeline* didn't tack side to side and was comfortable even when a swell rolled in.

The second advantage for me was that *Madeline* was still relatively light, so she didn't need big sails to move through the water. The rig was small, and easy for me to handle alone, whether on my watch or in the horrible event of Alec falling overboard. The smaller sails generated smaller forces, which meant smaller equipment could be used, reducing repair costs while increasing safety should something break.

Madeline drew less than three feet of water, which expanded our cruising grounds, increased our anchoring options and increased my confidence when navigating by sight. A rock or reef less than three feet under the water usually changed the water color, wave pattern, or current flow. There were a lot of other advantages, like a stable uncluttered foredeck, increased interior space, upright when beached and unsinkable if holed or capsized, but many of these factors depended on the specific boat's design.

With our lack of boating knowledge, Alec looked for a proven ocean-going catamaran design, by a manufacturer still in business. Prout Catamarans in England was the only company that filled these requirements. They had been building bluewater cats for over 40 years and their boats had crossed all the oceans of the world with only two capsizes reported, both when racing – or at least that's what they said.

The only disadvantage of a catamaran was that our budget didn't allow for such a high-priced craft. We'd put aside enough for a used monohull, and a suitable Prout was almost twice the price. Alec's father was keen on us buying a catamaran, hoping that we'd finish our escapade quicker and get back to our respectable careers sooner. Even after Alec had explained the realistic advantages of a catamaran, Jim kindly offered to make up the difference with an interest-free loan.

"Now I can see you made a good decision buying *Madeline*," Jim said before flying home from Montego Bay. "That was a great passage with you – I look forward to another one, perhaps?"

Panama was the next destination and our first major offshore sail. We read up on the passage across the Caribbean Sea, and the word "northers" kept appearing in the text. Sure enough, after a couple of relatively calm days and good fishing, the wind swung to the north and

accelerated. Little did we know that a major storm was spinning out of the Gulf of Mexico.

When we were in Florida and parts of the Bahamas, we received weather broadcasts on our VHF radio, but now we were out of range and Jamaica, like most places in our travels, didn't broadcast weather reports. A few of the low-budget cruisers had short-wave receivers. This was a cheap alternative because you could pick up good forecasts from great distances, if you knew the stations to listen to.

We had a saying that "the only weather you can choose is the weather you leave in"; the idea being not to set schedules. We had watched the weather reports on the Montego Bay Yacht Club's television, but everyday the forecast was "trade winds from the east", which matched the *Madeline* weather forecast. This was Alec's idea of forecasting and consisted of standing outside and looking at the sky and clouds and feeling the wind's direction, strength, temperature and humidity. It sounds a bit silly, but we were amazed by some sailors who insisted on the radio weather report, when the weather outside was quite different.

As the wind picked up from the north, we scoured our reference textbooks and quickly reread about these "northers". The adjective "boisterous" also appeared many times.

We rapidly shortened sail, until we had only our small mainsail up with one reef in it. To reef our mainsail, Alec would manually pull it down and tie it off, while I worked the lines in the cockpit. This enabled us to decrease its size once by a third, and if necessary, then by half of that, or as we would say, double reefed. To decrease the size of our foresail, or genoa, we simply pulled a line to turn our forestay. This rolled the sail up neatly, and we could change its size however much we wanted. I could do this job myself from the safety of the cockpit.

The wind and waves continued to strengthen. Gray clouds had filled in, but the sun shone through and I still felt comfortable despite the worsening conditions. The waves had built up quickly and they would loom behind us, threatening to break. At the last second *Madeline's* stern would rise up and the wave would pass beneath us. I was thankful the wind was from behind and *Madeline* raced downwind in the direction we wanted.

An enormous wave lifted *Madeline* and she started to surf, establishing a new speed record at 11.5 knots. The autopilot whizzed, struggling to keep *Madeline* from broaching as she raced down the wave front. We quickly reefed the main again. With the least possible amount of sail hoisted, we were still doing six knots, and a couple of waves broke on our transom, pooping the cockpit.

Two days previously when we were near the Pedro Banks we had seen fishing boats and freighters. Now, in the troughs of the waves I saw nothing. When we rose on a wave I could see mountains of water moving in the distance until the white and gray of the breaking waves melded into the turbulent gray of the sky. While on the peaks of the waves I would quickly scan the horizon: behind *Madeline* on the first wave, then to port, forward and starboard on the succeeding waves. Alec made a call on the VHF radio requesting a weather forecast. There was no answer.

Alec enjoyed the challenge, but I was wondering about the upcoming night. The high winds had increased all day; it was now blowing over 30 knots and the waves were often over 20 feet. I could see in Alec's eyes that he too was beginning to worry. He was at the chart table making various calculations and planning ahead.

"We're doing well," he said, trying to keep positive, "but, I'm not sure what effect this weather will have on our destination." We planned landfall at the San Blas Islands, a group of small reefs and islands sprinkled along the north shore of Panama, east of the Canal. "At this rate we'll be there tomorrow morning, and we'll have to make it into a channel between the islands. Our charts are not good copies and the area isn't accurately mapped in the first place. I'm not sure what effect the continental shelf and the reefs will have on these huge waves, but one thing I do know is that shoaling conditions and a lee shore is bad news."

I imagined huge curling waves and little *Madeline* surfing down them like at Seller's Cut, but ten times worse.

LEE SHORE

"WHAT ARE OUR OPTIONS?" I ASKED.

"We could put out the sea anchor to keep us here until the conditions change."

I was shocked. The sea anchor is a large parachute that attaches to the bow of the boat. It keeps the bow pointing into the wind and waves and was our last defense in extreme conditions. I suddenly thought that our lives might be in danger. I felt my face flush and then an icy tingling crept along the back of my neck. My muscles tensed as I aimed to control myself. I just had no idea what to expect, what *Madeline* could take, what extreme conditions would even look like.

"It would only be to stop us approaching Panama. We're not in survival conditions," he stressed.

"But we've never used the sea anchor before," I protested.

"We've never done any of this before!" Alec testily fired back. "Anyway, there's another option. We could head to the Panama Canal now. Surely we could enter the big ship breakwater in this weather. It would be well lit and we have a chart. Once inside, there would be protection."

We read through the instructions for deploying the sea anchor and pondered our decision. We really wanted to see the Kuna Indians who lived in the San Blas Islands. We agreed to put off the decision until later in the night.

I tossed and turned in my bunk, unable to block out the noises. The water outside the hull roared past my ears as I wrapped them with my pillow. The sounds were amplified inside the boat: the mainsheet groaned with the force of the sail, the hulls creaked as they flexed, and the wind whirred through the rigging. I couldn't help but listen, monitoring each sound. Was it getting worse?

Suddenly Alec woke me. "It's your watch," he said buoyantly. It seemed I'd been asleep only five minutes. "I think the wind is decreasing."

I got dressed, went out into the cockpit and stared into the pitch black and rushing water. The same noises seemed diminished now that I could see their source, but at night everything always felt worse. The darkness played psychological games with my mind.

Madeline's wake left a white frothy trail on the dark waves that were invisible except for the foam flecks on their faces and crests. The wind did seem less but the waves were still large. "You may be right," I called down to Alec in the bunk. "Maybe we can continue to the San Blas." The waves should die down by the time we sight land in the morning, I thought, and prayed.

By sunrise there were breaks in the low dark clouds. When we sighted the thin gray-green smudge on the horizon the waves were only six feet high. As we motored carefully into the channel towards Porvenir, the customs check-in port for the San Blas, I noticed something felt different with the boat.

Alec looked over the side and said, "Oh, the steering arm on the outdrive is disconnected. It must've vibrated loose in the storm. I must not have tightened it enough when I assembled the outdrive."

I couldn't help wondering if there were any other parts that he hadn't tightened enough. But there was little we could do about it now. We were both riding a high. We had survived our first storm at sea.

"I was frightened during the storm, but I'm pleased with how I reacted to the conditions. I did my share of the work and felt like an important member of the team. We discussed our situation as it changed, and made the decisions together. Sometimes I deferred to Alec, but I'm happy I'm not like many wives of sailors who make it out sailing only to lose confidence in their husband."

Small clusters of little islands speckled the distant water. The palm trees swayed in the still stormy wind. Ashore, short olive-skinned natives greeted us in Spanish at the rough stone pier. A lone telephone stood beside the weathered customs building, next to a little airstrip.

We called Alec's parents and they were relieved to hear from us. Down the crackling line Joan said, "We were very worried. The papers are calling it the *Storm of the Century*. A lot of boats sank in Cuba and the southern United States. In Florida, seventeen people were killed from tornadoes and a large freighter was lost in the Gulf Stream."

We hung up the phone elated. After five days and 600 nautical miles, we had made it to the San Blas, tired, but without damage to the boat or ourselves. The whole experience had instilled confidence in both of us. *Madeline* performed just as we'd hoped. She hadn't been challenged; it was the crew who had to overcome the frightful sounds and the relentless motion. The physical challenge lay in keeping a safe watch, staying rested and eating properly, so that when a decision needed to be made, the crew was capable.

Another sailor from a big, beautiful, dark blue yacht named *Aldebaran* was also visiting customs. He told us how they had tacked back and forth in front of the islands because they had arrived in the night and were afraid to enter with the high seas and strong winds. In the middle of the night their roller-furling headsail had broken off at the masthead and fallen into the water. They had wrestled it back on board as they ran the boat downwind to avoid losing the mast.

"What did you break?" he asked.

I looked at Alec as we both searched our memories.

"Nothing." I responded.

But I couldn't help thinking of the steering arm on the outdrive. It had just come unscrewed, but what if it had been something else? What would we do if our forestay broke? Could Alec and I wrestle that back on board?

We have a well-designed boat, I reassured myself.

While lying in a hammock tied between two palm trees on the beach, I looked out over the water, marveling at the beauty before me. The San Blas are a long string of tiny islands off the north coast of Panama and home to the Kuna Indians. The sandy islands are studded with clusters of palm trees and surrounded by reefs teeming with underwater sea life. The water color is a patchwork of pale, pale blues over a sand bottom, contrasting with deeper blues and other dark areas where the water deepens or covers coral patches. In the distance, perhaps two miles away, I could see five tiny islands. I could just make out the rainforest-covered San Blas Mountains on the mainland towering above the hazy horizon.

The Kuna had a unique arrangement with the Panamanian government; they had autonomous control of their islands and the mountainous mainland from east of the Canal Zone to the border of Colombia. The Kuna were among the last remaining descendants of the Caribbean Indians. Unique in their appearance, they were short in stature and rich in culture. However, as with aboriginals around the world, they were being influenced by Western consumerism.

The Kuna were willing to sell lobster, plantains and *molas* or to trade for clothes, fishing gear and staples such as sugar and rice. A *mola*, the traditional blouse worn by Kuna women, includes two intricately hand-sewn square panels joined together, one panel in front and one at the back. Traditionally the patterns were geometric, depicting lobster, turtles and godlike figures, but the new *molas* often had "San Blas" stitched at the top – the influence of tourist dollars. The combination of a *mola*, a gold nose ring, a black line painted down the nose, short cropped black hair, an orange scarf around the head and a brightly-colored skirt gave the Kuna women their distinctive and beautiful appearance.

While anchored at the outer islands, a *cayuco* would often paddle up alongside *Madeline*. This traditional dugout canoe was made from tree trunks and the Kuna used them to paddle or sail between their islands. Usually the first to greet us would be the women and children. They would have a bucket full of *molas* for us to look at. We learned a few words in Spanish, but often they spoke only their own language, so communicating was difficult.

Arriving at our first village, Ciedras, we anchored amongst six circling *cayucos*. We quickly explained that we were coming ashore and climbed into our dinghy to motor over. The women and children were shouting and waving for us to come. We were a little uncomfortable with our instant fame, and couldn't see anywhere to land. The entire island was only a few hundred yards long, and even less wide. As we passed close we could see that the village was very clean, with every square inch of the island taken up with housing. The toilets were little shacks on stilts out over the water. There was no way to get onto the island, but to arrive in someone's yard.

There were so many children! They stared at us, mouths hanging open. If I caught their eye, they would giggle, or shyly hide behind another. Alec reached out to shake a hand, and once one child shook, everyone wanted a shake! We walked through the village with a pack of about twenty children following us. Everyone was barefoot, and the youngest children hardly wore anything at all. They were jostling, playing, laughing, touching us and pulling Alec's leg hairs.

Everything was close together, and everyone walked freely, in and out of houses. We couldn't stand fully erect in the narrow alleys and our heads hit the thatched-roof overhangs. Inside the one-room homes there was a cooking fire in the middle of the floor. A few homes had beds with mattresses, but most had hammocks. There was no furniture, although in one home, a woman quickly dusted a log for us to sit on.

Both Alec and I found that while in the village, we felt socially uncomfortable, pleasantly awkward at best. It was as if we were invading their privacy – we looked foreign, we didn't speak their language, and everyone was watching us. Yet something about being with them was so enjoyable. The Kuna seemed amazingly unaffected by the 20th century despite being within a hundred miles of the Panama Canal.

As we left, the children were at the edge of the island, some in the water, all waving, cheering and whistling. "Adios, amigos!"

I could understand how cruisers spent months in these islands. At first I thought it was for the beauty of the islands, but now I was sure it was for the beauty of the people. Alec and I felt we were finally relaxing and starting to cruise together. This exploring thrilled us both, and it reconfirmed my desire to experience new lands and different cultures.

We left Portobelo, an enchanted little village east of the Panama Canal, with dolphins leading us out to a placid Caribbean Sea. We followed the coast for 20 miles and came through the breakwaters of

the Canal Zone at around noon. It was exciting to approach this feat of engineering we'd heard about all our lives, that would lead us into the Pacific Ocean. Never had I seen so many large ships in such a confined space, and I feared that any freighter might run us down.

Alec said to me, "Look closer. It's pretty difficult for a ship to hit us while at anchor!"

I relaxed a bit and became intrigued to see these monsters up close. They were all shapes and sizes and had so many interesting flags, cargo and destinations.

We had heard rumors of rampant crime in Colon, the city on the Caribbean side of the canal. Approaching the Panama Canal Yacht Club we could see at least eighteen yachts anchored out in the harbor. With only hearsay to go by, we chose to go to the yacht club, where we knew there was 24-hour security and a laundry room. We had heard rumors that we wouldn't see another washing machine until New Zealand, so I planned to wash everything we owned!

While Alec checked in with customs and about five or six other offices requiring hoards of paperwork, I scouted the clubhouse for the opportunity to go through the canal on another yacht. We wanted to assist as line handlers, so that we could get a feel for what the transit was about. Often, if you helped another boat, they would then reciprocate.

We were required to have four line handlers and a helmsman, plus an "adviser" assigned by the Panama Canal Commission. Alec would be at our helm, and I could act as a line handler, so we needed three more people. We could hire a line handler, either a local Panamanian or fellow cruiser – often teenagers – trying to earn some money, but the charge was US$40 per person, and three meals a day for potentially two days. The transit could be done in one day, but it depended on the freighter schedule and speed of the yacht.

There was a bit of a lull in the transient cruising fleet, and four days later I still hadn't found anyone who needed our assistance. We decided to find our own line handlers and book ourselves a date to transit.

At the last minute a couple from Vancouver canceled on us, but another couple, Sonny and Karen, from North Carolina, stepped in and offered their assistance. I ran down the docks and confirmed our third line handler, "Diamond Dan", who was on holiday, having sailed to the canal on a friend's boat.

We were all experienced handling lines, but not one of us had been through the canal before. None of us had even been through a lock! We felt that with common sense and good seamanship, there shouldn't be any problems, but the cruising grapevine was filled with horror stories of yachts being flung about in the turbulence and damaged against the rough canal walls. We needed four 100-foot lines to hold *Madeline* in the lock, and we double-checked each line to be sure it could take the stress.

We were given a start time of 0600, and everyone was aboard chatting excitedly and drinking coffee. There would be three locks up, a 35-mile sail across Gatun Lake and then three more locks down before safely reaching the Pacific. The only person missing was our adviser. After numerous calls on the radio, Fabio was dropped off four hours late!

We quickly hoisted anchor eager to discover what all the gossip was about.

INTO THE PACIFIC OCEAN

WE APPROACHED THE FIRST LOCK behind the biggest freighter I had ever seen. It was practically the maximum size for the canal: 105 feet wide, 38 feet deep and over 800 feet long. There was only an eighteen-inch gap on each side and a couple of feet of water underneath. There was more ship in the lock than water and I wondered what was keeping it afloat. Fabio explained that all ocean-going freighters were built to fit in the Panama Canal.

The freighter was eased into the lock by stout locomotives on rails next to the lock. Squeezed in behind the freighter were two tugboats, with one tied up to the wall of the lock, and the other alongside the first. After they were secured and stationary, Alec maneuvered *Madeline* to a position alongside the second tug, and we tied up to it.

The lock began to fill.

The turbulence was incredible and the tugs and *Madeline* swayed with the strain of the swirling water. The wire ropes connecting the freighter to the locomotives creaked and groaned. Huge tarpon jumped out of the muddy water feeding on the smaller fish flowing down from

the lake above. Within minutes we had risen to the top of the lock and we waited for the signal to move into the next lock.

"Keep the lines tied," Fabio warned us. "The ship will start the propeller." Moving his arm in a large circle, he explained that the locomotives needed the propeller's help to get the freighter moving.

The ship's engine roared as the propeller began to spin. Water rushed at *Madeline* and the current measured over five knots! Then the locomotives took up the strain and pulled the freighter forward.

We untied from the tugs and held back until they were in position in the second chamber. Struggling against the turbulence, Alec followed them into the next lock.

We repeated this same positioning once more without incident, and within an hour we were out in freshwater Gatun Lake, the largest man-made lake in the world. *Madeline* had never been in fresh water before, and she was now 90 feet above sea level.

Our group was a great team, and there was a party atmosphere with each little success. Out came the cold beer after our successful journey up the "up" locks. The anchorage was on the other side of the lake, about 20 miles away, and we motor sailed past jungle-clad islands that had once been hilltops before the valley was drowned. With our late start we would have to wait until the next day for the descent to the Pacific Ocean.

A boat picked up Fabio and the rest of us jumped in for a swim, ignoring our fears of the crocodiles that lived in the lake. We took great pleasure in washing and rinsing with copious fresh water – a small consolation for a two-day transit. Alec and I loved to entertain, and we served dinner by candlelight in the cockpit. Surrounded by tropical jungle, it was eerie to see freighters glide by in the darkness; the canal operated 24 hours a day for the big ships.

We had an early start the next day, and our next adviser, José, came aboard for breakfast. The first of the three "down" locks found us alone – so we went down in the middle of the chamber. Alec strategically placed Sonny and Karen together, as they already worked as a team on their own boat. He kept them at the stern, where Sonny's strength was there if needed. Going down, the water rushed out, so the most stress was on the stern lines. Dan and I manned the bow.

Other than a few missed throws by the Panamanian workers who tossed us thin "messenger" lines to retrieve our lines, we had no difficulties. It was easier going down, and when we shared the last two locks with a freighter, it was positioned behind us so propeller wash wasn't an issue. The day finished with *Madeline* moored on the Pacific side at the Balboa Yacht Club. After patting one another on the back, Dan left for the airport in Panama City, and Sonny and Karen hopped on the *Colon Expreso* bus back to their boat in Colon.

The next evening we took the 90-minute bus ride to reciprocate for Sonny and Karen. We arrived at the yacht club and found David Clark playing his clarinet in the bar. David would transit the following week, only too happy to play and earn some money at the club. We slept aboard *Tar Baby*, Karen and Sonny's immaculate 40-foot Swan sailboat, and their third line handler, Rick, joined us the next morning.

Everything began smoothly, but there is such a fine line between control and disaster. The adviser arrived punctually and clearly we were going to make it through in one day. Approaching the final locks, a decision had to be made how to tie up.

There were two yachts waiting from the day before, for a total of five yachts. Logically there would be a raft of two boats and a raft of three, however a big 100-foot yacht refused, leaving two rafts of two boats behind him. But to make room for the freighter, the two small rafts had to each go alongside a wall. Our adviser said it wasn't safe, but the only other choice was to spend a night anchored in Lake Gatun. The skippers pushed to continue on.

Panamanian workers on the lock walls took our lines and walked them to the next lock keeping pace with the boats as they motored forward. But as we moved into the last lock, it became apparent that our raft was moving too quickly with the current. The swirling water in the lock was sweeping the boats out of control towards the large yacht. The captains immediately put both boats in reverse, but it wasn't enough.

The adviser yelled out to the worker to tie off the stern line. He frantically gestured, shouting in Spanish. It was the last chance to stop the boats. The worker braced his legs and tried to physically stop the raft! He was quickly yanked into the canal, while *Tar Baby* swung around colliding with the stern of the other raft, bounced off and then smashed into the canal wall.

The bow line held the raft to the wall and just as suddenly, everything was under control.

The worker was safely dragged out of the canal and officials descended to investigate the damaged boats. *Tar Baby* had some scratches and the other boat's stern railing was smashed in.

Together we were lowered down the last lock and into the Pacific Ocean facing backward!

On April 8th we ventured into the Pacific Ocean. It lived up to its name, as the water was flat calm. We were in the doldrums, a windless region that circled the earth and, in this area, stretched from the Gulf of Panama south to the equator. We motored to the Las Perlas Islands and then hopped through the archipelago to the southernmost island, San José. At last a promising wind sprang up, but then it switched to the wrong direction and died. Our destination was the Galapagos Islands, almost a thousand miles to the west, through the doldrums and across the equator. We could not afford to begin this passage with our engine on, as we needed every last drop of diesel. We had bought three large plastic containers for a dollar each, and filled them with extra fuel just for this trip. Feeling tense about the long windless passage ahead of us, we sat in the cockpit quietly thinking of what to do.

"We aren't alone in the anchorage, the other boats are facing the same decisions. We've met many of them – all heading to the South Pacific, and I think of how exciting it'll be to see them again in our travels. In the cruising world, we're known collectively as the South Pacific Class of '93 and we're all pretty green. For most of the boats, it's our first time in the Pacific, and our longest ocean passage is soon to come."

At that moment, a white sailboat appeared on the horizon. Over the radio came, "*Madeline*, is that you?" It was Klaus from *Wado Ryu*! "It's Claudia's 32nd birthday today," he said.

"We must have a party," I radioed back.

"Of course, why not?"

We had met Claudia and Klaus, from Berlin, in the San Blas. They had told us that there was a "German guy" on Isla San José who would sell us papayas and pineapples. The day after celebrating Claudia's birthday we all went ashore armed with a bottle of rum and rang the bell as the sign instructed. Dieter came down to greet us at the beach, was happy to see the rum, and invited us up to his house to meet his wife, Gerda. He served us rum punch made from fresh-squeezed fruit he had grown himself.

With Claudia and Klaus to help in the translation, we learned that they had started cruising in 1980 intent on finding an island paradise. In 1983 they had arrived at San José and lived on their boat at anchor. The island was owned by another German, who granted them permission to farm an uninhabited slice of jungle. Eight years later they moved onto land, and built themselves a concrete foundation for a home that rested on a cliff overlooking the anchorage.

The view was spectacular, but their home was quite the opposite.

Gerda, Claudia, Klaus and Alec at San José

43

They had little money, and as a result, they lived in poverty, surviving off the land. They were living out their dream in their own way.

Dieter had hand-planted everything that grew there. They gave us pineapple, papaya, sour oranges, soursop and grapefruit. Dieter motored their sailboat to Panama four times a year to get supplies including grains, powdered milk and canned foods. They had a few chickens for eggs and ate the leaves of some plants for their greens. They told us of their life on the island, and entertained us with stories of scorpions, boa constrictors, alligators, vampire bats, crabs and mites.

Upon questioning the balance of their diet, they assured me they got plenty of protein from the local rats they trapped. There was little in the way of game on the island, so after the Smithsonian Institute in Panama had inspected the rats, they ate them regularly.

"What do they taste like?" I asked Dieter.

A smile broke his normally flat German façade and he said, "Like rats!"

After a lazy farewell over coffee with Claudia and Klaus, we motored *Madeline* away from the islands before setting the spinnaker in the light air. I spotted a lone Scalloped Hammerhead Shark, swimming beside the boat, and then a few minutes later we both noticed a large circle of turbulent water to starboard.

"Check the depth," Alec said.

"167 feet," I responded.

A fin, a blowhole, and then a huge hunk of flesh broke the surface. We were passing our first whale!

The Gulf of Panama, fed by the nutrient-rich Humboldt Current was full of sea life. The sea water was murky from all the plankton and little animals in it. The head, our version of a toilet, sucked in sea water for flushing. Alec noticed after he had finished flushing one time, that he'd sucked a cleaner shrimp into the bowl. It was tiny, the size of my fingernail, but it was happily swimming about, cleaning the scraps. Alec went on for the rest of the day that this was his new marketing idea. The business that would make us wealthy. No more nasty toilet bowl cleaning with toxic chemicals, just get the cleaner shrimps, and simply flush them out when the bowl is clean!

Dolphins provided great entertainment, hurling themselves out of the water doing giant flips, gainers and spins. I worried if they would bite our fishing lure, but they were smarter than that. Later, on our first afternoon out from San José, we caught a bonito tuna – enough for three dinners. The fishing was fun and rewarding, with simple equipment and no skill required. The next day we passed a fleet of huge tuna fishing boats, racing around under the direction of a helicopter which was tracking the schools of tuna and plotting interceptions. We

44

looked at our little rod and felt less guilty about our takings. It was sad to kill a beautiful animal, but we ate everything we caught.

During the moonless nights, we marveled at the dazzling phosphorescence in the water. Dolphins dove under *Madeline* leaving a sparkling blue trail like the exhaust of a jet fighter. The boat's wake bubbled and glowed as we slowly plowed the calm waters. Spooky large blue blobs swam beneath the boat. They never surfaced, so were not mammals, and seemed too big and round to be sharks. In the eerie calm, far from land, it was easy to imagine monsters or space aliens, but perhaps it was only schools of fish that caused the phosphorescence to coalesce when they all moved together. Strange white birds flew around us, briefly lit up by the navigation lights. I never saw them during the day, but often on my night watch I would suddenly hear a quiet flapping a few feet away in the darkness. A burst of adrenaline would jerk me to my feet.

A clumsy brown booby bird joined us on a couple of nights. He arrived at dusk and settled on the rail at the bow. In no time his head was tucked under his wing and he was asleep. One night Alec and I went forward to watch the dolphins play at the bow and perform their unique underwater phosphorescent fireworks display. Undisturbed by our excited whistles to the dolphins, the booby bird remained fast asleep beside us.

The sailing was straightforward and required very little of my time as the autopilot steered the course. Every ten to fifteen minutes I would look around for ships on the horizon, and check the sails, the wind, our position and our course. At night while Alec slept, I was more vigilant with this three-hour routine, as it was more difficult to sense what was happening. Soon we would clear the busy Canal-bound shipping lanes,

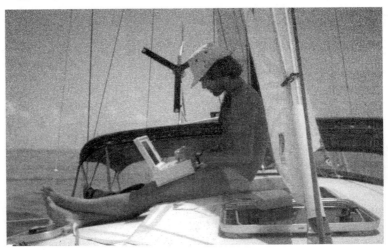

and freighter traffic would all but disappear.

I was thoroughly enjoying the passage and the time to myself. I slept well, ate well and I enjoyed occupying myself with all sorts of things. The calm weather and lonely watch routine gave me time to reflect on our new life.

"The biggest difference in our lives is that now we have time. Before, we were working so hard and never wanted to spend our precious time doing the menial everyday things. Now we do, because we can, and because we have to. Although completely out of character, it's fun...

While baking my first loaf of bread this morning, it dawned on me how domestic I've become. A good chunk of my day is spent preparing meals and cleaning. Another cruiser said that not only are cruising wives domestic, but domestic like 100 years ago. I thought of that while I carted jugs of fresh water from the river at San José back to our boat and then as I washed laundry by hand at the edge of the river. I can't believe I'm washing sheets and towels by hand, but there's no alternative. I joked with Alec that I want a washboard for Christmas – I saw another cruiser with a really nice plastic one! Who would have thought? I used to cringe at the age-old stereotype, but I now I find pleasure in doing all these things, including the cooking. I start reading recipes after lunch, and if we haven't caught a fish by three, I begin preparing something else for dinner.

Also out of character, I finished sewing a canvas cover for our life raft today, to protect it from the sun. And in each country we visit, sailing etiquette dictates we fly the country's flag from the starboard spreader, as a sign of respect. Alec is the designer on our sewing team, and I'm the seamstress.

Normally I prefer talking, writing, or doing something physical rather than reading, but I'm attempting my thickest book ever: The Path Between The Seas, by David McCullough. It's a history book on the creation of the Panama Canal, and I'm actually enjoying it! Dad would be impressed and pleased."

Alec and I had pleased our parents more often than not. We had similar family backgrounds, growing up in suburbia near big cities – he in Toronto and me just across the border from Detroit. Our parents had the traditional goals of owning a house, having a good job and raising a family. It's what was done, and what was expected. Our mothers, although they had professional careers of their own, had stayed at home to care for the children.

Alec's father was a Scot working in New Zealand when he met Joan and proposed four weeks later. They married in England, settled in Canada and enjoyed exotic travel. Although Alec's parents would have preferred that Alec continue with his career, they understood his desire to see the world and supported our trip from the outset.

My parents grew up on the prairies of western Canada. It wasn't until my father was in his twenties that he first saw a body of water where he couldn't see the other side, and this was tiny Lake St. Clair in Ontario. Although an able swimmer, he was awfully phobic of open water and especially boats. When he first heard of our plans to sail around the world, just six months before we left, he was shocked. He had an idea that Alec and I were becoming interested in sailing, but didn't expect this.

"I can understand your wanting to travel," my father responded, "but couldn't you *drive* around the world? You could take a Jeep."

I tried to convince him that driving was probably more risky than sailing. "Dad, it's not that unusual. All sorts of people are sailing around the world." The concept was completely foreign to my parents and I hoped they would gain comfort from knowing we weren't pioneers.

My father responded sarcastically, "Right! I bump into people everyday that are sailing around the world."

Before we left, he implied how concerned he was. "You know, Alayne, of all the people I have told about your trip, nine out of ten are *for* it. Isn't that incredible?" The one against was him, of course.

Being the oldest child, I stereotypically wanted to please, and it was difficult for me to follow our plan unaffected by his unspoken disapproval. Having his child sail away – something he perceived to be utterly dangerous – must have been difficult.

My mother never admitted to sharing his fears, although she wasn't pleased either. One of her friends had asked her, "How could you let your daughter go on a trip like that?" My mother reacted in the practical way she handled most things. "There's nothing I can do. She will live her own life, and all I can do is pray for her."

Our parents instilled in both of us a strong work ethic and set us goals to complete our education and get a job. We led conservative lives, active in sports, and both of us excelled in school. Alec was more of a rebel in high school, whereas I was a bit behind socially, being two years younger than my classmates. I caught up at university where we both partied hard, but all in all we remained pretty good kids and we both followed in our fathers' footsteps when selecting careers.

Our parents never gave any thought to alternative lifestyles. The house, the job and the kids kept them busy. Their weekends were spent on the golf course. Somehow, in the middle of all this main stream conservatism, both Alec and I had developed wanderlust, and a thirst for adventure. The love, sense of security and self-confidence that our parents continuously gave us, allowed us to dream and to risk our future.

But that was before we left on the trip. Now I questioned if my thirst for adventure equaled Alec's. Perhaps I enjoyed the menial daily chores on *Madeline* because I could control them, whereas the rest of my day was full of uncertainty and new challenges. With all the time we had on this passage, I found myself worrying about the many unknowns, despite the domestic idyll.

I had always been a "worry wart", as my mother called it. Even my kindergarten teacher had written on my report card, *"Very bright student, but worries a lot...afraid that her younger sisters are playing with her toys while she is away at school, and that they might break them."*

I wrote in my journal. *"Will we run out of diesel and wind? If there's no wind, I know we have enough food and fluids for six months, but would we get to land eventually? I just have to be patient, but again, patience is out of character for me.*

Will we bump into whales? Every life raft survival story I've read deals with being hit by whales on this same passage, but I keep telling myself that it shouldn't enter my mind any more than driving on the highway everyday fearing an accident. Just as with cars, a collision with a whale is not always fatal. These things happen, but not usually to you."

I began to see that I would be quite a different person after the trip. Even with all these unknowns, the unmitigated worrying and the potential hidden fears, I told myself that I was enjoying this adventure, more and more each day. Alec and I were getting along, but he didn't share my concerns. Could fear turn into excitement? I had to learn to enjoy the adrenaline rush, and have it work for me, not against me.

Ten days after leaving San José it felt like New Year's Eve as we watched the GPS count down to 0° 00'. I had been absorbed in a book all day and remarked how convenient it was crossing the equator at cocktail time.

Alec laughed, "Alayne, I planned it this way. We've been sailing parallel to the equator all afternoon!"

He cracked open a bottle of Guatemalan champagne and we ate crackers with cream cheese and caviar. We made some toasts, but it was an informal celebration, as all we were wearing was our cotton underwear. The combination of increasing temperature and fickle wind caused us to sweat profusely – we would have shed our underwear too, except that it kept us from sticking to our vinyl cockpit cushions!

The weather remained calm for the majority of the trip, with only a few rain squalls typical of the doldrums plaguing us in the last half. We arrived in the Galapagos, at the island of Santa Cruz, early on the morning of April 30th. We had spent the previous night slowly sailing around, waiting for the sky to lighten before entering the harbor. We rejoiced at completing what we hoped would be the slowest leg of our journey.

After breakfast, we pumped up our inflatable dinghy and began to row ashore. Immediately a Swiss couple we had met briefly in Colon offered a tow. It was fun walking through the seashore town on this isolated island, and bumping into so many people we knew! After being alone at sea the contact with these instant friends was very welcome. They had lots of information for us on what to do and where to find the post office, telephones, diesel, water, the bakery, the market, and Henry's bar. They also directed us to the harbor master and we paid exorbitant fees to the corrupt officials who granted us a four-day stay. Technically cruisers weren't allowed to visit the Galapagos without prior permission, but everyone did to replenish their fuel and fresh food supply. The officials knowingly used the law to pad their pockets, and the cruisers helplessly played along with the charade, claiming they were only making an emergency stop. After twelve days to travel only 960 miles, our definition of emergency was very broad.

But it was certainly worth it. We were exhausted from the sailing and unbearable equatorial heat, but excitement kept us going. At the Darwin Research Station, Alec and I happened upon a group of tortoises and had a few magical moments feeding them long green leaves by hand. The tortoises were huge; hundreds of pounds and hundreds of years old.

We paused for a refreshing midday drink at Henry' s open air bar, a popular place for cruisers and where we'd collect our beer from Claudia and Klaus for winning the race to the Galapagos. We watched the occasional tourist walking along the quaint cobblestone streets of Puerto Aorta. A tall, good-looking, young couple sauntered along, and I commented to Alec that they couldn't be cruisers because of how neatly they were dressed. The man was wearing a long-sleeved shirt, dress pants and loafers, while the woman wore a pretty flowered dress and sandals. At the local market the next day, Claudia introduced us to Nathalie and Robert – this same couple. Little did we know what a significant role they would play in our trip.

Nathalie and Robert were sailing on *Rode Beer* – translated as "Red Bear". They were our age, and had started their voyage from Holland

six months before we started ours. Both fluent in English, Nathalie had trained as a translator and spoke five languages, whereas Robert only spoke four! Nathalie and I connected right away, and by the end of the day my voice was raspy from talking so much. They planned to circumnavigate in the same time frame as us, but had chosen a much different boat: a steel and wood monohull.

Together, we arranged an island tour by bus and motorboat to see the world-renowned wildlife. The animals were so abundant and unafraid. We were entranced by the mating dance of the blue-footed booby birds, nearly stepped on marine iguanas oblivious to us, photographed beautiful swallowtail gulls and marveled at the big puffed-out red chests of the male frigate birds. For the last hour of the tour we jumped in the water and swam with the sea lions! The young seals could have played forever, while their mothers watched from the beach and the big grumpy males quietly slept. It was pandemonium and we were sorry to leave.

The next day the weather turned bad and the wind blew directly into the anchorage. All the cruisers stayed on their boats on "anchor watch", hoping they wouldn't drag. Being far from Panama and even further from Tahiti, we couldn't afford a mishap. Everyone cursed spending one of our precious and expensive days in the Galapagos bobbing about in an uncomfortable harbor.

Fortunately the weather calmed by the evening as Henry had invited us all to his home for a potluck barbecue. After the beer supply thinned out, the guys, led by Klaus, chanted "Nu-Ku-Hi-Va, Nu-Ku-Hi-Va", our destination 3,000 miles further west across the vast featureless Pacific.

Now came the big test.

23 DAYS AT SEA

ALL TOO QUICKLY IT WAS TIME TO LEAVE. Only three months after leaving Florida, we now faced the longest leg of our voyage.

The crossing from the Galapagos to the Marquesas Islands filled me with more anxiety than any other. Before, if something happened we were never more than a few hundred miles from land. Even if we had to get into our life raft, or if *Madeline* was damaged, we would be seen by another ship. But now, even though we knew there were others out there, our chances of seeing another boat were slim. Just as our chance of hitting a whale seemed slim, I still feared this awful possibility. What damage would we have? How would we cope?

David Clark said to us in Panama, "It's not the wind and waves so much as the breakdowns." Of course I looked at his boat and believed him, but another circumnavigator on a beautifully-maintained boat backed him up.

"Sailing around the world has very little to do with your ability to sail a boat. It's your ability to fix things that will determine your success."

These fears made it difficult for me to relax. My greatest fear was that something might happen to Alec, and I would have to handle things on my own. I felt reasonably confident in sailing the boat, but I knew nothing about the engine or how to fix things if they broke. I didn't believe I had his ingenuity.

With nonchalant goodbyes we lifted anchor. *Wado Ryu* had scammed an extension to stay at the Galapagos and as we passed them we yelled, "See you next month!" *Rode Beer* had left before us, and we could see their light and another boat the first evening.

We quickly lost contact with everyone, but in Panama we'd bought a small all-band radio receiver. It allowed us to listen but not talk. We religiously tuned in to one group of boats who talked each morning on the same frequency and called themselves the "Comedy Net". These boats were spread out between Central America and French Polynesia and although we only knew a couple of the boats personally, it was nice to know that we were not the only people out there.

Rode Beer talked with the Dutch and German boats on a different frequency, so we didn't know if they were close by. Sometimes, the sailors would offer information about the island they were visiting and we tried to put a face to the voice and imagine what their boat looked like. We talked about them on a first-name basis, and some we liked just for the way they spoke, hoping that someday we might share an anchorage.

For the first few days I felt seasick and tired. Our short stay in the Galapagos had been very busy and had left me happily drained, but I was feeling seasick in the exposed harbor even before we had lifted the anchor to leave. I wasn't vomiting, but I felt nauseous, apathetic and incapable of being my usual productive self.

There was no pressure from Alec, other than to take my watch, and he took over the preparing of meals, a chore we normally shared.

I tried various seasickness medications and began to feel better. I was sleeping a lot but never felt 100 per cent. We were making good progress on a beam to broad reach, but there was a large underlying swell that knocked *Madeline* around. At best it was annoying and at worst it made me ill. One boat on the radio described it as a "washing machine". Our poor autopilot was working extra hard to keep us on course.

The rigging was one area where Alec hadn't spent much time and he even admitted he wasn't sure how it would stand up to one month of continuous jarring and straining. "I've inspected the rig," he said, "but it's impossible to detect minute cracks. Other than replacing the entire rig at tremendous cost, there's little we can do, and even that wouldn't guarantee against a defect of some sort."

Feeling vulnerable now that we were out at sea, Alec would sit back laughing and marveling at the uncertainty and fear that surged up from his subconscious before he forced it back down again. They were exactly the same thoughts I was having, but he dealt with them so differently.

"Sure it'll worry you, if you let it," he sympathized, "but, there's absolutely nothing we can do about it now, so don't let those thoughts take over. "

I felt that a round of cards had been dealt, but I wasn't given a hand. We were the ante in a game between *Madeline* and Mother Nature and I was sitting in the middle of the card table, waiting for the cards to fall.

"What about Hank?" I asked. We had named the autopilot "Hank" after a co-worker of Alec's who was devious, yet always got the job done. We could constantly hear the clicking of the switches and the buzz of the electric motor. "What if this is too much work for him and he breaks? What if we have to steer day and night?"

Alec replied as he had before, "It's not *if* it will break, but *when* it will break."

"That doesn't help me," I complained.

"Look, those relays clicking in the autopilot must have a life of at least a million cycles." He brought out a calculator and said, "If they cycle once a second, 24 hours a day for 24 days then that is... oops. That's over two million cycles!"

"That was confidence inspiring. Thanks."

"All that proves is that I don't know much about relays," he retorted. It didn't seem to bother him that he didn't know every last detail. He was much more willing to wing it than I was.

I was also plagued by the thought of Alec falling overboard. It only took a few seconds to lose track of something in the waves; we'd already lost a bucket and a few baseball caps. Even if I witnessed it, which was unlikely due to our solo watches, would I be able to turn the boat around, manage the sails and find him? What if it happened at night? What if I was asleep? The thought of losing him made me shudder.

At first, we'd been very strict about wearing harnesses continually at night, especially when the other was asleep, but lately, we had been less obsessive. *Madeline's* cockpit was so large, deep and well contained that we no longer clipped in while sitting in it. But should one of us climb the arch to turn off the wind generator, go forward to change a sail, or do anything that took us out of the cockpit, then we would clip in our harness and let the other person know. At night this meant waking up the other person, so these activities were usually performed during a change of watch. Alec allayed my fears with regard to this aspect – he always wore his harness and consented to a ban on peeing over the side from dusk to dawn. Sailing myths claimed that many a man found drowned at sea had his fly undone.

"Aren't you scared?" Without something real to fear, I hadn't answered the question properly before we left. But now I knew more about the infinite number of potential misfortunes we could face, and I had to admit I was worried.

The first mishap occurred on the sixth day.

We had just sat down to a nice dinner of bratwurst cooked in beer, served with fried tomatoes and green beans when we heard a loud bang and the whole boat vibrated. We dashed outside just in time to see a black object fall into the water far behind the boat.

My mind raced as I tried to think what part of our boat was black. "The mast is black!" Alec shouted in horror.

Quickly we noticed the aluminum arch vibrating violently. We looked up to see that one of our three wind generator blades had broken at its base and plunged into the depths of the South Pacific. With a sigh of relief we realized that the mast was undamaged, and that the flying blade had not harmed the boat or us.

We'd already had some trouble with our batteries and the wind generator was used for charging them. The batteries provided electricity for our power-hungry autopilot, but also fed our running lights and navigation instruments. Alec assured me that our solar panels, and the occasional running of the engine, would keep our batteries topped up. The sailing had been good and we had an adequate supply of diesel.

I tried to think positively and not worry about things before they happened, but it did seem uncanny that we had just been discussing potential problems. Only that morning I had written, *"There's no sense worrying; that's wasted mental energy. But I can't help thinking – what next? Every little thing seems like a catastrophe, and I keep worrying about how I'll deal with something major going wrong."*

The next day I felt lousy after a restless night, probably due to my nerves. I tried to be productive with some cleaning and cooking. Alec was complaining about our slow speed, so we put up the spinnaker. After only two hours, the halyard chafed through at the masthead and the whole thing came tumbling down. There was no damage, except the broken line, but now our spinnaker was useless.

At least on the fishing front, our good luck continued. We only put out the line when we wanted fish for dinner. Alec had a memorable wrestle with our biggest catch ever – a ten-dinner tuna! We hooked a blue marlin, and this five-foot beauty gave a spectacular fight before escaping with our favorite green lure.

For a couple of days we made great progress. The wind blew from directly behind us though, making it difficult to set the sails efficiently. We had never really given much thought to how we would sail dead downwind. Most of the monohulls had elaborate rigs using two poles to hold out two large headsails. The poles kept the sails out as the boat

rolled from side to side sailing downwind. *Madeline* didn't roll as much, because we had no heavy keel under the boat, but Klaus from *Wado Ryu* had insisted we take his fourteen-foot oar to use as a pole anyway.

When the wind began to slacken, Alec tried fiddling with various sail and pole combinations to keep *Madeline* moving. I was sleeping one morning when he woke me to try yet another sail plan. I responded grumpily and he snapped back, setting the tone for the rest of the day.

I kept wishing my mood would change, but I was jumpy, depressed and finding the passage irritating.

"I'm not as productive as I'd like – the constant motion of the boat is so annoying. So much attention to the sail trim is draining us even though the autopilot does all the steering. Yet at the same time I have an urge to run around the block. Is it seasickness? Is it cabin fever? We're less than halfway, and I accept that it'll take a long time to get there, but Alec is constantly preoccupied with our progress. He's always mentioning how slow we're sailing and that we have too much weight aboard."

That night I didn't feel like reading, so I gazed at the southern hemisphere constellations twinkling at me in the clear sky above. The Southern Cross had taken over from the Big Dipper. But my mind was distracted and I brooded in the cockpit, waiting for my watch to end. Our interactions were bothering me and I decided to discuss them with Alec.

It was finally my turn to sleep, but I needed to talk. "Do we have to constantly agonize over the speed? After three weeks at sea, will another day really matter?"

"Sure it matters!" he responded. "An extra half-knot doesn't make a difference to the boat, but it could mean we get there two days sooner. I'd rather spend my time in paradise, than at sea. Anyway, it's not like we have other more pressing things to do with our time."

"But you're a grump. If the wind changes or something goes wrong you get angry and swear. That really bugs me." I was starting to cry.

"What bugs me is you don't keep the big picture in mind. You're always complaining about the little things, like the bouncing motion," he said, rising to my challenge.

"I thought this was supposed to be fun!"

"It should be fun, and you're right, I do swear too much. But I'm not really angry," he said calmly. "It's like how you cry when you get upset, I guess I tend to swear."

Just talking made me feel better, and we agreed to work as a team.

During my early morning watch, the winds strengthened and the waves built to ten feet. The boat was wildly racing along, and I became upset again. I finally broke with a long stress-relieving cry.

"I just want a break!" I sobbed, "I need an escape from the sailing, and a rest from it all."

Alec obliged me the best he could and rolled up the genny. We sailed quietly downwind with only the mainsail and he held me in his arms while I cried my heart out.

During breakfast, Alec made a list of downwind sail combinations. Together we discussed them and implemented the one we felt was best. After lunch we made love and I let him have a long nap. While he

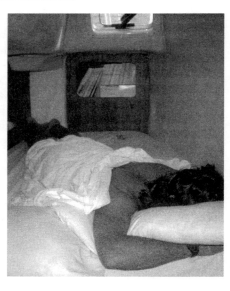

made dinner, I updated my journal with the events of the past 24 hours.

"Are you writing about what a nice guy I am?" he asked.

"I haven't reached that part yet," but admitted to myself that he was pretty good. *"He allows me to talk about my irrational fears, even though it frustrates him tremendously. Sometimes he finds it amusing and this morning he was laughing when I said I didn't want to be here anymore. I wasn't coping well then, but now I feel much better. I want to trust the boat, and to trust Alec, but this seems to be getting harder the longer we're out here."*

The wind inexplicably died early the next morning and I turned on the motor. Alec decided to go up the mast to rig another spinnaker halyard and find out why it chafed so quickly. Up he went in the Bosun's chair, with him doing more climbing than me hoisting. Even though there was no wind, there was the ever-present swell, and after an hour rethreading the halyard, Alec came down banged, bruised and exhausted.

We celebrated reaching halfway, and I rewarded Alec with a lemon meringue pie for his courageous performance. That night the moon shone down on me with millions of stars. With only their light on my page, I started a humorous list entitled, "Things you can do in the dark by yourself". We were sailing nicely on flat seas and the GPS indicated that the current was helping us along. It was such a peaceful and welcome break from the rough seas of only a day before. It was my kind of night and I felt proud of our achievement thus far. I looked to the stars and hoped for a successful second half of the passage.

The replaced halyard was more important than we thought. Just two days later we faced our biggest challenge. It was a beautiful morning with light winds steadily picking up after a few days of relative calm. After finishing a pancake breakfast, we sat down to our morning game of Scrabble, coffees in hand.

Suddenly, there was a loud flapping noise. The forestay had snapped at its base!

This wire supported our biggest sail and helped support our mast. Now with sail attached, it was swinging in large arcs before *Madeline*, bucking and bouncing in the wind and swell. The mast could come tumbling down, and we had to move fast, or my fears would be realized.

We dashed to the foredeck, ignoring our harnesses. Alec clutched at the flailing sail, trying to bring it under control.

"We have to roll it up," Alec yelled over the racket.

I grabbed the roller-furling line, but the sail wouldn't budge. "The lines are snagged at the top," I shouted back.

Alec indicated to the roller-furling drum at the bottom of the sail. "Sit on it!"

I straddled it with all my weight, keeping the bucking drum on the deck. "Hurry up," I yelled, hoping the wind wouldn't send me airborne.

Alec cut and removed a spare halyard, allowing him to roll up the sail. The racket ceased, and the battle was half-won, but the mast was wobbling without the forestay. It wouldn't fall down I thought, but might break off halfway up – not much better.

"We have to use the spinnaker halyard to tension the mast," Alec said. The only halyard left was the one he had replaced two days before. Quickly he tied the halyard down onto the anchor windlass. The mast was now stable and the crisis was over.

With over 1,200 miles to go, I mentally calculated how long it would take us to get to the Marquesas Islands with just our main and staysail, going three knots – another eighteen days!

Meanwhile, Alec was working out how he could fix it so that we could use the sail. To me, it seemed hopeless. A thick piece of stainless steel had broken right through where the forestay attached to the bow. Amazingly, Alec produced a spare stainless-steel plate and all day long he measured, sawed and drilled to fabricate a new plate.

By five in the afternoon the new plate, even stronger than the old one, was installed and we were ready to reattach the forestay. But the rolled-up sail was still heaving in the swell and the forces were so great that we couldn't pull the forestay forward far enough to reach the plate.

Once again the spinnaker halyard saved the day. We winched it down using our anchor windlass, so tight that you could see the rope stretch and hear it creak. It bent the mast forward, and we successfully maneuvered the forestay into place.

At last the roller-furling unit was firmly in place and we sailed into the sunset, which we did every night, because we were heading west! It was a great feeling of accomplishment. We cracked two cold beers on the foredeck and toasted ourselves. We both had pounding headaches, but I felt great. Despite my fears, I'd remained calm and helpful in a time of crisis.

For the next three days the wind howled and the stress of the incident lingered. I would usually take the first watch of the evening as Alec had no difficulty sleeping right after dinner and he would let me sleep late in the morning. However, I was finding the first night watch unnerving. The darkness amplified every sound and made everything seem worse. One night when I woke Alec at the end of my watch, I was in a frenzy, worrying about all sorts of potential disasters.

"We'll be okay," he said reassuringly, making me feel calmer.

"I think I hear a problem with the forestay," I said.

"Then let's try to sort out the noises." We went to the bow and peered at the repaired forestay listening for suspicious sounds. Nothing was amiss, and Alec reminded me the repair was strong.

At the start of my next watch I felt uncomfortable the minute he crawled into bed. I watched *Madeline* lurching and zipping along at six knots and decided to wake Alec to reef the mainsail. But when I told him I wanted to reef because I was scared, he refused.

"We make decisions on this boat based on logical rationale and issues of seamanship."

"But it will be more comfortable," I pleaded.

"Sailboats are not comfortable," he fumed, "and five knots isn't any more comfortable than six."

"Yes it is, and safer too."

"This boat can handle six knots, believe me."

"How do you know?"

"I know!" he yelled in frustration. "It's a catamaran. It's capable of twice this speed. But you're not talking about physical comfort, more psychological comfort."

"Both. Isn't my wellbeing important?"

"Don't you want to get there and end this?"

I got my way, but mostly because Alec couldn't be bothered arguing any more and wanted his sleep.

"My stomach is upset and I know it's not just from the continual bumping, rolling and jostling. It reminds me of school, when the fear of

58

final exams drove me to study night after night. But now there is nothing I can do but wait. This is the longest we've ever been at sea. You'd think I would have come to terms with this, but our previous passages were so different. For the twelve days sailing to the Galapagos we mostly prayed for wind and a chance to turn off the motor. When we sailed to Panama, we faced terrible conditions in The Storm of the Century, but that trip was only five days long. Now we have at least a week left, ample time for a disaster."

I awoke to see Alec poised over the chart table with the VHF radio mike in his hand.

"Alayne, guess what?" he asked. "There's a ship out there."

With a gasp, I sprang out of bed and into the cockpit to see the lights on the black horizon.

"And it appears to be on a collision course," he added.

I spotted two white lights almost on top of each other. I couldn't believe this was happening. The ship was coming straight for us. We were going to be run down in the middle of the Pacific Ocean. This was how our lives would end.

I panicked. "Gybe the boat!" I yelled. I ran down to Alec and back outside and then back down again. "Do something!"

"How about calling them on the VHF," he calmly suggested from his position at the radio. "Like I was about to do."

I struggled with my impulsive reaction to the situation, but I was shocked that he hadn't woken me sooner.

After three calls and no answer from the ship, Alec finally said, "Okay. I guess we'll gybe. But there's no hurry," moving extra slowly just to prove his point.

We gybed away from the ship, but passed close, seeing illuminated portholes and hearing the engine throb. If there had been people on deck, we could have waved. I thought we were a bit close, but could see Alec found the event exciting. He had seen the lights in plenty of time, but it was disturbing that they weren't even listening to their radio.

After fifteen days at sea we had been questioning the need for a watch. Day after day and night after night of scanning the same empty blue ocean made the thought of sleeping together for just a few hours incredibly attractive. Would we have hit? I couldn't say for sure, but now we were both thankful to be keeping a continuous watch, 24 hours a day.

"Only 160 miles to go! Less than 32 hours!" Alec was preparing blackened medium-rare tuna steaks with wild rice as the setting sun shone through the forward windows, bathing the cabin in amber light. Gourmet food and a sunset at sea seemed the perfect ingredients for a

romantic evening, but the dynamics between Alec and I were wrong. We had tried to identify our problem, but we just couldn't straighten it out. I tried to sort my thoughts on paper.

"The problem seems to stem from my complaining. I think of all those cruising wives who didn't last and went home, leaving their husbands with the boat. They must have all complained a lot too. Will I become another statistic? I always believed that complaining was a futile activity and it never had a place in my life. Until now. Either do something to change your life, or accept it and quit bitching! But when I try to do something about it – like change how we sail the boat – Alec doesn't accept how I present my argument. He says my crying and my emotions are irrational and illogical. But my feelings are real!"

The boat speed was still an issue. I found that going fast at night, in a good wind and moderate seas, as idyllic as it sounded, was difficult to sleep through. *Madeline's* hull was thin and the waves crashed against it with loud swishes, splashes and bangs. The waterline was right next to where my head lay on the pillow, and with each jolt and shudder I imagined the boat breaking up. At speeds over six knots it seemed we were bouncing from wave top to wave top. I found it uncomfortable and felt we were pushing the boat unnecessarily. During the daytime when we were awake and alert and could assess things better, it seemed okay. Not all problems would occur at full speed, but reducing the sail area reduced risk, in my eyes.

To Alec, this didn't make sense. If there was a nice 20-knot breeze from astern, six- to eight-foot seas, clear skies, and the boat could do seven knots easily, why not? *Madeline* was built to be sailed and every extra knot would decrease our passage time, reduce the chance of breakage during the trip and minimize the chance of running into bad weather. When I asked for a reef in the mainsail to reduce the sail area and the speed, he would say, "But you can't ask for better sailing conditions!"

Alec did have a level of caution, but it was different than mine. When conditions deteriorated, he became quite conservative and was quick to reef. I actually felt safer in rough weather because he would slow the boat down.

I asked him to look at it my way. "What's the big deal about a reef in the sail, if it would make me happy? Is cutting a little time off our passage that important?"

He said, "Yes, it may be important. You're just complaining and bitching, and that's not the way to make decisions. If we ever do have another boat, I'll put a big mast on it and sail with a reef perpetually in the mainsail, just for your psychological benefit."

I collected my emotions and tried presenting my requests in other ways, but it didn't work. I guess making me a little happier would have made him unhappy, but I didn't feel that the boat should have priority over me; that his happiness should have priority over mine.

"We're almost there, and I'm thrilled. I wouldn't trade this experience for anything. I regret being unhappy, uncomfortable, bitchy, and negative and wish I'd been better company. But we are good friends and it will get better. We both want to understand each other and to make each other happy. After 44 night watches apiece, we're both looking forward to sleeping more than three hours at a time. The sailing has been stressful, but now we have six months to cover the same distance as we have in the last 23 days. We have done the trip from Florida quickly."

Now the cruising would really begin. I anticipated idyllic anchorages, reunions with cruisers, white sand beaches, tropical fruit, snorkeling and the time to enjoy it all.

"We'll have more time at anchor, and without all the sailing, everything should be back to normal. I sure hope so..."

TROUBLE IN PARADISE

"WHY ARE YOU ALWAYS SUCH A PAIN?" Alec spat out.
"I can't take this," I muttered. I turned away, trying to get away. I
started to cry.
"What? Oh God, here we go again."
"I'm trying, but you make it so hard with comments like that."
"Look," he responded. "If you would just relax. You are so uptight.
You're not any fun. I am fed up with your complaining, your worrying,
and your fucking attitude."
"It's always me who has to change."
"Hey, I understood on the passage. Sure I wasn't perfect, but I did
my best to understand, didn't I?" Our arguments were developing into a
routine. We both had thought it would be better once we arrived in the
Marquesas. "Well, for Christ's sake, the passage is over!" he ranted.
"This is supposed to be paradise. This is where the fun begins. What's
the fucking problem with you?"
From past experience, I knew it was hopeless now. He was angry. I
was in tears. My mind was racing and I couldn't even remember what
had touched him off. He trudged out to the cockpit and sat down
heavily, sulking.
I tried to sort out my thoughts. He said I had to change. Could it be
all my fault? I was not as frustrated with him, as he was with me. Still,
it was difficult for me to accept all the blame. If I were to conform to
his wishes, I would have to change my whole outlook on things.
There was no hiding on a boat, no privacy, few private moments.
One experienced cruiser had told me, "It all comes out when you're
sailing." Now I knew what she had meant by *all*. Alec was gradually
moving away. I feared I had lost his respect and his desire.
I looked in the cockpit. Alec had his head in his hands and was
slowly shaking it.
He looked up. His mouth was downturned and just visible in the
corner of his eyes were tears. This was serious, I thought. I had been
with Alec for ten years now and had never seen him cry. I went to him,
but he pulled away immediately and glared at me with anger. Please
hold me, I screamed into my soul.
We had to resolve this. I just hoped it wasn't too late. I hoped that
there hadn't been too much damage to our relationship or to his dream.
I wanted to start over, from scratch.
"We have to talk," I said.

The breathtaking view from the cockpit distracted me momentarily. Dripping with green, the jagged peaks of Hiva Oa stood proud, timeless. We'd arrived at the Marquesas Islands three days ago. It still seemed incredible that we'd sailed our little boat across the Pacific. It had been difficult for me, but being anchored here was a spectacular reward. The huge surrounding mountains made me feel safe, and I gained comfort from having so many floating neighbors close by.

I couldn't let the argument end like this. He remained silent.

"We have to talk," I repeated.

"Well, I'm not going anywhere," he croaked. "This just isn't how I imagined it. I'm not enjoying my time with you."

"I know," I responded, "but I'm trying to be better. I really am."

"I know, but I've been doing some thinking. I guess I find that out here, out in the real world, I find it very difficult to work with you. Before, we only spent our personal lives together and we always had fun. Now we have to work together, through good and bad, through calms and through rough seas. I guess my expectations are too high. If you take my work as a management consultant as an analogy, then everyone worked bloody hard. Complaining and a lack of commitment were not tolerated. Everyone was expected to contribute positively and work together towards the goal, or... or out they went."

"In our situation that doesn't work. You're stuck with me."

"Exactly. I guess you could leave, but I would hope not."

"To take your analogy further," I said, "if someone was acting as if they didn't want to contribute, or if they weren't having fun, you couldn't respond with anger and frustration."

"No."

"No. To get the team working effectively you would have to understand why that person is behaving that way."

"Yeah, I'm not that proud of the way I've been acting," he admitted. "That's one of the things that gets me so down. I know I have to respond differently. But that's the difference. It's my response to your behavior. The root of the problem lies with you."

I felt my emotions, my insecurities surge up inside. Who did he think he was? Mr. Perfect? Even if he was, he was married to someone who was human – someone interesting, dynamic, unpredictable, exciting and even exasperating.

"So you think that the problem lies with me and I have to change?" I asked.

"Right, but I admit that I have to change my reactions to you. If I can stop it from bothering me, or make a joke of it, then we'll be way ahead."

"That sounds like a good plan," I said. At least he admitted he must also change.

"Yeah, it's always the same old solution. Alec controls his emotions. Alec deals with it. How about you dealing with it for a change!"

"I'm trying! What is it that irritates you? My complaining and talking about my fears?"

"That's a start, anyway," he muttered sarcastically.

"I just don't think I can hold back my fears. I have to talk about them."

"It's not fair or appropriate to share fears. I have no choice. If I shared my fears with you then you would be doubly scared. I have my own worries on a passage, and it brings me down to hear you constantly unloading negative thoughts. Specific concerns about a specific situation – that's okay, but general fears – no."

This sheds some insight on the problem, I thought. "But I must talk to someone. I need a girlfriend to talk with – to share thoughts with and agree with – really just to talk about ourselves. It makes both of us feel better and more confident."

"What about Nathalie? You seem able to talk non-stop with her."

I had quickly connected with Nathalie. She was lovely – warm and open. When we got talking I felt as if I was back home with one of my girlfriends. We agreed on most things and had immediately shared our life stories. There were some cultural differences, but sorting out these differences made life that much more interesting and exotic. Since our arrival in the Marquesas, we had spent a lot of time with Robert and Nathalie.

Three days earlier, Alec had bellowed, "Land Ho!" He had let me sleep as we'd sailed the last few miles to the Marquesas Islands.

"I don't see it," I mumbled, still groggy. Then I looked to my right and gasped at the unbelievably lush green cliffs towering above us. To know we had successfully crossed 3,000 miles of the world's biggest ocean and that we were going to be able to see and talk to people other than each other, filled me with excitement.

We'd had no radio contact with anyone for the entire passage, and didn't know whom to expect at the anchorage. Eighteen yachts were anchored behind the breakwater and as we came closer we saw the unique wooden mast of *Rode Beer*.

Nathalie and Robert had stood waving from their bow as we pulled up close to them to drop our hook. Robert rowed over to help with our stern anchor and then they both came over to share passage stories. Alec cracked open some beer and cranked the music.

Rode Beer had arrived late the day before and we both needed to check in. We headed into town together, excitedly talking and running down the road with bursts of pent-up energy. The walk was a long one, but it felt good to be on terra firma again. Every inch was covered in green! The island was so lush and beautiful, with big tall mountains poking holes in the clouds and deep valleys covered completely with palm trees. Flowers grew wild everywhere and strange tiny birds accompanied us on our hike up the hill. We greeted the smiling locals, testing out our rusty French and newly-memorized Polynesian greetings.

We found the *gendarmerie,* and the men conducted the arrival formalities while Nathalie and I chatted. The small stores carried few supplies, but we perused the shelves, just in case we found something we might need.

The phones were outside the tiny post office shaded under a large mango tree. I called home, but no one answered. Alec reached his parents and chatted for a long time. It was a collect call and must have cost a fortune. His mother was extremely relieved we were safe. "Call me once a week at least," she said. This was generous and kind, but impossible. We compromised by saying we would call once a month, and not to worry until two months had passed.

That night, we had cocktails on *Rode Beer*, but went home for a quick meal and an early night. We longed for our first solid night's sleep together in 23 days.

The next afternoon we hitchhiked back into the village. Robert had noticed our barbecue and he hankered for some meat after all those weeks at sea. We bought some frozen lamb together, which he offered to cook, but on our barbecue!

We tackled the phones again and I got the news that my sister had a Cesarean section scheduled in a couple of weeks. "We have to be at a phone then," I told Alec. "If I can't be there in person, then at least I can talk to her." Alec called his sister in Australia and she told him that they wanted to come visit. Then he called his other sister in Toronto and she told him that she was pregnant, and that they too wanted to visit. I was envious that he had spoken to his entire family and they all wanted to see him, whereas I had only left a message with one of my four younger sisters.

That night we uncorked a bottle of wine bought duty-free in Panama. We talked about where we were going to sail to next. Robert took over the galley, tasting this, adding spices to that. He whipped up a sauce for the lamb from scratch. I was amazed he didn't use mixes or recipes, and I displayed our large selection of instant sauce packages from Florida. "I don't think we have those in Holland," he said, "and definitely not at those prices." Our larder was full of a wide variety of food, packaged meals, canned dinners and interesting treats. *Rode Beer's* lockers were full of the basic building blocks, from which they could produce wonderful meals. They had been sailing longer and had last provisioned in Venezuela.

We had so much to talk about.

A few days after our big argument, Alec and I moved to a large bay at Tahuata, just a short sail south of Hiva Oa. Palm trees lined the deserted white sand beach that we shared with a handful of boats. We journeyed ashore and found banana, papaya, mango and lime trees

66

growing in the wild. Only the lime trees were bearing fruit and we took as much as we needed. The water was clear and the snorkeling good. No river emptied into the bay, which made for clean water and allowed coral to grow. We scrubbed off the accumulation of goose-neck barnacles that *Madeline* had acquired on the passage – a job more enjoyable in clear water where we could see any ominous creatures, rather than imagine them.

The bay was on the leeward side of the island and protected from the trade winds. Occasionally, some clouds would make it over the ridge of protecting mountains and race down the valley as a short-lived squall. We kept a watchful eye, and usually managed to dash inside, closing windows just before it drenched us.

Alec and I sat in the cockpit as *Madeline* gently tugged on her anchor in the breeze. He began sketching designs for a wind scoop for our main hatch that would allow us to keep the hatch open even if it rained. The canvas would keep the rain out while the scoop part would direct the wind down the hatch and help keep the boat cool. I was reading a book.

"What about the complaining?" Alec asked. "How can we deal with that?"

"I'm not sure." In the morning we had snorkeled around the coral and spotted a shark. I had bitched before we left that I wasn't in the mood and bitched during the snorkel that the water was too cold. I got really upset when we sighted the shark and complained all the way back to the boat.

"Well, it's really getting me down. It's just not enjoyable doing things with you."

"I've been thinking about it. I think we have different goals." I wasn't sure how to tell him that I just wanted to live comfortably. I was happy being productive, doing the domestic chores and hanging around the boat. Alec wanted to achieve. Mediocrity was not his game. "You're always wanting to go exploring. You want more adventure."

"Alayne, we've made a huge commitment. We outfitted this boat and sailed her for months to some of the most remote islands in the world. This is a fantastic adventure," his voice started to rise. "What do you want to do? Sit on the boat reading books? We are in the fucking Marquesas Islands! This is an incredible opportunity! Of course I want adventure! What did you expect?"

"I know, I know. You're right, and I usually like to explore too, don't I?" I had to confess I wasn't normally a bookworm.

"Exactly! That's what I don't understand."

"I don't know," I replied. "I miss my family. I miss being productive. I miss medicine. I need time to myself and time to write in my journal and time to write my friends and family. I guess all these things are causing me not to be what you expect. I'm sorry."

"You just don't like it out here." His voice was low and mean.

"No! I'm enjoying myself here and I like our adventures," I stubbornly insisted, "but my adventuring comfort level is lower than yours." I felt that admitting I didn't like it would be admitting failure.

"You do seem to enjoy my expeditions, even after whining your way through them. It's just that you make the process so bloody unenjoyable. What's the solution?"

"I'm trying to improve."

"Maybe you should fly home for a visit," Alec suggested. "Then you'll see which is better."

The thought was tantalizing. But when? It would cost too much.

"Okay, let's climb that hill over there," he proposed.

"But why?" I asked looking at the steep mountain overlooking the bay.

"Why not? It's there," he replied angrily.

Alec packed a knapsack and we dinghied ashore. The air was hot and thick and the hill steep and covered in rough bushy grass. I wondered if my scratched legs would ever be attractive again, but I kept the thought to myself. We climbed to the shade of an overhanging rock at the peak. Alec surprised me with a bottle of wine and hors d'oeuvres.

Further down the coast on Tahuata we invited a local teenager, named Ronald, aboard for a visit. He told me that the Sunday church service at the neighboring village was at eight, but I wondered if I was losing something in the translation.

"*L'église est Catholique*?" I asked.

"*Oui*."

I was impressed. I hadn't expected to receive communion in such a tiny village in the middle of nowhere. The strong French influence had blended with Polynesian traditions, and most Marquesans were Roman Catholic. Ronald explained that this Sunday was "*La Fête Maman*": Mother's Day! Being a mother was very honorable, and Ronald and others we met were surprised we had no children.

I'd been grappling with my Roman Catholic upbringing even before I met Alec. He was brought up without religion, but with high personal morals, and had challenged me on the need for organized worship at the beginning of our relationship. Alec was my only friend who would answer the religion question with "atheist" instead of the more diplomatic, "agnostic".

After we managed a compromise with our wedding, the issue disappeared. He was against the tradition of marriage and for him to agree to marry in my church was difficult. However, his parents loved the traditional church wedding, he being the only of his siblings to have one. On our wedding day, his mother commented to a groomsman, "It has been such a lovely wedding, especially considering it is a mixed marriage."

Confused, Dave asked, "What do you mean by a mixed marriage?"

"You know, between a Roman Catholic," Alec's mother replied, "and... well, a nothing!"

This voyage had not made the religion issue any easier. We spent long periods of time at sea, and when we did come to an anchorage, often the island was uninhabited or had only a small village. Under these circumstances, it was difficult, if not impossible, to attend a regular Sunday church service. When the situation was favorable, I did my best, but it was hard explaining this to my mother. She strongly believed that you're not a good Catholic unless you attend church *every* Sunday. Aboard *Madeline,* I had a missal and a bible and had become comfortable in my private relationship with God. Christopher Columbus brought his own priest on board, but that wasn't practical for me!

On Mother's Day Alec accompanied me to the church so that he too could see the locals in their Sunday best. The church looked new, with colorful half-Polynesian, half-Catholic designs and slatted windows to allow the breeze through. Beautifully carved wooden beams swept dramatically upwards to form the roof with large overhangs sheltering a concrete patio. Outside there was a procession of children holding fresh flower necklaces. The children led the way to the altar, followed by two men and two women in long white robes. After reaching the front, the children individually went to all the mothers in the congregation. A pretty little girl approached me, placed a necklace around my neck and then kissed me on each cheek. I guess at my age, she thought I must be a mother already. The fragrance from the flowers was wonderful and with every breath, I smiled.

One by one a man or a woman came forward from the congregation to do a reading. I couldn't understand them, and then realized they were speaking Marquesan. The singing was in French and words like "*le Père*" and "*le Fils*" were more familiar. Then came a song of "Alleluia" and I felt at home. The harmony was extraordinary and the children sang at the tops of their voices.

After a few more readings, the procession of four robed adults genuflected in front of the altar, and walked down the aisle. The service was over. I shouldn't have expected a mass with a priest, but it wasn't until then that I realized it. I discovered a priest visits only once every two months.

I walked outside to find Alec had stayed for the hour. He had been amused watching all the well-dressed fathers minding their small children. Tables were set up for a bake sale and they even had ice cream! I really wished we had brought some money, but a wallet was a thing of the past. We were off to celebrate at "*chez Delfine*", so it was better we didn't indulge anyway.

We had met Delfine two days earlier. I saw Delfine do a reading at the church, and her husband, Nicholas, was one of the two lay ministers. Alec and I were feeling part of the local scene. We weren't sure what to expect at the celebration, but we were almost certain there would be a lot of food. Judging from Delfine's size, we figured she spent a large part of her day eating. She was huge even by Polynesian standards, but a kind hostess and a great cook.

All the food was being laid out on a long table as we arrived. I helped in the kitchen, as Alec was promptly handed a beer and seated with the men. Delfine offered me orange pop! The food was delicious, each mound displayed in its own oversized bowl. There was rice, spaghetti, barbecued chicken, noodles with pork, raw fish in coconut milk, breadfruit with a sauce for dipping, sun-dried bananas marinated in a milk sauce, fruit salad, vegetable salad, watermelon that was yellowish-orange instead of red, and of course, lots of fresh bananas. The actual names and contents of certain dishes were unknown to us, but all were delicious.

Communication was difficult since nobody spoke much English and our French was rather rusty, but their repeated requests to "*Mange! Mange!*" were understood. They expected us to eat a lot and Alec and I obliged them. The women, children and guests ate first, while the men waited several hours before eating.

Bursts of song entertained us all afternoon, with ukulele, guitar and spoons in a beer bottle providing the music for numerous Marquesan songs. We felt so welcome and relaxed with this family, and contentedly we wandered home loaded down with pamplemousse, limes and bananas.

For the next week we enjoyed visiting several anchorages at Tahuata, some with *Rode Beer* and some without. I loved our time with Nathalie and Robert, often alternating dinner or cocktails on each other's boat. Yet we still did our own thing, coming and going on our own timetable, secure in our friendship. We didn't "buddy boat" as some cruisers did. These boats would travel everywhere together, talking on the radio and advising each other. *Rode Beer* and *Madeline* often split up, without the ability to communicate because we lacked a long-distance radio. But we knew each other's approximate schedule and at worst we could ask another boat if they knew where *Rode Beer* was, because Robert was often talking on their ham radio. We knew when Robert's parents were arriving in Tahiti, so we could always see them then. As it turned out, we anchored together many nights in French Polynesia, but it was the subtle aspect of freedom in our relationship that made it successful.

After a week or so, both boats headed to the north shore of Hiva Oa, to a large bay called Hana Menu. Looking at the shore from *Madeline*, we could see that there was no village, only a few huts. Two Marquesans rowed out, and invited us and two other boats to a barbecue on the beach that afternoon. Between our sparse French, a few English words and ample hand signals, we understood they were roasting the wild pigs that they caught in the mountains the night before.

Should we bring cutlery? Plates? Vegetables? Wild boar and beer seemed right, so we replenished our little 12-volt fridge and turned it up in anticipation.

Nicholas greeted us as we pulled our dinghy up the black sand beach. In English-smattered French he explained that for ten years nobody had lived at Hana Menu. Then, about a year earlier, he had come to work the coconut plantation and make copra, which is dried coconut meat. He was young, strong, handsome and lived alone, but one day hoped to have a wife and family. Nicholas gladly accepted a cold beer from us, and introduced us to his four friends who had hiked over the mountains to have a male-bonding holiday with him.

They led us over to a mound of sand and began to unearth our dinner. They carefully peeled back large green leaves, trying to keep dirt out of the food. Nicholas explained this was an *umu*, a Polynesian underground oven. Roasted breadfruit, taro and Marquesan bananas were plucked from the pit and tossed into a large bowl. They removed another layer of leaves, exposing a steaming layer of meat that was lifted out and into a bucket. They then showed us the hot rocks under another mat of leaves that had cooked the meat for several hours.

The table had been carefully placed on the beach to avoid any unexpected falling coconuts, and they encouraged us to dip the vegetables into a mixture of coconut milk, lime, salt and garlic. Our plates helped, but we mostly ate with our hands while standing around the waist-high table. A pack of sickly hunting dogs salivated underneath it. Crude eating and a little gritty, but delicious! After we'd eaten all we could manage, Nicholas entertained us with his guitar, singing songs he had written in his native tongue about Marquesan life.

Behind the neat rows of towering coconut palms the jungle took over. We explored this area and found mossy stone foundations and stone-cobbled roads amidst the tangled growth. These were remnants of the ancient Polynesian race that had flourished in the Pacific. When the

71

Marquesas Islands were first discovered, there was a prosperous warrior nation estimated at 80,000 people. The invasion of traders, slavers, whalers and missionaries destroyed the peaceful way of life and introduced numerous diseases. Tuberculosis, syphilis and others decimated the population and now only 5,000 people occupied the same islands. The population was growing again, but the young people were leaving to work in Tahiti and other countries.

We could see that a thriving population must have once lived in the valley. We asked Nicholas about the ruins and he went to his hut and produced an old bone. He said he'd mounted some bones above the door to his hut, until the *gendarmes* came and told him to take them down or they would put him in jail. He laughed.

"It looks human," I whispered to Alec, and then we both suddenly understood the warning that Delfine had given us.

When we were leaving the party on Tahuata, we had told Delfine that we planned to go to Hana Menu on Hiva Oa. She'd begun acting strange, warning us not to go. We'd asked her why, but in her excitement we had trouble translating what she meant. She kept saying Nicholas was crazy, that he was digging graves and eating the bones. At the time we were confused, because Nicholas was Delfine's husband, a lay minister! Only now we suddenly knew that she meant a different Nicholas. The person she had meant was standing in front of us waving a human bone! It was Nicholas at Hana Menu.

I asked Nicholas where he got the bone.

"*Le cimetière.*" He gestured towards the jungle. "*Beaucoup.*" He didn't want to talk about it anymore.

WILD HORSES

"WHAT ARE WE GOING TO DO?" I asked back on *Madeline*. "Should we heed Delfine's warning?"

"Wild horses couldn't drag me away," Alec hummed in response. He was having a great time and didn't care.

Nicholas' four Marquesan friends each planned to catch a wild horse while at Hana Menu to ride over the mountains back home to Atuona. Three were already caught, and they were keen to catch another. Nicholas had invited Alec and Robert to join them the next morning. I was just as happy not to be invited.

"For once Alec can have some serious adventuring without expecting me to enthusiastically participate. I get to do what I like – to have another long chat with Nathalie. Having her to talk to is really helping keep things in perspective for me. We're both experiencing this trip in a similar way that's different from our men. We have the same concerns and worries, and the same desire to chat idly about ourselves, our families or anything, significant or not."

The guys arrived on the beach at dawn to find the other "hunters" quite relaxed. Surprisingly there was another feast prepared, to precede the hunt. They served Polynesian-sized helpings of shrimp, crab, baguettes, rice, smoked fish and coffee. With all the food, Alec wondered just how strenuous this day was going to be.

Alec and Robert claimed that the hike up the switchbacks to the plateau was grueling, and their body odor afterward verified it. The rolling plateau was covered in dense brush, usually waist high, but often well over their heads. Hiking in the tropical sun was tough going but spotting the horses was wonderful. At one point they saw a group of five horses, four mares and one beautiful black stallion. Alec said they looked so majestic in the wild. The two groups watched each other for a moment and then the mares tossed their manes and trotted away. The black stallion, coat glistening and nostrils flaring, stayed back a bit and took one more look before they all disappeared into the brush. The men continued their search never getting close enough. Tramping through tall heavy growth, they decided to head back to the valley.

Suddenly, they heard what sounded like an avalanche – they had startled a group of horses from their resting place under a tree. The mare they had brought with them was quickly led through the bush to the wild horses. This horse had been washed down in the morning to remove any human scent and the plan was to use her as a lure. Alec had been carrying a long pole they'd cut in the valley from which a long rope was hung in a loop. One unsuspecting stallion took the bait and approached the mare. Nicholas took the pole and sneaked up from the other side of the mare, quickly placing the rope over the stallion's head. The horse went wild, bucking and trying to run, but the noose got tighter and tighter. The mare was rushed away while the guys desperately held onto the other end of the noose. They wrapped the rope around a tree, using it like a winch, and eventually the horse was strangled into submission.

"That was the dangerous part," Alec said, "but I couldn't imagine how the heck we were ever going to get this horse off the plateau and down the switchbacks to the valley." After a simple rope bridle was in place, Nicholas led the mare before the stallion, and amazingly, the stallion followed with little fight. "Stupid males," Nathalie commented afterward. "They're all the same."

Meanwhile, back in the valley, Nathalie and I had begun slaving away with the laundry, after a leisurely morning over coffee. Not far from the beach was a beautiful, crystal-clear, freshwater pool at the base of a waterfall. Chilly water poured from a spring about fifty feet up the side of the cliff. The whole area was nestled in lush bushes bursting with hibiscus and other tropical flowers.

Wearing bathing suits and standing knee deep in the pool, we scrubbed our clothes on the rocks. I could feel a pinching around my feet and on closer inspection discovered the pool was teeming with small shrimp. They were cleaning dead skin from our toes! We moved our scrubbing to the pond's edge and were having a pleasant day in this natural wonderland, when the wild horse wranglers came running and howling into the pool. They were filthy and covered with burrs and sweat. I couldn't blame these cowboys for cooling off in our laundry basin.

I asked Alec if he could feel the shrimp biting. "Yeah. They were delicious for breakfast," he replied. We managed to clean the clothes and the men, and then filled water jugs to take back to *Madeline*. Nicholas had rigged a hose direct from where the water poured out of the mountain; this hose ran all day long with pure spring water.

After more food, the Marquesans regaled us with a story about the last pig they had caught using the dogs to corner the pig while one of the guys sneaked up behind it and knifed it in the stomach. They produced the knife for the re-enactment, and displayed the jawbones that sprouted large tusks as the final proof of their success. Many of the dogs bore grisly gashes as testimony to the fight and I had noticed one dog skulking under a hut with a large belly wound leaking entrails.

Nicholas asked Robert and Alec if they wanted to go into the mountains to catch a wild boar. Alec and Robert were tempted, but exhausted, and when they learned the expedition would begin at midnight, they declined.

After five days and more feasts on the beach of Hana Menu, we decided to sail to Nuku Hiva. Two of the Marquesans came out to *Madeline* to wish us goodbye. We drank some beer and listened to music. Alec asked what music they liked.

"BO-ma-LEE," they responded automatically.

I was puzzled, but Alec immediately put on a Bob Marley CD. They were delighted. He gave a cassette tape as a gesture of our thanks to the young man nicknamed "Maman", because he did most of the cooking.

Maman bragged that he had many Bob Marley tapes and even some CDs back in his village. The Marquesas were strange in that way. The locals had ample food from the land and sea, and were fairly well off due to the money spent by the French government. But the islands were so remote that money was of limited value because there was hardly anything to buy. Thinking ahead before leaving Canada, we had brought every T-shirt we owned and the trading had been working well. From our materialistic viewpoint the Marquesans might be poor. But were they?

It was an overnight sail to the island of Nuku Hiva, the capital of the Marquesas Islands. Arriving at dawn, we scanned each boat in the large bay until we spotted *Wado Ryu*. We motored circles around them honking our horn, until Klaus came running out stark naked, yelling, "Nu-Ku-Hi-Va, Nu-Ku-Hi-Va!"

Over Panamanian coffee, Galapagos hard-boiled eggs, German smoked meats, Dutch cheese, and French baguettes, Klaus and Claudia related their difficult trip from the Galapagos. They had the misfortune of breaking their self-steering gear with 1,100 miles still to go. They hand-steered for more than a week, and were absolutely exhausted when they arrived. Klaus tried repairing the equipment, but without luck. Claudia found the steering wheel heavy and tiring, but kept up with her share of three-hour shifts, steering by the Southern Cross in the night sky. I admired her strength.

It was a business week for us in Nuku Hiva, filled with faxes, letter writing, bureaucracy, and phone calls. I was able to call home to hear the news of the birth of my sister Joslyn's second baby. Joslyn asked me to be little Matthew's Godmother, which I quickly accepted, but she also asked if I could be home for the baptism in a few weeks. It hurt me to tell her no, and although it was technically feasible, it was out of our budget. She had no idea of what we were doing, the places we were visiting, and how far away we had already sailed.

"She didn't ask me to be the Godfather, I hope." Alec said.

"No, she wouldn't put you through that. She did ask if I would come home. I would like to see everyone again."

"Maybe we should give that idea more thought," he replied.

We sailed to the island of Ua Pou, with its spectacular columns of rock resembling canine teeth projecting skyward from the mountains. They were the cores of ancient volcanoes that remained after the earth around them had eroded.

A cruiser approached me with questions about a local mosquito-borne disease called filariasis. Dan, on *Reverie*, had heard I was a doctor and wanted my advice as to whether he and his family should take the preventative medications provided free at the local clinic.

He said, "If you take the pills, we will too. We're waiting to see what you decide."

I hadn't heard of the disease and it hadn't been mentioned at our extensive travel clinic visits before we left Toronto. With Nathalie as my personal interpreter, we interrogated the young French doctor at Ua Pou. He was completing his military service, was full of information and eager to talk with us. Within an hour, both Nathalie and I had become the experts on filariasis for the whole cruising community.

Filariasis is a parasite that is transmitted to humans by infected mosquitoes. The disease is prevalent throughout the South Pacific, and one of the long-term complications is elephantiasis. For a short-term visitor, or tourist, the risk was quite low. The disease could only be transmitted by a mosquito that had first bitten someone with the active disease, before biting you. The handful of cases in the islands were mostly identified, under treatment, and therefore not infectious. Still, the doctor and I had difficulty deciding whether the risk aboard a boat was high enough to warrant taking the pills.

Alec joined us afterward over coffee in the doctor's lounge. When the doctor explained that elephantiasis could specifically affect the male genitals, with the scrotum becoming so large that it hangs down to ankle level, Alec's mind was made up! "Where are those pills? I'm taking them!" The chance of side effects was minimal, so we took the pills and Dan got on his long-distance radio to inform all the cruisers via the radio nets.

Months later Dan told us that a cruising couple had approached him after the filariasis episode had died down. "We heard that you're a medical doctor," they said apologetically, "but we wondered if you could help us with our sick cat?" The story ended happily, because although Dan had to admit he was not a doctor, he was an experienced cat owner and he solved their problem.

The Tuamotus are a group of islands barely visible from the sea as they are made up of coral and sand, with the tallest structures being palm trees. The Polynesian name translates to dangerous islands. In the past they were avoided by sailors because of the strong currents around them and the difficulty in spotting them. Arrival after daybreak was critical and often trips were timed to correspond with the full moon for improved visibility at night. The commonly visited islands were at the northwestern end of the chain, which allowed for a quick abort to the north if conditions weren't favorable. However, with the advent of GPS, a direct satellite navigation system that continuously updated our position, the Tuamotus were now more accessible.

GPS was more accurate than our charts, so we still had to be very careful, but with the confidence we had in this newly developed system, only affordable the previous year, we decided to travel off the beaten path to an island called Makemo. Our GPS, which Alec nicknamed "G-O-D", was one of the key reasons a young, inexperienced couple like us could now cross vast oceans. Alec claimed he could navigate by the sun and moon, but when he did dust off our plastic sextant to do his celestial shots, he was never very accurate. He could do it, but I was thankful that our lives did not rely on it, as they would have for sailors only a decade earlier.

The Tuamotus are much older than the Marquesas; ancient mountains that had receded into the ocean leaving only the surrounding reef. These atolls are circular rings of islands, each circle having an inner lagoon with one or two entrances from the sea, known as passes. The lagoon can be quite large, the larger ones upwards of 400 square miles. The infamous Mururoa, blown up with nuclear bombs by the French for decades, is an atoll in the southeast of the archipelago.

We had to time our entry through the pass with the tides, as the peak current running through some of them could be nine knots! We had the help of a guidebook called *Charlie's Charts*, with invaluable sketches of many anchorages in Polynesia.

Excitedly I spotted the palm trees on Makemo and called out to Alec. I was relieved that the passage from Ua Pou would soon be over. The wind had been stronger than the trip to the Marquesas and all our dishes from the past three days were stacked in the galley sink as a testament to the rough weather. We had been sailing on a fast beam reach, knowing *Rode Beer* would be soon following us. Despite my seasickness and the uncomfortable ride, it was only three days. Although many of the same fears plagued me, I could tough it out for a short passage.

I thought of a girlfriend of mine who had spent a year backpacking with her husband, spending 24 hours a day together, everyday. She had said there wasn't one moment when she wanted to be away from him. Envious as I was, our circumstances were vastly different. All my possessions, my lover and I were contained inside a tiny 33-by-15-foot boat, which was put to the mercy of the wind, waves and weather. The only certainties were that things would break and the wind would change. With an added dash of seasickness, a little thunderstorm or a ripped sail, a kind of stress was created that would cause even the most pleasant of people to get irritable. Alec and I dealt with crisis differently and this often aggravated things even at the best of times.

Alec calculated a moderate outflowing current, and when we reached the pass, we began to motor against it without too much difficulty. But at the end of the pass we entered into a large area of huge standing waves. They resembled moguls from a ski hill, the bumps the size of small cars, with lots of white froth all around. *Madeline* was wildly tossed about. Little yelps of panic were coming from my mouth. I screamed to Alec over the laboring engine. He was directing me from the bow, barely holding on as *Madeline* flung him about. The waves were angry, spewing foam and water all over the place.

"Keep going!" he shouted, raising his thumb indicating higher engine speed, while laughing and hooting. He wasn't wearing a harness, and I imagined him getting tossed overboard and then swept out to sea by the current. The sharks were always thickest outside the pass, and a struggling swimmer would make a nice snack.

Slowly we motored out of the rough water and into the lagoon. We began picking our way through coral patches towards the village two miles away. Alec stood at the bow scanning the water while I steered, following his hand signals. Many couples did otherwise, largely because the man did not want to give up the perceived leadership of being at the helm. Alec always offered me either job, but steering gave me a greater sense of control and placed him at the anchor where physical strength was more important. Even though I was at the wheel, I knew it was the person at the bow who had a better vantage point to spot submerged coral and who was truly responsible for the boat's safety.

Entering Makemo had taken its toll and I was very wound up. I felt trepidation over the last few miles to the anchorage and I eased the throttle back. I had to verbally release my stress and I couldn't help talking non-stop, constantly commenting on our progress. Alec indicated increased speed, and I reluctantly obliged. I could see his euphoria fading and he glared back at me a couple of times. He indicated left, and hollered back.

"Don't yell at me!" I responded.

He angrily stomped back to me. "If I don't yell, you can't hear me over the engine noise!" he yelled.

"You're still yelling." I said.

"Arrgh!" he was exasperated. "Look, I indicated left, but you didn't turn left!"

"But there's coral over there."

"That's about half a mile away! I'm more concerned about the coral patch in front of us! Who's driving? If you don't trust me, then *you* go to the bow and I'll follow *your* signals."

"No, I'll keep steering."

"So you prefer it with me at the bow?" I nodded. "Then work with me, and stop slowing the boat down. I can hear when you decrease the revs, you know."

"Why do we have to go so fast?"

"Five knots isn't fast. I want to get there. And the slower we go, the more the current pushes us in the wrong direction." He went back to the bow and eventually we dropped the anchor safely outside the village. I was exhausted.

After Alec finished putting the bridle on the anchor chain, he came back into the shaded cockpit. He removed his hat and sunglasses, and I could see he was still annoyed. "So what's the scoop with all this babbling?"

"I can't help it," I replied. "I release my stress by talking."

"Come on Alayne! When we try to anchor, something that we've done dozens of times, you turn into a babbling fool."

"It's a stressful situation. I'm scared."

"But you're an emergency room doctor! Surely you don't start babbling when they wheel in a trauma patient?"

"Well, no. But with the boat I'm afraid that I'm going to do something stupid. I'm going to mess up and create a disaster."

"But in a real crisis, like when we lost the forestay, you were great. You handle emergencies very well, just like I'm sure you did in the hospital."

"I did babble a bit when we lost the forestay," I responded, sitting down on the opposite side of the cockpit.

"It seems I have more confidence in you than you have in yourself. I know that if something goes wrong you'll manage fine. Why can't you have the same self-confidence?"

"I get excited. I can't help it. I thought you like that I'm excitable."

"I do, but not in these situations. It's the exact opposite of what I expect."

"I noticed. Is that why you tell me to shut up? You have just as hard a time controlling your temper as I have controlling my emotions."

"You start my temper going. In a crisis situation my first rule of thumb is to stay calm. And to quote *The Hitchhiker's Guide to the Galaxy*, 'DON'T PANIC'. I need quiet to think about the situation and then I take action."

"Yeah, you think and think and think. Those long pauses are painful. Why don't you tell me what you're thinking? That's what a woman would do. Your silence drives me crazy." In these situations silence made my mind race. I had to fill it by talking.

"Yeah, if I was a woman, we'd probably hit the coral, but at least we'd both feel good about it! Look at it from my perspective. I want to block you out. But sometimes you do tell me something important, so I must listen to you. But what drives me nuts is that I find myself responding when you're not really asking me a question, just talking!"

The village was two streets wide by half a dozen long, and we followed the main one past modest houses to an open square on the ocean side. We found the bakery, but discovered all the baguettes had been accounted for. We put in an order for the next morning. The village was preparing for the Bastille Day celebrations; booths were being constructed, costumes sewn and marching bands practiced each night. We met many friendly locals, and enjoyed their gifts of fish and coconuts. We gave them fruit from the Marquesas, which wasn't available on these dry sandy islands.

The wind was still strong and the anchorage was deep, on a lee shore and rolly. We tried to put the anchor on a sand patch, but some chain still grated on the coral bottom, making for uneasy sleeping.

A local told us of two small but beautiful islands about eight miles away on the windward side of the lagoon. Without a chart and only able to see a speck of a palm tree marking each island, we set out after a few days, with Alec again at the bow directing me at the helm.

With less coral patches to avoid, I felt more relaxed and Alec chatted with me while keeping a lookout. The lagoon was mostly deep, but here and there columns of coral rose to a few inches of the surface. Alec pointed out the patches as soon as he spotted them and we worked well together. As we got closer we saw that these little islands in the sun were a perfect private paradise. They were behind the lagoon's barrier reef, leaving us in a safe and peaceful anchorage. The full fury of the Pacific Ocean crashed continuously on the barrier reef, roaring it's disapproval and sending up angry spumes of foam, giving the anchorage a surreal quality unlike any other. Each island was only a few hundred feet long with a scattering of palm trees and bushes, and pink sand beaches. Immediately we dove into the transparent water and snorkeled the shallows, enjoying the greens, purples, blues, yellows and oranges of the coral.

The next afternoon our privacy disappeared with the arrival of an Australian boat, *Juslookin' 2*. We had to put our clothes back on, but we enjoyed the visiting. We used *Juslookin's* SSB radio and found out that *Rode Beer* had entered the lagoon at the other pass.

The next day we chased the whitecaps across the lagoon, past the village and towards the other end of the atoll. We were dodging coral heads for most of the 25 miles but it became difficult to see as the sun crossed the sky and reflected into our eyes. I could feel my stress level rising, but Alec counteracted it by making jokes and deflecting my silly questions. It worked so well that he coaxed me into anchoring under sail next to our Dutch friends. We dropped our hook in eight feet of sand behind a palm-laden beach. I loved knowing that *Madeline* was absolutely secure and we could sleep deeply and untroubled. We dove off the boat, swam past captivating coral and climbed onto *Rode Beer*. Nathalie told me they had just celebrated their first wedding anniversary. The two of us talked until sunset.

The coral in front of *Madeline* was full of fish, including delicious grouper. Alec decided it was time to try spear fishing. It was a moral dilemma because we both enjoyed snorkeling for pleasure. In places where spear fishing was common, the fish were skittish and timid. In remote places such as this the fish were often curious, coming out of hiding to look at us. Spear fishing sometimes seemed akin to clubbing baby seals. Although trolling for fish was often gory, the mind rationalized it differently. The fish initiated the process by taking the hook, and you landed the fish in your environment. With spear fishing, however, you were in the fish's environment watching it swim along, and then violently shooting a pointed rod through its body.

Alec found spearing fish to be more challenging than spearing lobster in the Bahamas, and there was some primal satisfaction he felt in living off the sea. He enjoyed the thrill of the hunt, but we only caught what we could eat. More importantly, it gave both of us an appreciation of what we ate and where it came from. Before, we were

far removed from the process. When I bought packaged boneless, skinless meat in a supermarket, it was easy to forget that an animal had lived and died. I now felt more appreciative.

Lazy days were passed snorkeling, exploring ashore and socializing. The focal point was Alec and Robert's daily trip to the coral heads to get lunch and dinner. I had lost count of all the meals back and forth on each other's boats.

Juslookin' 2 and *Rode Beer* hoisted anchor and sailed for the western pass out of the lagoon. We followed behind shortly after and I noticed how different each boat was. There was a ferrocement ketch, a steel sloop and a fiberglass catamaran; each capable of sailing around the world. We made it through the turbulent pass, the current pushing us out quickly.

Instead of going to Tahiti like the others, we headed to another atoll in the Tuamotus called Fakarava. It was a difficult sail because it required weaving between the atolls at night. The atolls blocked the normal ocean flow causing strong unpredictable currents. Just after midnight we lost sight of the other two boats. We turned north, sailing between the islands, carefully checking and rechecking the course Alec had plotted on the chart. The GPS would calculate immediately when the current pushed us off track and we tweaked the autopilot to bring us back on course.

The seas were calm because the islands blocked the swell. There was a nice breeze and *Madeline* was sailing beautifully. During my night watches I was constantly scanning the horizon for breakers and listening for surf crashing on the reef. I used all my senses for any information – with sounds becoming especially important. Staying awake was easy that night.

When we arrived at the village anchorage, a large 160-foot Navy boat was our only companion. We thought they were customs officials, and within minutes of our arrival, a group of six approached us in their dinghy. Alec groaned as we reminisced about our U.S. Coast Guard experience. One of them spoke English quite well, and he said the group was going into the village to play soccer with the locals. "Maybe we'll see you later," he said.

At the pier we saw the group again, and Alec began a conversation with the same English-speaking guy. "What's your position on the boat?" Alec asked.

"I'm the Captain," he stated. I thought he was joking; he looked so young. He told us his name was Bertrand and when he invited us aboard for cocktails that night, we gladly accepted.

Our outboard had died despite numerous attempts at resuscitation by more knowledgeable cruisers. We rowed everywhere now, which was fine, until an oar went missing one stormy night at Makemo. Alec constructed another oar out of a mangrove tree, which looked pretty funny, but worked. So here we were, at Fakarava, rowing over to a French Navy ship with a huge gun on its foredeck, using our mangrove oar. The crew watched from the deck while we laughed at ourselves. I grabbed onto the rope ladder and scaled the fifteen feet up to the deck, glad we had a long painter on the dinghy. Alec followed me up full of smiles and the crew tied our dinghy behind the ship. We had found the long rope on the beach at Makemo while searching for our lost oar. I thought of how resourceful we'd become, finding a use for everything and making do with what was available.

Bertrand, the captain, introduced us to the three other officers and we were eager to get first-hand information on anchorages in Tahiti and the rest of the Society Islands. We found it quite amusing when Bertrand left the room in search of his own personal guide to these islands, to share with us, and returned with *Charlie's Charts*! It was the same guidebook all the cruisers used, but even more astounding was that his was photocopied. After a pleasant visit in the officer's lounge, Bertrand asked if we would like to join them the next day for a tour, "à midi". Why not?

Once again I was in a situation where I had no idea what to expect. I faced this everyday, but at least this time, it turned out better than I could have hoped. We rowed back over to the ship at noon and were led to the lounge for cocktails, and appetizers of chips, nuts and pizza. Next we moved to the dining table, complete with white linen, china, silver and crystal water goblets. We were served smoked swordfish with fresh lime on the side and a chilled Alsace white wine.

The steward then came in and asked how we would like our steaks! Alec's face lit up; we hadn't had red meat in months. A bottle of Bordeaux was opened and the steaks arrived with *frites*, accompanied by warm Roquefort dressing. All this was followed by an assortment of cheeses, including Brie, Gouda, blue, and fresh baguettes. My favorite part was a crunchy praline-coated ball of vanilla ice cream with a meringue center. We moved back to the lounge for coffee, before the tour of the ship. I felt I had just eaten at the finest restaurant in French Polynesia.

As parting gifts, they gave me a locally-weaved hat and Alec a regulation, French Navy oar, in battleship gray. Alec was in heaven and his attitude towards Navy boats had changed forever.

The wind on our next passage was strong initially, but gave us a very pleasant downwind sail, and we spotted the lights of Tahiti on the second night. The high island was visible even though we were still far away. The wind died completely early in the morning and we motored the rest of the way into Papeete's harbor. This was Alec's dream come true. "I can't believe we're actually here," he said.

He wanted to tie up at the quay, but I was not keen on all the maneuvering with everyone watching. "We are in Tahiti," he explained. "That's just what is done. You have to tie up at the quay in Papeete. It's one of life's moments."

We motored up and down the line looking for a spot, waving to the boats we knew. The quay was full and only the beach was available, which meant inflating the dinghy and a lot of motoring in reverse while a long line was taken ashore. We watched all the motor scooters and cars racing along the street next to the quay, spitting out smoke and noise. Alec conceded and we motored another five miles down the coast to anchor off the Maeva Beach Hotel. I was much happier, especially because *Rode Beer* was there.

We took *Le Truck* into Papeete, the capital, and after checking in with customs and immigration we found the American Express office. Three large packages from home were waiting for us. I checked the contents and chose a letter to read immediately on a bench in the shade. When we got back to *Madeline*, we opened a bottle of wine and sipped while alternately reading the letters to each other. Taking a break, we invited ourselves to *Rode Beer* for dinner. We brought freshly caught marlin and they cooked it. After dinner we stayed up late, savoring more mail. I loved hearing what everyone was up to.

"I've been thinking more about a trip home," I told Alec.

"Me too. I think the best time for you to go would be after we get to New Zealand. Probably after Christmas, in February. Of course that is winter in Canada," he laughed.

"I want to see my family, my girlfriends and especially my little Godchild, but I'm also worried about my medical skills. I already feel like I've forgotten everything. If I worked while at home I could polish up and make enough money to cover the airfare and expenses. It wouldn't affect our cruising budget."

"I think we have enough frequent-flyer points that you could fly free." Alec had accumulated points through his credit card.

"I could work in Windsor, and stay with my parents." My father and two of my sisters were doctors in my hometown, and I was sure they could find me work.

"Actually, a little earned income would be favorable from a tax standpoint," Alec reasoned.

"But, what would you do?"

"I'll hang out with Betty-Lou, Lady Jane, *Madeline* and all the other boats! Seriously, that is when I would haul out *Mad* and work on her in a boat yard." Our list of maintenance jobs for New Zealand was already growing.

"Should I write home and have them book me some work?"

"Good idea."

Suddenly I felt much better. *"What's changed? I don't miss my family anymore. Just knowing that I'll see them in six months makes everything different. Waiting three years would have been too long, with too much uncertainty and death-defying sailing before I'd see them again. But now it's decided. If they won't come to me, I'll go to them."*

Wild horses could drag me away, but I was much happier for it.

INTO THE CRUISING LIFE

BEEEEEEP, BEEP! BEEP! The motorcycle weaved by, leaving me with the smell of coco butter, hibiscus and burning oil. As much as I loved nature and the outdoors, I got a certain thrill from being in the bustling city of Papeete. We were well into the cruising rhythm, and the best part of Tahiti was the friendliness and the neighborly feeling we had with the other boats. We had become part of a close-knit community of about 200 people. We couldn't go anywhere in town without running into another cruiser, and if anything exciting or especially dangerous had happened, everyone was buzzing. There was a lot of gossip of course, and it could go full circle, until someone was telling you a story, about yourself!

It was our third wedding anniversary, and this year it was my turn to surprise Alec. We rode rented mountain bikes along the coast, stopping for a picnic lunch, and then riding fifteen miles out to swim in wonderful waterfalls. Just as we finished a private skinny dip, a group of 20 tourists arrived! The day's exercise felt great on our thinning thighs, and we topped the celebration off with a rare dinner out.

A week quickly disappeared as we visited the ship's chandler and made some major repairs on *Madeline*. Alec bought a toggle for the forestay and reworked the repairs he'd done en route to the Marquesas. We purchased a new outboard motor, since we knew we couldn't row everywhere once our guests arrived.

Pat Helps, the owner and skipper of the boat we raced on during our Toronto summers, joined us for two weeks with his friend Della. After cruising north through the Society Islands, Pat and Della flew back to Tahiti from Bora Bora. They were great guests, very easy-going and keen to explore with Alec and to chat long hours with me. They brought us mail, wind generator parts, countless gifts and goodies from home, as well as many presents from each of them. We enjoyed having them on board, but there was an extra tension between Alec and me.

"The most obvious problem with having guests is the lack of privacy. Clearly there's a lack of sexual privacy on our open-concept boat, but there's also less opportunity to talk through our problems. We're still sorting out our cruising relationship, and having guests is disrupting the progress.

There are some clear benefits – our petty arguments have ceased. There's always someone to talk to when we're anchoring and this cuts the tension. Alec is less frustrated because I'm not bothering him, and he's in good form because he has an audience."

The vacation atmosphere was a welcome change, but after two weeks I was ready to continue passage-making on our own.

The Cook Islands is a separate country that receives protection and aid from New Zealand. Because of that influence, the local people speak English with a Kiwi accent. It would be a pleasant change to converse easily with the locals.

It was an enjoyable four-day, downwind sail from Bora Bora to Aitutaki in the Cook Islands. We safely negotiated the long, narrow, turbulent pass. There were only a few boats in the tiny inner harbor, and we laid out multiple anchors to reduce swinging.

Once *Madeline* was secure I could relax and take in the scene. A thin white line of surf separated the turquoise waters of the lagoon from the indigo ocean. The shore was lined with tall, graceful palms blowing invitingly in the steady trade-wind breeze. Our past few months had been spent enjoying the predictable weather in the tropics, with blue skies, scattered puffy white clouds and a gentle southeast wind. During our first trip ashore we phoned Alec's parents.

"How's the weather?" Alec's mother asked. It seemed an odd question at the time, because after so many sunshine-filled weeks I had come to take it for granted.

We went for an evening of local dancing at the hotel, and arrived back at *Madeline* after midnight – well past our usual cruising bedtime. The boats had spun around and *Madeline* was in a completely different place. Jurgen, from the neighboring *Bullwinkel,* dinghied over when he saw us return.

"There is a storm coming," he said. "The wind shifted and your stern anchor must have dragged, so I tied a line from your stern to my line on the shore. You'll be okay now." Cruisers were great that way. So helpful, and friendly, when we were practically strangers. I felt negligent, as we weren't even listening to the weather forecasts anymore. Sometimes the wind was more or less, but had always been from the same direction.

We left things as they were, but as the wind increased, we were awake checking our position every hour. The next day was dedicated to anchor watch for all the boats in the little harbor. We played anchor roulette with the howling wind as it clocked through all the points on the compass. During the worst, *Madeline* was exposed to waves coming across the lagoon, and she rocked back and forth, pulling the lines taut. She shook in the gusts and we crossed our fingers hoping the anchors would hold. Jurgen stood on deck leaning into the wind with his hand-held anemometer. He yelled to us that the wind was over forty knots.

It took several days for the weather to settle so we rented a scooter and had fun with a young couple who were backpacking. I was getting anxious to leave, as we'd heard so much about our next destination, Palmerston Island. Finally by Friday, the thick clouds lifted and the sunny trade-wind skies were back.

"You shoulda nevera leava ona a Friaday!" said Lauretta, shaking her finger. Lauretta was a wonderfully Italian cruiser from the boat *Messer Polo*, traveling with her husband, Vincenzo, and their sixteen-year-old son, Marco. There were six yachts at Aitutaki for most of the week, with three of us leaving for Palmerston Atoll once the weather was right.

"We're not going to let an old superstition interfere with our good judgment," I told Lauretta. "We've been waiting for this weather all week. It's a perfect day to leave on a passage." Many of the cruisers wouldn't set out on a Friday for fear of bad luck. Lauretta went on to tell us that in Italian tradition, they didn't leave on Tuesdays or Fridays. "No wonder *Messer Polo* often spends weeks, even months, at anchor," I whispered to Alec.

As we stowed away our gear in preparation, we watched the cargo ship anchored outside the pass. Containers were being unloaded onto barges. In turn, these barges were towed by tugs into the harbor. Since the pass was so narrow, we had to time our exit when no barges were coming or going.

We started up the engine, and began to gather the mess of anchors still in place from the storm. They were all well embedded in awkward positions. We hoisted the last anchor and quickly turned to follow a barge out the pass.

Our engine suddenly sputtered to a stop. We were halfway down the pass. Alec quickly tried to restart it, but it wouldn't fire. He peered into the engine room, and yelled, "I don't know what's wrong with it!"

My mind raced as the current rapidly swept us down the reef-lined pass. "What should I do, Alec?" Without the engine we couldn't steer! There was no time to hoist a sail. "Should I drop an anchor?"

"Yeah. Do that. Drop an anchor!"

The engine refused to start, but the anchor took hold, spinning us around in the strong current. I glanced back to see the next tug heading for the pass. If the tug got up to speed in the pass, there would be unpleasant consequences. I called on the radio to *Messer Polo*, asking for help.

Young Marco dropped his father off at *Madeline*, and then raced to head off the tug. Unable to speak English, Marco frantically signaled to the tug skipper and got his message across. In the meantime, Alec got the engine started again, and we picked up the anchor and beached *Madeline* at the edge of the narrow pass on a patch of white sand. Vincenzo ran an anchor out with his dinghy, to make sure the current didn't push us back into the pass.

I breathed a sigh of relief. Both Alec and I were perplexed that we had purposely driven *Madeline* aground, but it was the only alternative. Vincenzo quickly discovered a lot of water in our fuel filter and after draining it, the engine roared to life. Alec changed the filter; the water was likely from the fuel we had bought in the islands.

"We are ready – once again – to leave for Palmerston," he declared.

Lauretta had joined the confusion aboard *Madeline*, and she shook her finger at us. "Ia tol' you, nevera leava ona a Friaday!" She insisted we now wait a day, enticing us with an authentic Italian meal on *Messer Polo*. Maybe she was right, but the weather was absolutely perfect.

We made it through the pass, but the standing waves on the ocean side buried the bow in water two or three times as *Madeline* rode up and down the roller coaster of turbulence.

We refused to believe this episode had anything to do with a Friday. "Things always break on a boat, and misadventures always occur. That's what makes it fun!" Alec said, although I didn't exactly see his logic. I couldn't resist searching our logbook to see if we'd ever left on a Friday before. Remarkably, there was only one other time, a few days before we had ripped off our outdrive in the Bahamas. Coincidence?

"This is Palmerston Island to the sailing vessel approaching Palmerston." After two days at sea, we could barely see a smudge on the horizon, so we wondered how they could see our sails. "Will you be calling in at Palmerston?"

Assuming it was us they were calling, we answered. "Yes, we're looking forward to it."

As we came around the south side of the atoll, we doubted our position. There was a beautiful island covered with palm trees and surrounded by white sand beach, but it looked uninhabited. However, a skiff approached, as the man on the radio had promised. David, Bill, Goodly and Goodly's youngest daughter Nano boarded *Madeline*. They were eager to have us sign their guestbook and we discovered that out of hundreds of cruising boats touring the South Pacific, we were only the fourteenth to come that year. They were pleased we would stay, because as the guestbook attested, many deep-draft monohulls only stopped briefly.

On June 16th 1774 Captain Cook discovered Palmerston Island during his second voyage to the Pacific. He named the island in honor of the First Lord of the Admiralty, Lord Palmerston. He didn't land on the island until his third and final voyage in 1777. Although the atoll was uninhabited at the time, ancient graves and other evidence were found indicating previous habitation.

The story of the current residents begins with a man named William Marsters. There's more than one version, as the tale has changed over the years, but it's generally accepted that he was born in 1821 in England. At the age of fourteen he ran away to a life at sea, working as crew aboard a ship. Eventually his travels took him to the South Pacific, where he jumped ship at one of the Northern Cook Islands. There he married the chief's daughter and, in good Polynesian polygamous fashion, took along her cousin as well. They and some others came to the uninhabited Palmerston Island in 1864, hired to plant a coconut plantation. Eventually the cargo ships stopped coming and for many years they remained isolated, but continued to work the plantation. The owner of the island had passed away, and in lieu of wages owed, the estate gave the island to Marsters. He took a third wife, when her husband deserted her there. Thus, the Marsters family began: three wives, with three separate families, all apparently living in harmony. William Marsters had seventeen children in all, with 54 grandchildren and so on. There were now sixth generation Marsters on the island.

William Marsters was a strict man – with rules regarding everything, including inbreeding. Many of his children and grandchildren married people from the other Cook Islands, and as a result, the now over 2,000 Marsters lived elsewhere, many in New Zealand and Australia, with only 50 or 60 still on the main island of the atoll. When William died in 1899, he left Palmerston Atoll divided equally among the three families. There are 35 small islands that circle a central lagoon eight miles across. The main island is about one mile long by half a mile wide and is also divided into three, with the

"windward, middle and leeward" families still living in separate sections.

Apart from the island's beauty and unique story, the hospitality and the generosity of the people were unmatched. It began that very first day. While we were finishing up with refreshments aboard *Madeline*, the four Marsters asked if they could show us their village.

I asked Alec if he could grab my sandals, and Goodly Marsters said, "Why do you need shoes?"

His question surprised me. "Aren't there corals or rocks on your beach?" I asked.

"No," he responded, "it's all sand."

Sand it was. Fine and soft, the kind bare feet love sinking into. It didn't stop at the beach – the whole village was on pure white sand, including the streets, the gardens, the houses, the church and even the graveyard. The streets were meticulously manicured – they raked them daily. They had planted the palm trees carefully and new shoots were neatly boxed in. The people loved their island, and it showed. Clear water, white sand beaches, glorious colors of coral and curious fish in all varieties made it truly a paradise. Few see this paradise, as there wasn't an airstrip, and to anchor in the safety of the lagoon you needed a shallow draft like *Madeline*.

As we walked by the church, Goodly told us more of the island's story. William Marsters had left them with religion, and all three families strictly adhered to Sunday services and daily prayers. I noticed they practiced the Presbyterian faith, and I asked if William had been

Presbyterian. "We don't know for sure," Goodly answered, "he could have been anything!"

William's son built the church at Palmerston at the turn of the century, using the remains of a shipwreck. The window shutters were made from ship cupboards and two ship companionways with brass handrails led to the pulpit. The church was barely standing, supported by struts, having survived many summer storms. In the 1926 hurricane, it blew to the other side of the island, and they rolled it back on logs!

Many of the islanders felt that in its present condition, the church wasn't safe. Democratically, the decision had been made to build a new one at the same location. The monthly cargo ship arrived while we were there and relatives from afar disembarked with the building supplies for the new church. We attended the final Sunday service before the memorable old church was dismantled. This was quite a day for the people of Palmerston – some happy for the new, but most sad to say goodbye to the old.

Our interaction with the Palmerston Islanders was unlike any we'd ever had. Alec chummed with Goodly and Bill who did much of the fishing for the island and for export. I befriended 65-year-old Inano, William's great-granddaughter, who shared all the stories and secrets of Palmerston with me. She told me of the worst hurricane, when she had been only a little girl. Waves washed over the entire island and everyone had taken refuge on the highest point, "the hill", only six feet above sea level. They had lost everything: food, clothing and shelter.

"But we made do. For months we ate fish and coconuts," Inano recounted. "We wove clothes from palm fronds. We were fine."

Eventually, a German yacht arrived. They unloaded their boat, giving everything they could. When other yachts came, they also contributed canned food, tools and clothes. "We will never forget the generosity of the yachts."

Each night the family expected us to eat with them. "While you are here, you are part of our family." They insisted that their guests ate first, while the children served us and waved the flies away with palm fronds. After a week of this, I asked three of the teenage girls to join us on *Madeline* for lunch, so that we could serve them. The Marsters adhered to strict old-fashioned values of discipline and obedience, so it took some coaxing before Inano allowed the girls a two-hour break from their daily chores. The girls were thrilled to be able to look back at their island from *Madeline*, as they rarely got a chance. The boats and fishing were the domain of the men.

After a week we mentioned to David Marsters that it was time for us to move on. "Why leave?" he asked. "Why don't you stay for a couple of months, a year?"

"But hurricane season is approaching," Alec pointed out.

"No problem. We can roll *Madeline* up onto the beach on logs using one of the tractors. We'll tie her down and build a thatched roof over her so you can live on her. With your catamaran it'll be easy."

Alec was captivated, but we both knew we had promised to meet his sister in Tonga. The forced schedule was a drawback of having people visit us. We could never predict when we'd find a wonderful place such as Palmerston.

The next morning the Marsters guided us out over the reef. We'd shared a short chapter in each other's lives, and it was a unique experience. The Marsters had taken us in and had treated us as family – and this was a very special family to be a part of.

"See you later," we called.

"Everyone says that, but no one ever comes back to Palmerston," Bill responded. But I had made a promise to Bill's daughter that we'd write to each other. I wanted to learn what the future would hold for a young girl on an island like this. Maybe someday we would be back.

Three days after leaving Palmerston we arrived in Alofi, the main village in Niue. We called home, picked up duty-free beer and explored the limestone caves for which Niue was renown. The island was a raised coral atoll, still a low island, but higher than a true atoll like Palmerston. Cliffs encircled the island and without rivers to cloud the water, we could see the bottom 150 feet below. The sea was full of tiny, brown, yellow-ringed, venomous sea snakes that the locals said had mouths so small they could only bite you between the fingers or on the earlobes where the skin was thin. I swam with my hands closed tightly and cupped over my ears!

Alec calculated we had just enough fuel for the two-day trip to Tonga, so we departed even though there was no wind. Alec's sister and her husband were due to arrive in a few days, and we were excited to get going, even if it did mean motoring.

Another boat also on a schedule, *Kick 'em Jenny*, left at the same time. We'd met briefly, and had heard via the grapevine that they were both German doctors. They had a friend on board who was flying home from Tonga. We talked on the radio once or twice that afternoon, and we could see their masthead light all night. One of us would try to sail in the light zephyrs while the other boat motored past and vice versa. There was just no wind.

In the morning *Kick 'em Jenny* was ahead of us, but facing in the wrong direction. All her sails were up. Alec called them on the radio asking what they were up to. No answer. We called again and again. Nothing.

Scanning with the binoculars, we realized that *Kick 'em Jenny* was not moving at all. The sails were limply hanging and flopping; there was not a breath of wind. The boat was bobbing aimlessly, lifelessly.

Here we were, two boats in the middle of the South Pacific Ocean. It was dead calm.

One boat was idle and apparently unattended. They were not answering their radio and I couldn't see any sign of life on deck. "They have a friend with them," I commented. It all seemed a little weird.

"We can't motor past," Alec said. "We have to check it out." We changed course and headed straight to them.

We were getting closer. *Kick 'em Jenny* wallowed in the slight swell. My cheeks flushed. I peered through the binoculars looking for a clue.

We both jumped when the radio sprang to life. "*Madeline*," it was Bernd talking. "We're okay. I can't talk right now. I'm using the Ham radio to talk with Germany."

There was our answer! Many boats must shut off their engine and electronics so as not to interfere with reception. This explained why their VHF radio was off. It wasn't that their psycho guest had killed them after all.

With that sorted out, we turned *Madeline* back on course. Zzzzzzzip! The fishing line peeled out and I knew we had a big one. Alec ran to the foredeck for the battle, while I frantically steered *Madeline*. In the meantime, *Kick 'em Jenny*'s crew had come back to life and motored over to join the fun. They were circling *Madeline* as I chased after the fish. It was chaos and they were taking photos.

After fifteen minutes, Alec had the fish close to the boat. It proceeded to zigzag across our bows – to the port, to the middle, and finally to the starboard bow. I dashed to the foredeck and the comedy routine began. I held the gaff ready while Alec worked the rod, but the fish wouldn't give up. Alec and I did about six circles around each other as the fish swam back and forth on either side. We smashed into each other, laughing, yelling in hysterics and smiling for photos all at the same time. Alec pulled the fish closer, we switched gear and he quickly gaffed the fish.

Alec hauled up. "Uh oh."

"What?!"

"I can't lift it over the rail!"

Hand over hand we gave a giant heave-ho together and with a thud there was this amazing yellow-fin tuna on our foredeck. We looked up to cheers and applause from *Kick 'em Jenny*. The fish was five feet long and very thick in the middle. We grinned at the cameras, while the fish gasped.

Whack! Whack! Whack! The tuna thumped the foredeck with short powerful bursts from its tail. Blood sprayed the sails as Alec struggled to pin the fish with the gaff before it bounced off the boat. I poured tequila shots in the fish's gills, hoping to sedate it and speed its demise. The death struggle finally ended before the deck was pulverized, and once again we smiled at our success.

Bernd was an experienced sport fisherman, and he said it weighed at least 60 pounds. Alec cut eight large pot-roast-sized fillets and I sliced each into ten steaks, some plate-sized – an 80-dinner tuna.

The next night we arrived in Vava'u. We gave a slab to each of the officials from customs and immigration, making for an easy entry into the Kingdom of Tonga, and we invited *Kick 'em Jenny* for a celebratory dinner, sending them home with another slab. Not only did we still have fish for Alec's sister and husband, we fed all our friends anchored in the Tongan harbor!

Sally-Ann and Andrew arrived carting not only all our mail, but an 80-pound wind generator assembly and numerous spare parts. We loved our visit with them, catching up on all the news and seeing Sally-Ann six months pregnant with their first child. I particularly enjoyed the connection with home and our previous lives, and it confirmed my need to fly home and see my family too.

"Having guests was easier this time. Alec and I have eased into the cruising life, but are still having arguments. The difference now is that we've learned to ignore our differences, and with Sally-Ann and Andrew we lapsed into our holiday routine, pretending we have no problems at all. But now the computer is broken – it started to smoke one rainy night. I realize how much I've been using it for writing – to express my feelings and keep in touch with home. I can't go on without a computer, just as I know I can't ignore our difficulties for the rest of the trip."

"Tonga! Where the hell is that? Sounds really primitive!" This was the response I got when I called my family and told them where we were. I couldn't blame my sister Tamara for her reaction, as not long ago I would have said the same thing.

The islands are raised coral atolls; formed by shifting of the earth's crust. They are rocky with dramatic cliff faces and intriguing caves. The pattern of the islands is random and without tricky passes or currents to battle, they made for great exploring. As was usual for the Pacific, the water temperature was lovely and we spent many days snorkeling as well as scuba diving.

The Kingdom of Tonga is the only South Pacific island group never colonized by a European power. It continues to be run as a monarchy, with King and Nobles. This royal government has been criticized for being corrupt, but the people loved their King.

The missionaries made an impression, as the entire country was Christian. Numerous denominations were represented, sometimes as many as a dozen different churches in the tiniest of villages. The competing harmonies could be heard across the anchorages as the children sang their hearts out on Sunday mornings.

As we traveled from village to village, the portrait was the same: pigs, grass mats, and cemeteries. Pigs were everywhere. They were raised and eaten as food, but also seemed to become part of the family. They were inside as much as they were outside people's homes, and you couldn't go very far in a village before one crossed your path. A successful life was measured by the number of pigs slaughtered at your funeral. Over 30 pigs and you were very important.

The locals wore a traditional woven grass mat over a skirt. Skirts were popular with men as well, likely because of the heat. There was

often a familial significance to the mat, and it would be worn anytime a situation called for more dressy attire. Schoolteachers, bank tellers and other professionals would wear their mat over their work clothes. On Sunday, everyone wore one.

The cemeteries were also numerous and stuck out like sore thumbs. Gaudy, tacky signs above the graves boasted all sorts of colors and materials – often looking like a clothesline with garments hanging. A popular poster over graves was the scene from the Last Supper, accented with tinsel and flowers all around. The actual grave itself was simply a rounded hump of rocks or coral. The most outrageous gravesite of all was that of the recently-deceased Roman Catholic Bishop of Tonga. He was the first Tongan-born Bishop, and as evidenced by his ornate and lavish grave, he must have been well respected. Probably a 100-pig funeral.

We would often eavesdrop on the radio, especially if we knew the boats involved. Although against an unwritten rule, the urge was irresistible and everyone did it. We listened to conversations about the Ha'apai group – sketchy information going back and forth about uncharted reefs and poorly protected anchorages. Of course Alec heard all this and said, "Let's go!" He was continually searching for ways to get off the beaten track, and knew that if there was perceived danger and risk involved, then the area would be less visited.

Originally we had planned to go from Vava'u to Fiji, but we unanimously agreed that we'd like to hang out in one place for a while, without a tight schedule.

The Ha'apai group turned out to be just the kind of cruising Alec had hoped for, and I had to admit I loved it too. The fears of the other cruisers were unfounded. Navigating was no more difficult than in the Tuamotus, and we always managed to tuck behind a sand island, even when the wind switched. There were only a handful of yachts, friendly locals, no tourism and absolutely spectacular underwater life. The corals and the fish were among the best we saw on our whole trip.

I turned down the squelch on the VHF radio and could just hear our friends aboard *Windrose* over the background static. They were at a large volcanic island, about 30 miles away, called Tofua. On our chart, it was the size of a penny.

"We anchored on the northwest side," I heard Warren say, "and we climbed to the rim of the volcano today. Over."

"Roger, what was the trail like? Over," Alec responded.

"There is a small village, but no one was living there. We followed a path from behind the village east and then you see the path up the mountain. There is no vegetation because of the fumes from the cone, so it is easy to spot. Over."

They gave us the GPS co-ordinates of where they'd anchored, and we wished them a safe trip onwards to Nuku'alofa, the capital of Tonga. We were at the island of Ha'afevu, and were not eager to leave the magic of the Ha'apai. We'd already hooked a giant Blue Marlin that got away, seen humpback whales breaching in the distance and explored virgin coral reefs. But Alec began to thirst for even more adventure, and when *Windrose* had mentioned the idea of exploring Tofua, he was keen.

In 1789 the *HMS Bounty* was near Tofua when Christian Fletcher cast Lieutenant Bligh and his supporters adrift in a few longboats. Bligh sailed for Tofua where the natives promptly killed one of his men. Bligh set back out to sea and sailed over 3,000 miles to the island of Timor in Indonesia and into the history books.

We left the anchorage at two in the morning, sailing out between the reefs using a compass bearing we had taken before sunset. Another boat in the anchorage, *Querida*, joined us. The chart showed no reef or rocks around Tofua, but little else as well. We kept a good watch as we approached at daybreak.

The wind was different than when *Windrose* was there, so we sailed around to the other side for protection. We anchored in the lee of the vast island in dangerous rocky and coral-strewn waters. Alec jumped in and snorkeled the anchor. In the swirling winds behind the island the chain could wrap around a rock and become taut. If the wind changed or swell rolled in, the anchor chain could snap under the quick snubbing motion. To protect against that situation, we tied a long bridle of stretchier nylon rope onto the chain. *Querida* was too worried to leave their boat, but we carried on, secretly happy that they would watch our boat also.

The northwest corner of the island was barren, but the coastline on our side was cliff-lined with jungle-covered slopes up to the crater rim. By mid-morning we landed the dinghy through the surf and onto a steep lava-boulder beach. As we pulled the dinghy over the rocks, we heard shouting. Three large Tongan men stepped out of the jungle.

They smiled and shook our hands, and I wondered if Bligh's initial greeting was the same. They had spotted our yacht and had run a couple of miles to greet us.

We explained – with the usual broken English and hand signs – that we wished to hike to the top. They thought we were crazy *palangi*, or white men. We started into the jungle but they signaled for us to wait. One man had to run back and get his machete, as they had appointed themselves as our guides.

We hacked our way through the jungle, crossing ravines on huge felled tree trunks, feeling like Indiana Jones. As we climbed, I grabbed trees for support, often looking up to see them loaded with ripe papaya.

We discovered our guides lived on Tofua for six months to harvest *kava*. They showed us the plant, a small bush in the pepper family. Drinking *kava* is the national pastime of Tongan men. The ground root combined with water makes an awful-tasting, slightly narcotic drink. We had participated at a weekly *kava* club in Vava'u and had heard that the Tofua *kava* was very potent.

Tavenga, one of the guides, was a huge strapping lad who was particularly concerned about me. He literally cleared a path for me as he went along, knocking down plants and uprooting small trees. They told us that Tavenga went to the Seoul Olympics on the Tongan rowing team! We knew that the King of Tonga had taken up rowing a few years back to lose some of his 300-plus pounds, so perhaps Tavenga was an Olympian. His only contribution to the conversation was to repeatedly point at me, and say "hungry". We had a good laugh about this, but all I could think was that my small frame didn't measure up to Tongan standards.

We finally reached the summit, despite our trusty guides twice getting lost, and our reward was a spectacular view. It was impossible to see while standing amidst the trees, so we climbed to their tops. Inside the original crater was a smaller volcanic cone spewing smoke, surrounded on three sides by a freshwater lake!

We stumbled back down the valleys, crashing through thick decaying vegetation. Concerned that some of the lava run-off gullies might be too smooth, and provide too fast a descent, the Tongans carefully selected our path and we slid down, whooping and laughing.

Back at the boat, we exchanged gifts with our new friends. We gave them canned food, T-shirts, an old pot, and sandals, and they loaded our boat with papaya and drinking coconuts.

As the sun was setting we said goodbye, which included lots of kissing and hugs, to Alec's astonishment. It was too risky to spend the night at this unprotected rocky shore. Tired but delighted, we set sail overnight for Nuku'alofa, home of the King of Tonga on the island of Tongatapu.

On November 10th we moved out of the muddy small-boat harbor at Nuku'alofa to a pretty island just off the capital city so we could finish preparing for the trip south to New Zealand. We had filled our freshwater tanks and hand-washed our clothes, and now only scrubbing *Madeline's* hulls remained. *Windrose* had greeted us when we first arrived in the harbor, but they'd already left. Many boats were leaving.

The cyclone season would officially begin December 1st and the winter storms peeling up from Antarctica were slowing down. It was the optimum time to make the trip south. The problem was that this passage would take us out of the tropics and into the temperate zone. Instead of steady predictable trade winds, the wind strength and direction would be determined by the high- and low-pressure systems that crossed the area. By knowing the location of these systems you could figure out the wind direction swirling around them and predict your weather. "It's the best time of year for this passage," Alec assured me after reading our reference books, "but it still means variable conditions and one gale per week, on average."

The next morning we tuned into the "Comedy Net", listening to the weather and trying to time our departure. We heard *Rode Beer* report to the group that they were en route to New Zealand and Robert sent us a quick message. He knew we were probably listening, and said he finished the book we'd given him for his birthday in Vava'u. It was a long time since we'd been together, and I looked forward to seeing them in New Zealand.

The winds were light, but we decided to leave. I dinghied over to the boat beside us, because the woman on board had talked on the radio that morning, and I asked her to relay to Robert that we were leaving. She was happy to pass on the message.

I was ready to go, but some simple math was bugging me. We had 1,100 miles to sail to Auckland, which would take over a week. I guess that meant one gale.

NEW ZEALAND BOUND

SOMETIMES I FELT THE TRIP WAS CHANGING ME and I was becoming a new and stronger person, but lifting the anchor and leaving Nuku'alofa made me feel as if I hadn't changed at all. I was reactive, defensive and downright negative in my responses to Alec while he directed the boat through the reef from the bow. All went well in the end, of course, but I was so panicky and negative that he got mad and I promised to stop, yet again. It had become a habit.

Fortunately, the episode did not seem to bother Alec and I was able to quickly get over it too. We cleared the land and made wonderful love on the foredeck with the colorful spinnaker billowing above us.

Overall, I believed my confidence had built over the past couple of months. I had learned a lot about boat handling and navigation and leaving Tonga was just a slip-up caused by the anxiety of the upcoming voyage. I wanted to learn more and take more control of the boat.

"I've been sort of a back-seat driver and let Alec make all the decisions and then I react with irrational fears. My main problem is that I haven't felt comfortable making the decisions or taking on responsibilities. This isn't right – either I should learn to shut up and let Alec be the captain, or I should start making some decisions for us as well, and not be so damned afraid of the consequences, or of fucking up." Considering we'd sailed over 8,000 nautical miles together, it sounded funny that I was finally ready to take on more responsibility.

We planned on breaking up the trip with a stop at North Minerva Reef, where we would hopefully sit out the weekly gale. It was a circular reef, similar to an atoll, but there was no land – only reef. There was a large pass into the lagoon and the lobstering was legendary. The reef was claimed by Tonga, and a few years before, when a Fijian commercial lobstering boat was there, the King sent a Tongan warship to assert their sovereignty. They arrested the Fijian boat and towed it back to Nuku'alofa.

Our first day out the winds were light but enough to keep sailing. Late that night the wind died and we started motoring. On and off we motored the entire next day and night. I was pleased, writing and baking in the calm, but Alec was concerned about our diesel. After Minerva Reef we still had over 800 miles to Auckland and he didn't want to deplete our fuel supply. Four other boats were in VHF radio range, which helped ease the monotony.

The wind picked up from the north and we tried to sail. The current wasn't favorable and we quickly saw that we wouldn't make it to the reef before nightfall. It was a painful decision. Do we use the fuel and motor sail to increase our speed, or spend another night out at sea?

One of the boats in radio contact, *White Tunny*, was an Israeli motor-sailer. They carried a lot of fuel and could motor the entire way to New Zealand if needed. Ahmi was behind us, but determined to make it to Minerva that night for the sake of his pregnant wife and baby son. He did not want them to spend another night at sea.

One of the thirteen boats at North Minerva overheard our conversation and he offered to guide Ahmi and us through the pass at night using his radar. His radar screen showed the waves crashing on the reef, with a blank area indicating the pass into the lagoon. He would see our boat when we got closer, plus we had GPS co-ordinates for the middle of the wide pass.

We had always believed that you do not enter a new place at night, especially a poorly-charted reef in the middle of an ocean. Despite knowing we'd probably be fine, we decided against relying on all the electronics and agreed to spend another night at sea. The wind died again and we bobbed in the ever-persistent swell.

It was my watch when I noticed the sails flapping lightly. The wind had finally picked up and I went out into the darkness to start sailing. Without warning, the wind dramatically shifted and intensified, backwinding the sails and causing *Madeline* to wallow awkwardly. I struggled to get her going again, but the genoa snagged on the baby stay and I couldn't free it. The wind howled as I wrestled with the lines in the cockpit, beginning to feel desperate. I could figure this out on my own. Stay calm, I told myself.

The sail was flogging loudly. If I didn't get it under control, I knew it would tear. The wind was now 30 knots and screaming. Short steep waves were quickly building, knocking *Madeline* sideways and shooting sheets of cold water through the cockpit. I couldn't hold down my fear any longer.

"Alec!" I hollered over the din. I cursed myself for panicking, but kept yelling for him.

He groggily stumbled into the cockpit. I backed away from the lines and he calmly tamed the genoa. The waves continued to smash into *Madeline*; the spray whisked away in the wind. Tears were streaming down my face.

Alec trimmed the sails and then suggested we reef the main. He hooked on his harness, climbed up on deck and hauled down the sail, while I eased the halyard and mainsheet. He unrolled some of the genoa and then we reefed the mainsail a second time. *Madeline* was sailing well once again.

At the chart table, Alec figured out our course, but the news was bad. The wind was coming straight from North Minerva Reef, only 25 miles away. It was blowing 35 knots steady, with gusts to 40, 45 and 50 knots. The sea was foamy; eerie against the black sky. I turned *Madeline* to a beam reach, trying not to lose ground away from the only shelter in hundreds of miles. In the gusts, the sails vibrated and the mast creaked. The rigging shrieked as the wind whistled past the thin stainless-steel wire holding up our mast.

We both stood in the cockpit watching the waves, the wind and the sails. "I can't believe I got so upset," I said, wiping back my bedraggled locks.

"This wind is nuts, and you're doing really well now." Alec braced his legs and gave me a hug, "I wonder how long this is going to last?"

Three long, sleepless hours later and now 30 miles from North Minerva Reef, the wind dropped. It was still blowing over 25 knots, but the terrifying gusts had ceased and the seas were more even. We turned the boat into the wind, brought the sails in tight and began beating into the waves towards the anchorage.

Our speed on the GPS was low as the big waves were stopping *Madeline* and trying to push her downwind, the opposite direction to which we wanted. Without the heavy keel of a monohull *Madeline* did not have the momentum to carry her through the mountains of green water. We needed more speed and I reluctantly unfurled more sail while Alec winched the sheet tighter.

Madeline leapt off the wave crests smashing into the troughs below, her rig shaking violently. Inside, I anxiously listened to the hulls creaking and the sea hammering her amidst a cacophony of sounds. My whole house was flying through the air, and then free falling, coming down with a crash. Wave after wave she flew over. Everything shuddered and shook. It was relentless.

Once the sun was above the horizon, we called the other boats and found they were experiencing similar problems. *Sanyassi* was a couple of hours behind us. *El Gitano II* had ripped their mainsail in a gust and would be out for another night. The last boat was out of our radio range. They had been blown so far away that they were now carrying on to New Zealand.

The constant beating was like a slow drum march, but *Madeline* was making progress. We took turns carefully monitoring the sails and course, knowing we'd need all day to reclaim the lost miles and to claw slowly upwind.

We eventually made it through the pass late in the afternoon, and motored across the lagoon to the other cruisers. Someone called on the radio and jokingly welcomed us to the Minerva Reef Yacht Club. We anchored in 40 feet of clear water over rippling sand. *Madeline* was covered in a salt layer, thick like snow. Exhausted, we ate, showered and fell into a deep sleep.

The next morning we cleaned out the boat. There was a nice wind to dry our clothes and foul-weather jackets, but it slowly decreased to a dead calm three days later. From the bow of the boat we could see the anchor buried in the sand below us. We could see little fish swimming around and every ripple in the sand. The fish were plentiful and the coral beautiful, and I was thankful for this idyllic respite in such a unique anchorage, ringed by open ocean and crashing reef.

We found lobster immediately and ate it every night. The dreaded shark stories that were circling seemed unfounded. The only ones we saw were sleeping blacktip reef sharks, often hidden inside coral heads. Before spearing a lobster, Alec always took a good look to make sure he wouldn't rudely waken a shark.

I had seen a lot of sharks by now, but only harmless nurse sharks or timid whitetip and blacktip reef sharks. The latter had gray bodies with the tips of their dorsal fin and tail fin colored. Bill Marsters at Palmerston had explained his shark safety rules, "If you see a large striped shark, a tiger shark, get out of the water. If you see a yellowish shark, a lemon shark, get out of the water. If you see a gray reef shark, which has no color on its dorsal fin tip, and you're spear fishing, get out of the water. Whitetips, blacktips and nurse sharks are safe." The real danger was when spear fishing. Gray reef sharks, which are normally considered safe, accounted for most shark attacks in the South Pacific – all when spear fishing.

To illustrate, Bill and Goodly had taken Alec out to the reef one day at Palmerston. They had planned a big barbecue to celebrate the last church service and wanted to spear about 150 small reef fish. There were thousands of these little fish in the coral. They had brought a young boy along to string the speared fish through the gills. The boy stood on a big coral head. The water covered his plastic sandals. Bill, Goodly and Alec started spearing around the coral head, taking the little fish off the spear and handing them to the boy. As they exhausted the fish at one spot they moved on. It was becoming inefficient to hand the fish to the boy. Bill and Goodly would take the fish off the spear and bite with their teeth between the fish's eyes to kill it. Then they could throw the dead fish to him. They encouraged Alec to do the same, but he declined.

Then the sharks came. Four whitetips started circling the coral head, trying to swim up on it. The smallest was about three feet long and the largest seven feet. The string of fish bled into the water attracting more sharks. Unconcerned, Bill and Goodly kept spearing more fish, but Alec was still transporting his speared fish through the sharks to the boy.

"Ahh, what about these sharks?" Alec asked.

"Oh don't worry about them. Just give them a hit if they get too close," Bill Marsters responded.

The sharks moved away if Alec approached, but he'd had enough of swimming through them. He tried biting the little reef fish, but the first one he bit swam away. He bit the next one harder. "You just bite until you hear a CRUNCH," he told me afterward, as if I might try it myself one day.

Inside the lagoon at North Minerva Reef, the sharks weren't abundant, but two boats anchored at the pass reported hundreds of sharks, including more dangerous pelagic species like the mako. Even Alec was not bold enough to suggest we check it out, but I knew it wouldn't be long before he too would want to dive the passes.

Peter on *El Gitano II* had been sewing his mainsail for a couple of days now. Pushing the large sailmaker's needles through the heavy canvas with a leather palm was a slow process. Most of the boats left in the calm weather and *El Gitano II* invited the remaining three boats over to celebrate their completed patch, but more importantly Peter's 50th birthday.

Val and Peter had been living aboard and cruising for seventeen years. Peter was German and Val was British, and they somehow could afford to raise four children on board. Sven was 13, Michael 10, Zoë 7 and baby Neils was only 2. The children were excited about the party, but very adult-like, as cruising children usually are. They prepared the appetizers, baked the cake themselves and politely passed the dishes around, except for Neils who was climbing the rigging in his birthday suit.

I asked Val how she managed it. She said that when the gale had hit them a few days earlier, just as it hit us, she was a nervous wreck. Her teenage son tried to reassure her, saying, "It's going to be all right, Mom."

"I felt a bit stupid with this scrawny kid hugging me, trying to comfort me. It had always been the other way around!"

Al and Lisa on *Sanyassi* also experienced the gale, and the women all commiserated. Al was a solo long-distance racer and had done quite well in some transatlantic single-handed races. He was a breed apart, and was completely comfortable sailing their boat alone. Although Lisa had a lot of racing experience and had now sailed across the Pacific, she had moments where she lost it and was completely incapacitated. Her fears overcame her and she would retreat below while Al would sail the boat by himself. She enjoyed most aspects of the cruising and loved Al. She could see Al was so happy out cruising that she decided to live with her fears. There were many similarities to my experience.

During the gale, Al had called down to Lisa, "What is it? Why can't you explain it? What is it that frightens you – is it the roar of the wind? Is it the zigzag of the lightening? Is it the relentless pounding of the waves against the hull?"

Lisa, as I too had found, could not always explain her feelings. "It's everything!"

While the women supported each other, Peter, Al and Alec all laughed and shook their heads a lot. Peter admitted, "It drives me mad!"

Although it was a serious problem, everyone spoke openly about it and the other boats seemed to accept it as a compromise of cruising. It gave me hope that Alec and I could improve our working relationship.

A few days later, we decided to leave for New Zealand. The winds were light and as we passed South Minerva Reef, we gave in to the idea that snorkeling would be more fun than sailing. South Minerva Reef is a figure eight shape and lower in the water than its partner to the north. At North Minerva Reef the lagoon got choppy at high tide for about an hour from the ocean waves pouring over the reef, causing me to get mildly seasick. At South Minerva the rough period was for about six hours, but the coral and fish were reported to be more spectacular.

It was usual for me to tow the dinghy during our snorkeling expeditions. When spear fishing, it was important to get the wounded fish out of the water as quickly as possible before any sharks arrived. When Alec caught dinner, having the dinghy right there meant he didn't have to swim back to the boat. This arrangement suited me fine, because it also meant I could get out of the water quickly. When Alec could hear me speaking clearly to him, then he knew I was likely out of the water and thus, there must be a shark around.

We anchored *Madeline*, donned our fins, masks, wetsuits, and dove in. Immediately we noticed that the coral was older and that large, ponderous, coral heads had grown to the point that some had tumbled over with their own weight. There were creepy caverns and dim tunnels under the coral heads. Any lobsters were well hidden in those recesses.

"Look!" Alec grunted through his snorkel. I followed his pointing arm and froze when I saw a pack of young gray reef sharks. There were about ten sharks in a vee formation like a deadly squadron of fighter planes. They took no notice of us and swam past in the distance. I'd heard that where there were no blacktip or whitetip reef sharks, then the gray reef sharks took over. They cruised by again, still taking no notice. The pillars of coral appeared more menacing in the lengthening shadows of late afternoon. We returned to *Madeline* dinnerless.

The night was calm and we were happy with our decision to stay. The next morning, we looked for shallower water where shark packs would be less likely. Right in the middle of the figure eight was perfect lobster coral, and within ten minutes we found several. Alec speared one and put it in the dinghy. Then I spotted a five-foot gray reef shark swimming towards us. I jumped into the dinghy. The shark came close and then veered away, disappearing into the distance. I tried to remind myself that a five-foot shark eats fish much less than one foot long. He was just as afraid of me as I was of him, I convinced myself.

"It's clear," Alec said. I got back in the water, took the spear and speared my first lobster. I removed the lobster and handed the spear back to Alec. I'd had enough and I stayed in the dinghy. There were just too many sharks around.

"Here comes another one!" Alec said as he turned to face the shark. It was another gray about seven feet long. I could see the dark body through the water, the fin breaking the surface as it approached over the shallow coral. Alec tensioned his spear, arm outstretched at the shark as he slowly swam backward to the dinghy.

My God, I thought, he's going to spear the shark! With deliberate side to side motions, the shark swam closer. About three feet from the spear tip the shark turned slightly, swimming past. Alec rotated with the shark, spear poised.

He scuttled into the dinghy. "Shit! They must be able to sense when we spear the lobster. Two lobster are enough. Let's get out of here!" I was perfectly willing.

The wind was favorable, though light, and we sailed slowly but comfortably on calm seas, south to New Zealand. Crossing into the eastern hemisphere the next day, we watched the GPS count up to 180 degrees of longitude. It then switched to east 179 degrees and started counting back down. We had already crossed the International Date

Line en route to Tonga. The King wanted to be the first in the world to experience each day so the dateline artificially jogs eastward to include Tonga in the same time zone as New Zealand.

The third day was studded with weather fronts passing over. The low ominous band of clouds indicating a front usually brought a wind shift and rain squalls. These dramatic cloud bands looked like bridges over *Madeline*, casting shadows as we sailed under. After numerous changes in the sail plan, we ended the day becalmed.

We had to conserve fuel, but we also had to run the engine to recharge the batteries. Diesel engines prefer to be run under load, so we took advantage of the calm and put the motor in gear, making some distance during the night.

The wind picked up, but directly from New Zealand. We tried a port tack and then a starboard tack, calculating which was favored. We monitored Keri Keri radio in New Zealand for weather information. Alec ate his criticism of the weather fanatics in the cruising fleet and started plotting the highs and lows on a map.

The head, or toilet, stopped pumping properly in the morning. Alec dismantled it, but he didn't have the right spare parts on board. He grabbed a bucket and declared it our new toilet.

Dark gray clouds covered the sky and the wind shifted around the compass. Compared to the tropics and their trade winds, this was extremely frustrating sailing. At least the changing conditions kept me busy, and I was coping well so far, but our progress was so slow that I knew we'd still be sailing when the next gale showed up.

The wind dropped off yet again. The seas were still running and we bounced around in the uncomfortable slop. On went the motor, but we were really beginning to run low on diesel. Four hours later we turned off the engine and just bobbed in the calm.

I looked up from my book, shocked to see Alec climbing down the swim ladder rather than use the bucket. He wasn't wearing a harness and I immediately imagined him falling in and me losing him. I ran outside yelling, "Alec, what are you doing? Please use the bucket, or put on a harness!"

"Alayne, take a look around you," he said. "If I fell in, I'd be more concerned about landing in my own shit!" He was right. The sea was a glassy calm and the sails just hung limp from the mast. It was an opportunity not to be missed.

"Calling any ship, calling any ship. This is the sailboat *Madeline*." Alec was feeling bored and restless, and put out a random call on the VHF radio.

"Hi *Madeline*, this is Jurgen on *Bullwinkel*." Another boat! We had first met *Bullwinkel*, a 42-foot schooner, in the Galapagos and had last seen them in Tonga. They had shared some of our big tuna. They were about 20 miles away and were also finding the sailing frustrating.

"But you will get wind soon," Jurgen said. "I got a weather fax over the radio and there is a low approaching that should give us very strong easterly winds."

His prediction was correct and during the night the wind slowly built. By the next afternoon the wind was blowing over 20 knots. A cold rain blew into the cockpit all day. *Madeline* was surfing down the waves, often sailing over ten knots. Even I didn't mind the speed because we were finally making progress to New Zealand.

We gathered around the radio and listened to our fate predicted. It reminded me that we weren't the only fools enduring such hardship. We heard that boats just east of us had winds of 40 knots, so we reefed the mainsail in preparation for the blow. The wind continued to build until it was a full gale, over 35 knots. The genoa was fully rolled in and the small staysail stowed away. Only the mainsail was up, double reefed to the size of a small tablecloth.

I lay in my bunk trying to sleep. There was a loud sound. I jerked awake, muscles tense. Something was wrong. "What was that noise?" I yelled to Alec through the small hatch into the cockpit.

"It's nothing," he said calmly. "Try to get some sleep."

I couldn't; the noise inside sounded awful in contrast to the dead calm and windlessness of 24 hours ago.

The cold, gray and rain continued into the next day. The wind was howling and the seas had grown to over ten feet. We would be at the coast in less than one day at this rate, and ironically, I hoped the gale would hold. But the wind had started to clock again and we knew that if the low pressure passed above us, the wind would be against us once more. The barometer had dropped and now was holding steady. Was the low passing?

We listened to the radio again. The forecast was for the wind to shift that night to the southwest. Dammit! We were so close.

We sheeted in the sails some more, but couldn't hold the course to New Zealand. *Madeline* crashed over the waves. The swell was confused with some waves coming from the northeast and some from the southeast. When these waves combined they towered over *Madeline*, often breaking and roaring underneath her.

I sat in the cockpit, breathing the crisp air and watching these monsters sneak up. *Madeline* always rose to the challenge and let the waves pass beneath.

"Do you want to beat into this all night?" Alec asked.

"No! I wish I could beam myself out of here." It was turning into the trip to Minerva reef all over again. Only this time we were 120 nautical miles from an anchorage, not 30 miles.

"Well, I don't want to do it either. Let's deploy the sea anchor. Why beat if we don't have to?"

We had spoken to a trimaran sailor in Aitutaki about parachute sea anchors. Rather than reserving it for emergencies, he used his all the time, whenever he wanted to take a break. We decided to give it a try.

I turned on the engine to help maneuver *Madeline*, while Alec attached one end of his tether to his harness and the other end to a long piece of webbing attached at the bow and stern. This allowed him to walk around the deck while remaining attached to *Madeline* should he be tossed overboard.

Alec climbed forward, using both hands to hold on. I turned the boat into the wind and a wave broke over the foredeck washing his legs out from under him. On hands and knees, he crawled to the anchor locker and dug out the sea anchor. Carefully he attached the lines to the cleats on the pitching bows, knowing he couldn't afford to tangle them. With a quick glance back, he threw it over the side. I let the boat drift back and the parachute quickly filled, hanging under the surface. Alec slowly payed out 300 feet of line and *Madeline* swung into the wind facing the waves. It was done! We were anchored in the middle of the ocean.

We checked the GPS and we were slowly moving backward, downwind, at less than a nautical mile per hour. We wouldn't lose much distance, and *Madeline* rode the waves well. I felt prepared to face anything the storm could dish out. Exhausted as I was, I took the first watch. We were at the mercy of the sea – and any passing ship.

On the third attempt Alec snagged the trip line with the boat hook and he hauled the empty parachute up onto the foredeck. During the night the wind had continued to shift, a sign the low had passed. It was still blowing 25 knots but we hoisted sail, psyching ourselves up for two more days of beating. The seas had calmed down from the gale and *Madeline* began the now familiar smashing through the waves. Spray flew over the boat and Alec monitored the sails from behind our vinyl windshields.

"Check this out!" Alec called. I pulled on my cold, damp, foul-weather gear and stepped outside as we sailed under a low ceiling of dark clouds. Just beyond, a clear, cloudless, bright blue sky stretched for miles. The dividing line was distinct and unlike anything I had seen. We cheered that the low had passed, and the sunshine on my face felt wonderful. The barometer nudged upwards slightly and so did my spirits. On the radio, they said the low was an early tropical storm, whereas the gale at Minerva Reef was a late winter storm. It seemed we couldn't win, trapped between the two seasons.

Late that night I heard *Bullwinkel* on the radio talking to a freighter, and I was pleased we were still close to them, even with eighteen hours on the sea anchor. It wasn't only us having difficulty.

We kept beating all the next day, and I was tired of the tacking, the broken head and everything. Alec brought some grog out to the cockpit before sunset and I snuggled up to him as best I could – not fully relaxing, but bracing my legs against the motion. We didn't have much food or water left. We had finished our last fish and only had rice, pasta and various unappealing cans of food. Our supplies had lasted for the ten months since Florida. We had planned almost too perfectly.

Even so, this was my favorite time of day. For most of the past eleven days we talked only briefly, in passing during our watch changes. But at cocktail time, if weather permitted, we talked about all sorts of things: our past together, our childhood, or the latest book we had read. The recurring topic was how frustrating the weather was.

"It seems the majority of the time has been spent beating into the wind," I said.

"And the only good sailing was during the gale," Alec said. "That was the only time we sailed off the wind and made progress to New Zealand!" He took a swig of his rum and water.

I pointed at the sun as it descended into the ocean. "Conditions look perfect for a green flash." When the sun sets on a clear horizon it distorts and appears very red. At that point the sun is already below your physical horizon, and what you see are the sun's rays refracting around the earth's atmosphere. In perfect atmospheric conditions, when there are no clouds or obstructions on the horizon, the sun turns red and then possibly flashes green as it disappears. The theory is that green light refracts through the atmosphere slightly further than red light, causing the green flash. We often watched for it, although Alec claimed the source of the elusive green flash was only retina burn from staring at the setting sun.

This night we tried not to look until the sun was almost set, and then... there it was, unmistakably.

The green flash!

Ten seconds. I timed the interval between the flashing of a white light on the horizon. I returned to the chart on the navigation table. This corresponded to the light on Burgess Island, a ten-second flashing light visible for 25 miles. "Land Ho," I whispered proudly to myself. I tacked south and we were finally on course towards Auckland. The full moon sparkled on the wave tops, improving visibility and making me feel less tense.

The predawn sky lightened, streaked with delicate pinks and yellows. Groups of birds visited *Madeline* and I spotted the distant jagged silhouettes of the islands before us. *Madeline* was close-hauled and sailing well. It was December 1st, springtime in the Southern Hemisphere, and even though the air was cold, I was enjoying the sail while Alec slept. I was so glad to be close to land again.

As we entered the Hauraki Gulf the wind increased, and *Madeline* dashed over the small waves, spray flying. We were close reaching, heading into the wind as usual, but on course for Auckland. One last race against the darkness and then this constant motion would come to an end.

Mid-morning, Alec was watching the battery voltage as the autopilot whizzed. "I think we have to run the engine and charge the batteries. Bit of a shame, considering the good speed we're making."

I turned on the engine and after fifteen minutes, I noticed a funny sound. "Alec, listen to the engine. And look – there's gray smoke coming out of the exhaust."

Alec opened the engine compartment and smoke poured out. "Turn it off! It's overheating."

Alec peered inside. One of the raw water cooling hoses had split with the heat and was emitting smoke. Alec replaced the hose and then began the awkward task of removing the raw water cooling pump. He grappled with the unseen bolts in the oily bilge as *Madeline* jostled over the waves.

"The battery voltage is too low for the autopilot motor," Alec said. "You'll have to hand-steer until I fix the engine. It shouldn't be long now." His voice was filled with his usual optimism.

He removed the impeller from the pump, but was surprised that it looked perfect. "No need to replace that," he muttered. He reassembled the pump and dug out his engine reference books. We tried the engine again, but Alec watched the exhaust and no cooling water spat out, so we quickly turned off the engine. He went back to work, head stuffed into the awkward compartment.

I sailed into the lee of an island and was having difficulty steering the boat in the swirling winds. The prospect of anchoring under sail was eating away at me. I accidentally tacked the boat when the wind swung around. "I can't do this!" I cried. "You take over, Alec."

Alec looked up peevishly from the cockpit floor. "I have enough problems here. Can't you just steer the bloody boat?"

"You wanted to go behind the island. I wanted to tack around the other side," I argued.

Alec sat up and displayed his filthy oily hands. He tried to change his tone. "I can't help you right now. You've been doing really well. Look, it's just a few more boat lengths and then the wind will settle back in."

Persevering, I got *Madeline* through the wind shadow and she began bouncing over the waves again. I put on the autopilot briefly and checked the chart. We had some rocks awash to avoid, but it also appeared that we were losing the race against the clock.

I brought the chart to the cockpit and examined alternatives as I steered. I checked the coastal weather report on the VHF radio and then convinced Alec that our best bet was to sail to Waiheke Island where we could anchor for the night. Legally we could stop along the coast, if we didn't go ashore. I plotted our new course and entered a waypoint into the GPS. We would get there just before nightfall.

Late that afternoon Alec replaced the impeller anyway, after having checked everything else. We started the engine and cheered when the cooling water flowed like normal. "I don't know what's wrong with the original impeller," he said. "All that matters is it works."

We raced towards Waiheke Island at seven knots and sailed into the small harbor I had picked. Alec wanted to anchor under sail just to prove we could have done it. I pointed out the dark, cloudy water and our little chart showing reefs around the bay. "You're the captain today," he said, agreeing to motor the last bit amongst the local boats.

I was so relieved the passage was over. Sheep were grazing the hillsides and a small neat town lay at the head of the bay. Deciduous trees lined a brown, rocky beach. The orange rays of the setting sun warmed my face. The sheltered, calm, pastoral scene enveloped me. My energy was sapped. Perhaps we would cook a meal, have a celebratory drink, or maybe have a shower. I was thankful to be safe and sound, but I just sat there, numb.

Alec came back from anchoring at the bow. He was both annoyed and excited. "You know the toggle on the forestay that I installed in Tahiti? It's broken. The clevis pin jammed in the chainplate, and is holding the whole rig up! I wonder how long it was like that."

I felt sick at the thought of it, and then even more happy that we had arrived safely. If the forestay had come loose while we were beating, we would have lost the mast.

Alec continued to list other problems. The anchor guard had been bent by the waves and a hinge was broken on the anchor-locker hatch, both minor compared to the broken toggle. He went to get a rope to secure the  forestay and found one locker inside the boat completely full of water. He began removing things and cleaning out the locker. He found a small hole where the propane line entered. "Water must have been forced through this little hole from the waves washing over the deck," he yelled out to me. Then he began cleaning up the mess from fixing the engine.

I was baffled. Our most grueling passage was finally over and he didn't even stop to acknowledge the accomplishment. His way of releasing tension was to do something about it. His "to-do" list had gotten too long, and now that the boat had stopped moving, he seized the opportunity to solve these problems.

My way of releasing the tension was different. I cried. I sobbed. I begged Alec to stop. I wanted to relax, to sit still, to celebrate and to be held.

Alec compromised. He worked feverishly for another few minutes to satisfy his own needs and then appeared in the cockpit with drinks and an appetizer of artichoke hearts on crackers.

We had a nice candlelight dinner. We made love. I cried some more. We fell asleep, bodies entwined.

BOOK TWO

THROUGH ROUGH WATERS

I STEPPED ONTO THE AIR NEW ZEALAND FLIGHT at Los Angeles airport. Sitting down with my magazines, I prepared myself for the long flight back to Auckland, *Madeline* and Alec.

I cherished my visit home and had accomplished more than I set out to. I was glad to see that everyone at home was happy and healthy. Knowing that they were still thinking and talking about me, allowed me to feel better about being away. I no longer had the dreaded feeling I might never see them again. I was also relieved that working as a doctor came back to me quickly, and it was more rewarding than messy work in a New Zealand boat yard.

It took time to absorb all the emotions seeing everyone created. I found it overwhelming at times: the hectic pace, the cold weather and all the attention. It took time getting used to showering every morning, putting on make-up, and wearing clean clothes, socks and shoes. I cut my scraggly hair and soon looked like the old Alayne. Many at home commented I was just the same. However, my thoughts had clearly changed, and my perspective was now different.

I grew up competing with my four younger sisters. We were all very expressive, and during dinners together we talked loud and fast, vying for attention, trying to get our point across. Now I watched the action, ironically not feeling able to share. As excitable as I had appeared on the boat, I was now patient and relaxed compared to my old self. I was less image conscious than before, constantly looking for substance behind the issues.

Many of the older cruisers said they were tired of the rat race, the big cities, the pollution, and all the people. I thoroughly enjoyed my trip home, my friends, and my work, and it reminded me that our reason for leaving was not to escape.

I took a blanket from the stewardess and snuggled into a comfortable position for the long flight home. Going back to *Madeline* was going "home", and that felt good. I looked out the window and down over the Pacific Ocean, and thought back to all those long passages across that great expanse. The last one to New Zealand was the most trying of all, but it had been worth it for the exhilaration of entering Auckland Harbour at last.

When we had arrived in Auckland on December 2nd from Waiheke Island, we'd checked in at the customs quay and then docked *Madeline* at Westhaven Marina. A cruiser said he thought *Rode Beer* was somewhere in the marina, but over a thousand boats filled the horizon. The marina office had closed for the day, so we left a note on the bulletin board telling *Rode Beer* our slip number. That night Alec was turning off the wind generator when a woman called from the pier.

It was Nathalie! The night air was cool and she was wearing narrow yellow pants on her long legs and a multicolored fleecy. She jumped on *Madeline* and gave us kisses on alternating cheeks and long tight hugs. "The Dutch give three kisses," she said reminding me.

Robert sauntered up wearing his usual non-typical cruising attire of collared shirt, dress pants and loafers. "So good to see you," he said, dragging out the words with a mockingly formal accent. He shook Alec's hand vigorously and gave me five kisses. "The Dutch give five kisses to beautiful young women!"

Cruising scuttlebutt had informed them that we had been heard on the VHF radio. This reunion cemented what I knew was going to be a special and lasting friendship. We talked and drank late into the night.

A few days later we went with them to a car auction. We would be in New Zealand for five months during the South Pacific hurricane season, and like other cruisers we planned to do some touring. It was cheaper to buy a car and sell it later, than to rent one. Robert, whose family was in the car business in Holland, was a great help selecting an ancient Toyota Corolla that we fondly nicknamed "Rusting Matilda".

We spent our first week running errands around Auckland, the largest city, home to 1.5 million people. Everything we could possibly want and need was available, from fast food to engine spares to half-price movies on Tuesdays. Alec fixed the head and the forestay before his sister and her husband flew over from Sydney, Australia. We cruised for two weeks in the Hauraki Gulf, and had a memorable Christmas aboard *Madeline* with Gillian and Dugald. Boxing Day was spent back at Westhaven Marina partying on *Rode Beer*.

The next day we hopped out of *Madeline* and into Matilda. We dashed south, breaking it up with camping and visiting Alec's relatives along the way. His mother grew up in New Zealand, and her whole family still lived there. Leaving the beautiful pastoral North Island, we crossed to the majestic snow-capped mountains and lupin-covered valleys of the Southern Alps. We arrived at his family's cottage in Wanaka for New Year's Eve and spent a week celebrating with Alec's aunts, uncles and cousins, before returning north for my mid-January flight to Canada. Just before I left New Zealand, we moved *Madeline* to a boat yard north of Auckland.

The in-flight movie started, and even though I still felt video-deprived after the busy visit home, I was too absorbed in my thoughts to be interested. I decided to write in my journal. *"Our trip around the world doesn't seem so large and all-encompassing to me now as it did a year ago. Our day-to-day life on board Madeline is drastically different from what it was in Canada, but I'm starting to see it as a trip, and not as a lifetime."*

There were two things that had made my adjustment to cruising difficult. *"Our journey itself – the very nature of it – is unusual, isolating, risky, potentially dangerous, but very exciting. This has been a lot to deal with, yet it seemed so much more trying during the first year than it does in retrospect from my seat here in the airplane... Experience helps – I've now sailed over 10,000 miles. That should build some confidence."*

The second thing was being away from my friends and family. Initially I had thought I was just homesick, but now I saw that the support group I'd had my whole life had been absent during the most challenging part. *"At home, there are countless ways to alleviate stress and life's frustrations – phone calls to friends or family, people to visit, aerobics classes, movies, shopping – all sorts of diversions and escapes. I depended on my support group for my happiness, but on the boat, I have limited resources to counterbalance the irritations."*

When I had arrived in Canada, my parents had been anticipating all sorts of strange things. They had thought that I would be malnourished and sickly, and hoped I would tell them I wasn't going back. They were surprised to see me so fit and tanned. They saw a woman who was confident and pleased with her decision to sail around the world. I even sensed pride in my father's voice when he said to a friend, "She is sailing around the world *and* working as a doctor. She's doing it all."

I felt satisfied that I had taken care of the main reason Alec and I were having so many problems. I had been feeling out of my element and lacking the confidence and self-esteem that were normally bolstered by my career, my family and my friends. Seeing the trip from the perspective of home and my family – that it was such an amazing adventure and a wonderful opportunity – gave me the boost I needed. Alec encouraged me, but I couldn't expect him to fill all my needs.

Of course when Alec was calm and I was panicking, I was disappointed in myself. There would still be challenges, but I felt stronger now. I was refreshed and ready to tackle the rest of the trip with a new spirit. I had great hope for our future together on *Madeline*.

Alec met me at the Auckland airport. We had so much to talk about. On *Madeline*, we shared every little event during the day and were almost always together. Now we had six weeks to catch up on. We talked for hours at a little café in the fashionable Ponsonby area of

Auckland. I told him of all my visiting, my work and our families. He told me of his troubles at Gulf Harbour Marina.

While I was away, Alec had made the decision to paint the hulls on *Madeline*. He had the time, the costs in New Zealand were low, and we had been wanting to do this at some point during the trip. He had hired an outside contractor to spray paint *Madeline*, only because the boat yard's painter was too busy. This had unfortunately embroiled him in yard politics and he was fed up with the egos and unprofessional yard management.

In the meantime, Alec had taken *Madeline* apart and put her back together again, with extra attention to the rigging, the rudders, the engine and the bottom. One more coat of paint was all that was left before we could escape.

A week later we sailed back to Auckland and reunited with *Rode Beer*. We spent every evening together, catching up as well as planning our next stage of cruising. Our plan was to head west to Australia whereas *Rode Beer* was sailing north to Fiji, but we made arrangements to meet up in Indonesia at the beginning of August. The Indonesian authorities required us to submit an itinerary of the islands we intended to visit. Not an easy job, as with over 13,000 islands, this was the largest island group in the world.

Nathalie, Robert and Alec had read guidebooks and had planning sessions while I was in Canada. The problem was that, of the foursome, I was the least adventurous. They all immediately agreed that the goal was to get off "the beaten path". Alec had read about some cruisers who had sailed around northeast Borneo, skirting one of the last areas of piracy, the Sulu Sea and the Filipino Sulu Archipelago. It didn't take Alec long to convince Nathalie and Robert.

It took a little longer with me. Our prepaid, stamped and official Indonesian itinerary took us up the Indonesian coast of Borneo, so I didn't have much choice, but we all agreed that we would re-evaluate the plan as we uncovered more information.

Soon it was time for yet another goodbye with *Rode Beer*. Such was the nature of our friendship. It seemed we had just said hello again, when the goodbyes reappeared. I could never be quite sure when, or where, or if I would see them again. So much could happen to change a cruiser's plans.

We sailed up the northeast coast of New Zealand during the day, stopping each night to anchor. The weather was perfectly sunny and warm with just enough wind for smooth sailing without any ocean swell. Our first town was Whangarei, where we found dozens of overseas boats that we hadn't seen since Tonga. There was an end-of-season party for cruisers, thrown by the town, and we managed to get ourselves invited.

It was a completely social time, saddened with numerous goodbyes. Most of the overseas boats would spend another season in the South Pacific going to Tonga, Fiji, Vanuatu and then returning to New Zealand or Australia for the next hurricane season. Only *Rode Beer* and *Kick 'em Jenny* were continuing on as we were, into the Indian Ocean. We bid farewell to our Canadian friends from *Windrose*; they were heading back to Vancouver, on the final leg of their South Pacific voyage.

Continuing north, we sailed to the Bay of Islands, the most popular cruising area in New Zealand. The remainder of the overseas boats spent their season there, and again we made our goodbyes, this time with our German friends from *Wado Ryu*.

Following the passage to Jamaica, we had asked Alec's father when he would like to join us next. Jim asked what would be our toughest, most challenging passage of the trip. The response came quickly: "The Tasman".

Between New Zealand and Australia, the Tasman Sea has a well-earned reputation with sailors. Rather than brave its waters, most yachts travel north to the tropics instead of crossing directly from New Zealand to Australia. Seasoned Kiwi sailors would quip, "Head north until the butter melts, then turn left." But Alec's sister lived in Sydney, which is at the same latitude as the northern tip of New Zealand. From the time we first planned our circumnavigation, we had intended to cross directly to Australia.

After we arrived in New Zealand, Jim raised the subject again. "I completely understand if you decide to do it by yourselves," he said over the phone. We weighed the benefit of an extra crew to sit watches, versus the disruption to our sailing routine. We didn't foresee any problem, so we committed to meeting him in Picton at the top of the South Island.

Going to Picton would give us a better sailing angle to cross the Tasman Sea with its predominant southwesterlies. But it meant crossing the notorious Cook Strait between the North and South Island, more notorious than the entire Tasman, though only twelve miles wide. I feared getting caught in one of the horrendous gales that the Southern Alps funnel through the Cook Strait. The ferocious winds and violent seas have toppled huge car ferries that ply the strait.

Alec planned our journey to Picton with adequate time to wait for weather windows, and we knew the weather forecasting on the VHF radio was frequent and reliable. The best approach, depending on who we spoke to, was to sail down the west side of New Zealand, so we sailed north on our social trip trying to time the weather to round the top and dash south down the west side.

When we resumed sailing north from the Bay of Islands, large dolphins guided us out to sea. Just as we could make out the steep cliffs protecting Whangaroa Harbour, the wind sprang up from the north. We reefed down the sails and started the painful, deafening beat to windward.

As an unconscious reflex, I suddenly lost control, crying and complaining to Alec. In turn, he snapped at me, "Deal with it!"

I was more upset with myself than the conditions. These past weeks had been the absolute best that cruising had to offer. I was so happy back on *Madeline*, sailing and with Alec again. I thought that the trip home had worked its wonder, filling all my needs that weren't being met aboard *Madeline*. I had a renewed sense of confidence. I had erased all the doubts and fears that had plagued our relationship throughout the South Pacific.

Then why was I acting this way? Why was I ruining it? If I couldn't handle this, how would I manage the Cook Strait, the Tasman Sea and everything else? Alec had reacted with his quick temper, with his typical unsympathetic replies, trying to solve my "problem" and fix me like a broken piece of equipment. He couldn't understand me. Who would help if I really needed it in the months to come?

The wind was now blowing 30 knots and a short steep chop had built up. Alec turned the boat downwind. "We'll find shelter elsewhere," he offered.

I appreciated his sympathy, but convinced him to keep going. "No, you're right, I can cope with this," I said. We motor sailed the last hour into the narrow entrance of Whangaroa. The green steep cliffs ringed the myriad of little bays in this large harbor. Like a walled fortress, inside it was very protected and enchanting. I was glad we had continued on.

"There was a band of steep breaking waves about a quarter mile wide extending off Cape Reinga for a couple of miles out." The cruiser described his trip around the top of the North Island. "We ended up sailing through it, but I was sure glad it wasn't at night."

The mixing of currents from the Tasman and the South Pacific could produce strange conditions and Alec read about a catamaran that flipped in nice sailing conditions when a rogue wave hit them in this area. After an early celebration of Alec's 30th birthday, we left Whangaroa in good weather hoping to round the top. We anchored south of Cape Reinga as night closed around us, waiting for the evening weather forecast.

The planning, the waiting and the uncertainty made me tense, but the forecast was perfect, so we agreed to go for it. Sailing past Cape Reinga, I could see the historic lighthouse blinking in the night. We both stayed up, closely watching the water, but there were no breaking seas or violent rip currents. Our timing was right.

The water was like polished glass. There was not a breath of wind, nothing to ripple the surface. The only movement was a gentle swell that flowed underneath us like pouring molasses. I was mesmerized, almost hypnotized. The glowing orange and fiery red-stained clouds of the sunset were perfectly reflected on the mirrored surface in front of *Madeline*. Behind, the churning motor left a bubbly wake.

The weather had stayed perfect, almost too calm, but one more night would put us in New Plymouth, our last stop before the Cook Strait.

Two small land birds frenetically circled *Madeline*, reminding us we were not alone. They settled on the port lifelines close together and puffed out their plumage in preparation for the night.

Just below the water's surface, thousands of tiny sailing jellyfish poked their translucent pink sails through the reflected sky. The folding swells created shadows on the distant surface, playing tricks with our eyes and games with our minds. But it was no illusion when Alec burst out, "Whale!"

The broad back of a whale surfaced before *Madeline*, breath and spray blowing skyward.

The back and dorsal fin surfaced again, as the whale expelled more air. It was moving very slowly and our gap was quickly narrowing. The smooth gray flesh surfaced in almost the same position. The distance from the blowhole to the dorsal fin was wider than *Madeline*.

"Cut the engine!" Alec called back. I put the engine in neutral and ran forward to join him. Twenty feet in front of *Madeline* the whale surfaced and arched its back to sound. There was a large gasp as it took a final breath and then disappeared into the dark water. We stood silently in awe, a barnyard stench wafting through the air. *Madeline* glided up to where only moments before the huge whale wallowed.

Far to starboard another whale surfaced sending a spume of water into the sky. Were they always there, like the jellyfish, but only seen in the calm? I wondered how many times we had been this close, but had not known it. I'd heard whales had a blind spot with their echolocation, but the theory was they could hear you if your engine was running and still avoid you. If I hadn't shifted into neutral, would we have hit the whale? What would've happened? Would it have gotten angry and attacked us?

I hoped to never find out.

A few days later in New Plymouth a local sailor hollered from the barge we were tied to, welcoming us. He told us that few foreign yachts stop in New Plymouth, or even leave the sanctuaries of northern New Zealand. This pleased Alec, but made me wonder why so few venture south. It was getting cool as winter was approaching and when I saw a penguin in the harbor, I knew we were too far from the equator.

As with sailors around the world, the conversation swung to future plans and the exchange of helpful information. We picked this sailor's mind for advice on crossing the Cook Strait and anchorages in the Marlborough Sounds. We had some charts, but local knowledge could be a lifesaver. He told us of weather forecasts and weather patterns. A few hours later he came back with a guidebook for the Sounds. "Just mail it back to me when you are finished with it," he said.

We left New Plymouth with a light breeze behind us, and the prediction of it building to 20 knots. It was only a 24-hour hop across the dreaded Cook Strait and into the Marlborough Sounds. At midnight Alec woke me for my watch.

"Listen to this," he said with a laugh. He turned up the VHF radio so I could hear from the warmth of my sleeping bag.

Over the static I could hear the Kiwi weatherman, "The regional weather center in Wellington has issued a gale warning for the Cook Strait and Marlborough Sounds."

I groaned. Our weather luck was short-lived.

"I can't believe this," I muttered, pulling a sweater over my head.

Alec laughed with excitement. "At least the wind is from behind."

Two hours later I woke Alec to further reef the sails because we were sailing too quickly and would arrive before sunrise. At dawn the building wind chased us into the sounds, and as the sky slowly lightened, the islands ahead were veiled in an eerie orange-colored cloud. The wind was over 25 knots and rain squalls were pummeling us, momentarily blotting out the surreal landfall. I said, "It looks like we're approaching hell."

Alec responded, "Yeah, I guess this is what you see as hell, Alayne. Sailing towards a group of unknown islands with zero visibility and a Cook Strait gale on your stern. None of the usual fiery stuff!"

I didn't like the scene at all, but as the sun rose, the wind seemed less and the land less foreboding. Escaping before the worst of the gale, we sailed into Pelorus Sound, and were sheltered by tall fjord-like fingers of land that project into the Cook Strait. The steep cliffs were green with bushes and small windswept trees. The wind quickly calmed and we unreefed the sails to keep the boat moving.

Bullets of wind frequently screamed across the water with little tornadoes being sucked from the surface. There was scant warning and we had no time to reef the sails so we let out the sheets and the sails flapped wildly until the gust passed. After each gust, the wind was nonexistent. We struggled to sail until the next bullet descended upon us. Soon we called it quits and motored into a large bay.

The bay was very deep and steep and there was one valley in the bay where the wind was funneling down at double the speed. Whitecaps started at the shore, and we could see that choosing the right place to anchor was critical. We hailed the only other boat, a Kiwi sailboat, and they pointed to a couple of mooring buoys on the other side of the bay. "Those belong to a local cruising club and they are in the best spot. If no member takes them before nightfall, you are free to use them."

Alec always resisted taking a mooring and trusting someone else's work, preferring to rely on our anchor. In this case, it seemed that the moorings were there for good reason. Late in the day we motored over and took one.

We had a week before Jim arrived and we slowly sailed to Picton, which is nestled in the head of Queen Charlotte Sound. Some areas had the deforested, sheep-grazed look common to New Zealand, but most of the Marlborough Sounds were rugged and untouched. We spent a couple of cold foggy evenings in magical little coves surrounded by lush pine forests. Many mornings we woke to see our breath hanging in the air and I would pull on my long underwear while still in my sleeping bag, before layering on shirts and sweaters.

We were noticing many older, more traditional yachts with classic lines, tan-colored sails, wooden masts and ample baggywrinkle in the shrouds. Baggywrinkle are clumps of material resembling feather dusters that are tied along the wire shrouds to protect the sails from chafe when they rub against the rigging.

A local fisherman stopped us, and asked us about our boat and our trip. With a tone of certainty he said, "Surely you couldn't have crossed an ocean with that boat!" I prepared to counteract the usual comments about catamarans flipping, when he went on, "She's not salty enough. You don't have any baggywrinkle!"

In Picton we met some local sailors, Les and Zoey, who offered us their mooring in the crowded harbor. We happily accepted this safe and cheap alternative. Les also invited us into the yacht club and we had a nice evening over cocktails.

There were a couple of foreign boats in Picton, but we were the only multihull, foreign or local. Many of the sailors were skeptical of multihulls and thought we were either brave or foolish. Alec tried to show how popular catamarans were becoming, especially in Australia and even north in Auckland. They shrugged their shoulders saying that sailing was different in these waters.

Once again we discussed local sailing conditions and our plans to cross the Tasman. They told us Picton

was no longer a customs port, which meant we would have to sail to Nelson before leaving New Zealand. We could sail back across the Cook Strait to Wellington, the capital, to clear out of the country, but that meant a lot of sailing in the Cook Strait, something I was determined to avoid. The trip to Nelson, however, meant going through "French Pass", a narrow section of the Sounds where the tidal currents race through at seven knots or more. Les assured me it was no problem if you went through at slack tide, but it was critical to approach at the right time.

Alec's father had booked a month for the Tasman. The distance across was only 1,200 miles, or ten days of good sailing. Thirty days seemed more than adequate, but headwinds, gales and a possible stop at Lord Howe Island in the Tasman would increase the actual passage time. Now there was a trip to Nelson and possibly a week's wait for the right weather window before we would leave. Alec's sister Gillian, in Sydney, hoped to have time with her father before he left too, so all these pressures were adding up.

Alec assured me we would consider the safety of *Madeline* and her crew first and if the schedule was missed, his father could always book a different flight home. Money was expendable, our lives were not. We monitored the weather religiously, trying to better understand the weather patterns so that once Jim arrived we could predict our departure. Alec was constantly rethinking the schedule.

While we waited in Picton, Alec's cousin came to visit with his wife, small child and dog. They drove from Christchurch to see *Madeline*, and to share a weekend of fishing and barbecuing. I told Richard that we had to go to Nelson, which meant taking French Pass. He looked to Alec and said, "French Pass? You're a brave man."

"Have you been through?" Alec asked.

"No, I've just heard the stories about it," Richard said.

The next day I asked Alec what he thought Richard meant by his comment. Richard was an airline pilot and had served as an officer in the army. He was not someone to be easily impressed.

"He's just having some fun with you and trying to make something out of it," Alec said. "With every danger there are anecdotes, some personal and some passed through the grapevine. But you don't make decisions based on one-time occurrences where you don't have all the details and don't know the people. You make decisions based on taking precautions, being prepared and being aware of what usually happens statistically. I'm sure hundreds of people travel French Pass regularly without a problem."

"But you didn't even know about this until we got here!"

"So what? We do now." Alec countered. "I have a tide table and we'll plan to arrive at the pass before slack tide. Then when the tide switches and there is no current, we can motor through. Don't worry," Alec repeated his mantra to me. "It'll be no problem."

These calm and logical discussions helped redirect my fears and prevented them from escalating. Yet there was always a thread of doubt. Alec almost enjoyed leaving that doubt in the equation. That was what made it exciting. For me it would continuously nag until the situation had passed.

Jim arrived in Picton after a turbulent flight over the Cook Strait from Wellington. We spent the first evening chatting, opening gifts from home and reading our mail. Alec and I dinghied to the yacht club to finish our laundry and have a last long hot shower.

It remained cold, even in the sunshine the next day, while we sailed to a bay five miles from French Pass. After we had tied to a mooring, Alec brought out the tide tables. "Slack tide is around eleven in the morning which is perfect," he announced. "See? I couldn't have planned it better," he teased me.

The night was very chilly, and we closed all the hatches as well as our perpetually open companionway door. In the morning the walls of *Madeline* were dripping with condensation. After breakfast, we motored under a clear blue sky to Elmslie Bay, next to French Pass. We made the climb to the top of a small cliff face to have a look at the infamous pass.

It was a spectacular day. The rugged landscape of the pass was stunning, reminiscent of a Canadian river, with a racing current and white frothy overfalls. In the distance was the panorama of the snow-capped Southern Alps. I was relieved there was no wind, thankful there was one less force of nature to battle.

Perched at the lookout was a historical placard describing how d'Urville had been the first explorer to traverse the pass in the 1800's. Alec nudged me as Jim read aloud that d'Urville went through the pass under sail. "It'll be easy for us. We have an engine. No problem." Alec knew that I didn't always trust our engine, because the few times it had failed had been unexpected and almost disastrous.

Scanning the water below, we could see the flow slowing before our eyes, until it practically stopped. That was our cue. A wave of anxiety washed over me, as it did when I first heard of French Pass.

Alec had switched his tone that morning and was talking up the danger to his father, like when we had made our weekend camping jaunts back in Canada sound like a colossal battle against nature. Exaggeration had been fun then, as we tried to make our safe lives seem more exciting, but now I tried to block it out because I was so negatively affected by the comments. My life was exciting enough.

I knew from my discussions with Alec that there should be no problems. He had explained the dangers of the pass and our plan to get safely through it. I ignored any thoughts of catastrophe, and downplayed the whole event in my mind. I coped much better when I did that. Quietly I started the engine as Jim unhooked the mooring.

Tension filled the air aboard *Madeline* as we rounded the headland. Jim brought out his video camera to record our death-defying challenge. I could see where Alec got his lust for adventure.

We uneventfully motored through the absolutely calm pass. Jim came back to the cockpit shaking his head, saying, "That was a dead loss – a real non-event." Alec remained quiet, but I was sure I caught an "I told you so" glance. I said nothing, but couldn't help smiling, feeling elated that we made it through without a hitch and without heroics.

We lay at anchor in beautiful Abel Tasman National Park. A large high-pressure system had begun to cross New Zealand augmenting the area's reputation for moderate and consistent sunshine. Close to the Cook Strait but under different meteorological influences due to geography, Tasman Bay is an agricultural paradise with numerous fruit growers and vineyards.

The sun shone brilliantly in a dark blue sky warming the golden sand beaches. The park was deserted at this time of year other than a few hearty hikers and a couple of sea kayaking groups. We hiked the trails and found a large pool at the base of a waterfall to bathe in. Returning to *Madeline,* we were clean and invigorated. We were poised to venture across, to challenge, the Tasman Sea.

A few days earlier in Nelson, our last visitors to the boat had been a woman and a man from customs. I thought they were just a couple Alec

had met in town, and I couldn't understand why they were forcing their reluctant yelping dog onto our deck. The man had told Alec, "We like to dog the boats before they leave Nelson."

Before full comprehension of the verb "to dog" sunk in, the spastic canine was sniffing frantically through *Madeline*! All the dog found with his nose was Jim's backside as he bent over his berth making his bed. I'm not sure who startled who more. The customs man smiled and winked as he said, "Everything grows here."

With our customs clearance in hand, we sailed to Abel Tasman National Park. Here we monitored the weather, looking for the right signal to hoist anchor and depart.

Ironically, this beautiful sunshine wasn't what we wanted to leave in. Our intent was to leave as a low-pressure system was passing so that we could sail *into* a nice, calm, high-pressure system in the middle of the Tasman. Generally the systems alternated between high pressure, then low pressure, then high, etc. But the location and direction of the system also influenced the wind. All these factors made the decision to leave difficult and I waited in dreaded anticipation as the days dragged.

During our conversations with cruisers and local sailors over the past few months, they would inevitably ask us about our plans after New Zealand. When we told them, they would give us a concerned and pensive look, searching our eyes for confirmation that they'd heard us correctly. This was followed by a pause, and then the usual, "The Tasman, eh? Hmmm..." or the other more dramatic, "Ahhhh, the Tasman..."

Judging by the curiosity and questions evoked, I translated their comments to, "Are you guys nuts?" Again I found myself being influenced by what other people said. I couldn't help but listen to all their hearsay and anecdotes, and I omitted common sense and logic when forming my opinion about the Tasman Sea. The result was a negative mind-set for me about this purported awful stretch of water.

I expressed my concerns about the Tasman to Alec privately. He didn't get angry, but neither did he give me sympathy nor understanding. He joked about my fears and refuted them.

"What about the French Pass?" he asked. "You got all worried about that. What happened?"

"Nothing, but..."

"What about the Cook Strait? Or, the breakers at the northern tip, at Cape Reinga?"

"It all worked out," I acknowledged.

"Or the turbulence in the Panama Canal, or the passes in the Tuamotus? Everywhere we go, there is a horror story about the next place."

"Okay, okay, I get your point."

"Or the length of time needed to get to Picton. You were all worried about the weather. When did we get to Picton?"

"We got to Picton a week early, but we never waited long for weather."

"I'll admit the weather was good, but we did wait. We waited in Whangaroa, briefly at the top and in New Plymouth. We had a week to spare, because we'd planned for it. We had a good trip because we were careful and we sailed at the right times."

"But this seems different," I said. "The Tasman is so many more miles. I just want to get it over with."

"I know waiting is tough. I'd rather just get out there too, but we must leave with the right weather."

"I know. You're right."

I couldn't argue his impeccable logic. His careful planning had resulted in our successful crossing of the Pacific. Our track record should have given me more confidence.

But there was something else. A few days earlier at a payphone in Nelson, we'd called our families and told them we'd be leaving soon, but refused to give a date of departure or an anticipated date of arrival in Australia. Our weather would be unpredictable and we were wary to set expectations. The calls were fun and positive, but later Jim told us that both Alec's mother and his sister dreaded the trip and had visions of losing almost half of their family.

My mind was unsettled. I was scared too.

THE TASMAN

"ARP! ARP!" TO ALLEVIATE THE BOREDOM of waiting, we sailed to Tonga Island to see the seals. Our guidebook warned about being nipped, so we watched the youngsters wrestle in the frigid water from the safety of our dinghy. The gorgeous sunshine was ending; a fast-moving low was to the north. At lunch time we listened to the weather forecast and Alec decided we could leave.

A school of dolphins joined us, performing their impressive underwater acrobatics at the bow. Alec had always been tempted to swim with them, and decided to give it a try. I stopped the engine and he jumped in, wearing his wet suit, fins, mask and snorkel. The dolphins swam by him, a group in formation, and Alec was thrilled. He played with them as long as he could stand the icy cold and then he insisted I try it.

I was reluctant to jump into the open ocean, but talked myself into climbing down and holding onto the swim ladder. Endless murky green filled my vision. I felt exhilaration at just hanging over the bottomless depths and my heart pumped wildly to warm my shivering body. As I waited expectantly, searching the watery void, two dolphins slowly came into view. My muscles froze. They swam closer and then turned past me. Wow!

The wind built in the afternoon. We were close-hauled and fighting a current, but the boat was handling well. We had finally started, but I was on edge and could not shake my apprehension. I found myself being curt and impatient with Jim, but couldn't understand why. I told Alec I was feeling tense and that I needed to talk.

"I don't understand, Alayne. For a week you've been wanting to get going, and now that we're finally underway, you're upset."

I turned to my journal and page after page of bottled up emotions poured out. *"I'm worried about our decision to rely on Jim. He has such little experience, and yet he'll be doing an equal share of the watches. Our Caribbean passage with him a year ago was wonderful, but everything's different now. The Tasman is more treacherous, and I'm afraid...It's strange that I'm angry Jim is enjoying himself. He's seeking thrills and adventure and more than once he's said, "Isn't this exciting?" His enthusiasm is getting to me... Now, more than ever, I want to downplay the significance of this crossing. I need someone to commiserate with."*

The usual dynamics between Alec and me, our intimacy and our discussions, were stifled by the presence of a third person. There was the obvious loss of privacy, but I also felt I couldn't be myself. I had long ago given up trying to impress Alec, but I felt I needed to impress Jim, and I was reluctant to expose my fears.

I wanted Alec for myself. But he had more roles to play on this passage, and given the choice, it was clear that Jim was being better company. This angered me even more. I felt myself competing with Jim, not only in ability to handle the trip, but also in time with Alec.

Although my frustration seemed justified, I still had a long passage ahead of me. "*Where is my normally sharing, giving, pleasant self? Do I want to give in to being selfish and rude?*" After discharging my negativity onto the pages before me, I tried to be positive, concluding, "*I have a wonderful life. This is a great opportunity and I can embrace it with high spirits or I can mar it with a bad attitude... What do I have to gain by being a pain? I have so much more to gain by being good-natured.*"

For the next two days, I was positive and pleasant. We remained close-hauled, but were making reasonable progress. The bumpy seas made everyone uncomfortable. The days passed quietly, with all of us reading, sleeping and dealing in our own way with the awkward motion.

That evening the wind really picked up and we reefed the mainsail twice and took down the staysail. Rain squalls buffeted *Madeline* with gusts. Fortunately I had made some stew during the day and I made sure everyone ate, even though appetites were low.

Keri Keri radio said a cold front was approaching. The winds increased to 30 knots, but within a few hours the skies cleared. The wind eased as the front passed, but we were still left beating into 20 knots.

The sailing improved slightly the next morning; the waves were even and the wind angle was better. I had lost my appetite and was mentally exhausted after the previous night of beating. Even Alec admitted frustration and a headache, and we all agreed it would be a long and trying passage. I just hoped that we would come out closer and better friends, rather than enemies.

The horizon was full of birds and we cracked opened our seabird identification book, in an attempt to learn and differentiate the subtle markings and shapes. A Black-browed Albatross and two Yellow-nosed Albatrosses followed us for much of the morning. Most of the birds would slowly work their search pattern across the waves and then soar in the draft of *Madeline's* mainsail, curiously eyeing us. A huge

134

Wandering Albatross floated above our silver arch momentarily, before soaring off without a flap. Its wingspan was the width of the boat.

I tried to be competitive in a Scrabble game, but the concentration and jiggling tiles made me woozy. At noon the rain squalls began again and we quickly reefed down the sails. Low, dark clouds loomed on the horizon and whistling gusts over 30 knots kept our progress to a minimum. The seas picked up and *Madeline* smashed through the waves, yet again. After four hours the clouds passed and Alec predicted a wind shift. The wind began to swing south and the barometer started to rise. Alec stir-fried dinner and afterward, I fell deeply asleep.

"It's your watch." Alec stroked my head to wake me, and said, "I've got good news. The weather report said there is a huge high-pressure system in front of us."

"Congratulations," I said. "Just as you planned it. I can't wait for some calm weather."

"The bad weather lasted longer than I hoped, but it's all working out now." He took off his clothes and we traded places. "Oh, I heard a whale spouting beside us on my watch," he added.

Sitting in the cockpit, facing the stern, I watched the star-studded sky slowly decrease in intensity as an orange luminescence radiated upwards from the horizon. I knew what was coming, so I grabbed a chocolate-covered granola bar and a glass of milk for the show. I snuggled into my seat and watched in awe, as the orange and then pink light grew brighter. Like a slice of watermelon, the moon began to magically hover over the black horizon. It was a magnificent performance for an audience of one. I experienced a rush of gladness.

After my watch I had a solid sleep even though *Madeline* raced along, careening down the swells. The wind was from behind and the barometer was still trending upward. We needed to make distance now, before the wind disappeared. At dawn the sky was mostly clear except for the puffy cumulus clouds, indicating a high was approaching.

My appetite returned and I cooked gourmet pizza for lunch and did a little housekeeping while Jim did the dishes. He had volunteered to do all the dishes on the passage rather than kill us with his cooking. We played Scrabble in the afternoon and I won. A couple of rain squalls buffeted us, but the wind stayed from behind and the sailing was tolerable.

We ran the engine and played a CD while Jim and I brought our journals up to date. We compared notes and both agreed that the weather had been pretty poor up until now. Our personal interpretations of the trip, however, differed vastly.

"Jim is hanging in much better than me, and of the female contingent, Madeline is also coping better. She's built for heavy weather, whereas I'm not. Physical seasickness and my emotional fear are still a struggle. Positive thinking helps, if only I can keep it up... I keep telling myself that the Tasman Sea is just another body of water, and we've crossed lots of bodies of water. I know that the heavy seas and rough weather will return, but I have to remind myself that we're crossing at the safest time, we're monitoring the weather obsessively and we're doing exceptionally well. Although it's been a very rough ride, I have to admit it's not that bad. Nothing is unsafe. But, whether it makes sense or not, I'm still scared to death. I can't wait to get into warmer, calmer and seemingly safer latitudes. It's all in your state of mind, and in this, I have a lot to learn from Jim."

Jim viewed the trip from an entirely different perspective. He had joined us for the excitement and challenge of the passage, neither of which were lacking. He suffered little from seasickness, quickly adapted to low-maintenance grooming and was content with simple foods like sandwiches and pressure-cooked potatoes. He took to the sea naturally. His father and his father's father had been fishermen in the north of Scotland, and he had traced their roots back to the Vikings that raided from across the North Sea. Jim grew up when the herring stocks were rapidly dwindling. Discouraged from following his ancestral vocation, he became the first from the fishertown to go to university. Although his recreation was spent on the links rather than in a boat, the sea salt was still in his blood. It made perfect sense to him that Alec would be attracted back to the sea.

I admired Jim for his eternal optimism, his apparent lack of fear, and his ability to block out the plethora of noises when we were beating. He was able to chat, eat and sleep as if the body of water next to him was his backyard pool. I could now understand what Alec's expectations were modeled on; Jim made it look so easy.

"Now, I'm glad Jim is experiencing this with us and feel he adds something special. My hopes are coming true – we've developed a sailing style, pace and teamwork. I wonder if my impatience a few days ago was just seasickness." It had taken Alec and me our entire first year to learn to deal with each other, especially during times of stress and

seasickness-induced irritability. I wondered if Jim was seasick or stressed, but I knew he would never say.

The next day proved great sailing. It was noticeably warmer as we'd moved up four degrees of latitude. Like many mornings, the decks were covered with large flying fish and squid. Alec took the deck brush and cleaned off the scales and ink. We created funny skits for Jim's video, feeding dead flying fish to the albatrosses and sending a message in a bottle to Gillian and Dugald in Sydney. We played Scrabble and I did some writing on our new computer. There was a big swell running, but the waves were hundreds of feet apart. When *Madeline* slowly reached the peak of a long swell you could see the ocean undulating into the distance like giant sand dunes in the Sahara.

Lord Howe, an Australian island about 400 miles east northeast of Sydney, was north of the direct path to Sydney. We had purposely sailed closer to it just in case we needed to take refuge in an emergency. A cruiser had given us an aerial-view postcard and had marked the pass through the reef. The island was a spectacular sight with jagged peaks and a partially protected lagoon.

We were 620 nautical miles from Sydney versus 400 nautical miles from Lord Howe, plus an additional 400 afterward from Lord Howe to Sydney. We were reaching the point where we had to decide if we would go to Lord Howe or proceed to Sydney.

The weather forecast indicated a large area of light westerly wind. We were getting the high-pressure system we wanted, but the light winds would be against us. Alec felt we could motor to Lord Howe, get more fuel and then wait for another good weather window for the last passage to Sydney. We didn't have enough fuel to motor to Sydney and maybe we could sail straight to Lord Howe in the light westerly.

Alec was favoring Lord Howe and asked for opinions. Jim opted for Lord Howe just to see it. A remote island landfall was high up on his adventuring scale. I pointed out that this meant extra nautical miles at sea, but assuming I would be out-voted, I agreed to Lord Howe.

That night on my watch I was furious. My foul mood matched the light fluky winds alternating with annoying rain showers. I could not believe that Alec would take a vote. Why would we delay our journey to Sydney? Why would we spend longer on this awful sea? I couldn't believe I had agreed to go to Lord Howe. I knew this diversion would be a big mistake – I could only maintain my composure for so long.

The morning was dramatic with rainbows and albatrosses everywhere, but my foul mood remained. *"I'm ready to be finished with the Tasman, and I can't get enjoyment from this stark beauty. For some reason the weather is unsettled and I'm tired of the gusts and the sound of surf under Madeline. I have cabin fever and want this jerky motion to stop. Where's the high pressure?"* Everything was black for me, and the island of Lord Howe now embodied all the dread and fear I had been harboring since leaving New Zealand.

In an effort to keep my spirits up, I made a celebratory halfway chocolate cake with chocolate sauce for dessert that night. I should have been happy for our success so far, but as we sat down together, all sorts of emotions bubbled up. "I don't want to go to Lord Howe. We're increasing our total time on the Tasman Sea," I said, tears in my eyes. "Prolonging this passage feels like we're pushing our luck."

"But we're doing well so far," Jim said.

"I know, but the sooner we make it to Sydney, the better."

"We're making good time, and the wind is best for Lord Howe," Alec argued. "It'll be a unique landfall in an out-of-the-way place, and more importantly, you'll get a break from the sailing."

"And it's a chance for me to contribute with the cooking," Jim added. "Dinner ashore will be my treat."

Later Alec spoke to me privately, apologizing if I thought there was a vote on whether we would head towards Lord Howe. "The final decision is mine," he reminded me, "but your opinion is always considered. We're still making progress to Sydney, so if you have good reason, we can continue on non-stop."

"I just want the Tasman to end as soon as possible." I poured out my feelings of dread and doom. "I see Lord Howe Island cloaked in an evil fog. I see disaster."

"You're being ridiculous," Alec countered. "We've been through this before. You've agreed that your emotional outbursts and irrational fears don't justify changing the way we handle the boat."

"Please," I pleaded with him.

"Look Alayne," he snarled, "state your concerns in a logical and comprehensible fashion and they will be considered."

I was angry. I felt very alone. I had lost my sense of control over the situation.

As if to confirm my premonition, the wind increased in strength all night and the next day. The seas grew steep, gray clouds rolled in and the barometer fell significantly. Alec was perplexed. "Southerly winds over 25 knots. That's not what was predicted." He tuned into the weather forecast with headphones to help him hear the now distant station. He took notes as Jim and I patiently waited to hear the verdict.

Alec removed the headphones with a concerned look on his face. "At least that explains our weather. Remember that large area of light wind? The forecast was completely wrong. Now they say it's a late tropical storm! And it's right on top of us!"

LORD HELL

ALEC WANTED TO RACE FOR LORD HOWE, and we had to maintain an average of six knots to get there before dark the next night. Speed was not a problem, as there was ample wind to push us along. The waves were steep and *Madeline* crashed over them much faster than I liked. Two or three wave patterns created big sloppy and confused seas with the occasional large tumbling peak of water when the swells converged. Squalls continually passed over us, but Alec was reluctant to reef, wanting to keep up the speed. I was tense and tired, and we started our usual argument about the boat speed.

"It's better to get there and re-evaluate things then," he insisted. "We have good wind direction now. Let's take advantage of it, because our weather could change. You never know what may happen with this storm and we may be really thankful to be anchored at Lord Howe rather than spending another night out at sea."

"You forget I don't want to go to Lord Howe. All you're doing is pushing the boat and increasing the risk of something breaking," I retaliated. "You are always the same. It's so frustrating!"

"Oh Yeah?" Alec countered. "Yesterday you wanted to end the trip quicker, but today you want go slower and make it last longer! *You* are always the same. Talk about frustrating, ARRGH!"

We kept up the speed, but the constant motion and crashing made sleep difficult. In conditions like this the greatest enemy was fatigue, so we kept to a watch system of two hours on, four hours off. We arranged the watches so that Alec got more sleep because he was constantly being woken when the wind shifted or the sails needed reefing.

When Jim was on watch Alec and I slept together in our bunk, a luxury for a passage, but little consolation in these conditions. I suddenly woke, feeling the boat accelerating down a wave. I elbowed Alec, "There's something wrong!"

We both stumbled out into the cockpit where Jim was monitoring the sails. The wind had increased and was blowing well over 30 knots. The swells had built to ten feet.

"We're making great progress!" Jim bellowed enthusiastically.

Madeline was in the trough of a wave. Slowly the next wave lifted her. She increased speed, starting a long fast surf, maintaining her position on the wave. Alec peered at the dim light of the knotmeter.

"We're going thirteen knots!" He turned to his father yelling over the roar of the wake, "You're supposed to wake me up when things change! I didn't want to go *that* fast!"

We quickly reefed the mainsail and brought *Madeline's* speed down to a safer six-knot average, only going eight knots when slicing down the waves. Remarkably, the autopilot had handled the high speed.

By next morning we'd covered a record distance in 24 hours. The wind was screaming and *Madeline* continued to charge along under heavily-reefed sails. The gale-force winds were still blowing although blue sky now peeked occasionally through the dark clouds. This would be *Madeline's* trickiest landfall. There were 40 miles to go and no sign of the weather abating. It was difficult decision-making, but Alec felt there was too much wind and sea to attempt going through the reef at a late hour in the day.

He went to the bow and deployed our sea anchor. The fifteen-foot diameter parachute opened in the water and *Madeline* drifted back, bow into the wind. All was secure within a matter of minutes and we hovered there in the sea, tugging at the parachute.

Alec cooked a big brunch of scrambled eggs while Jim videotaped the blustery scene outside. I went into my room and hid. Periodically a breaking wave pounded us, roaring underneath the boat like a train, and I cringed as *Madeline* staggered drunkenly.

Alec listened to the weather forecast describing the tropical storm, and then announced, "We'll go ahead tomorrow and try to get through the reef."

I couldn't believe my ears. Why was he so insistent on going to this island? I expressed my disapproval.

"I thought that the ominous forecast would make you want to duck into Lord Howe," he said.

"The southerly winds and swell could make the entrance impassable," I countered.

"If it *is* dangerous, we will change plans *then,*" he said. "What do you want to do? Start beating towards Sydney now, in 35 knots of wind?"

"We could sail to any port on the coast. Like Coff's Harbour or something further north and easier to get to. We could miss Sydney," I responded.

"True," Alec said, "and we could still do that after waiting one night on the sea anchor. We have time."

"It's not that bad out there," Jim said, poking his head in from the cockpit.

His comment maddened me more, because I knew it wasn't *that* bad. I was enraged that my emotions were not being considered. I felt I had no control over my destiny. Again, I retreated to the solace of my bunk and my journal. I couldn't believe the two of them were calmly and happily setting up a game of Scrabble.

I thought of a *Cruising World* article where a man wrote, "What seems normal and logical to me scares the hell out of her." This was true in our case, but what could I do? I had so few choices. I gathered my thoughts, and considered my options, tears streaming down my face.

"I could carry on, keeping my fears to myself and obeying the orders. I could act as one of the team, contributing the best I can. This is how I've been for most of the Tasman, but my reserve is waning. I feel myself weakening, crumbling and sick with fear. I'm disappointed in myself. I thought I was made of pretty tough stuff, but I have to accept I'm not like the men. I'm just not cut out for this.

My only other choice is to stay in my hideaway – refuse to participate. Alec and Jim could probably get the sea anchor up and manage without me. Why should I leave my bunk when I don't agree with the plan and I don't want to be in this situation?"

My writing made me feel better, but then Alec poked his head in and made a sarcastic joke about my crying, leaving me even more upset. Burying my face in my pillow, I bawled. Regardless of my choices, I just needed someone to comfort me, someone to hug me and tell me it would be all right. Where was my daddy? Where were my girlfriends when I needed them? Did the safety of the boat include the morale of the crew? At least Val had her son to put his arm around her. I had never before felt so utterly sad.

Again Alec came into the cabin and this time he sat down beside me. I couldn't talk without loud sobs and I didn't want Jim to hear me, so I had Alec read my latest journal entry.

After a few minutes he sighed and said, "You're right Alayne, it's rough out there, and maybe we should skip Lord Howe. Come here." He held me close. "It's gonna be all right."

The wind had eased to 25 knots.

The next morning I woke feeling less tense. Stepping outside, I scanned the circular horizon, noting the waves, the wind and the clouds. Everything was calmer and once again, I agreed to go to Lord Howe Island. I made everyone breakfast and then we lifted the sea anchor.

We sailed past Ball's Pyramid, a towering rocky obelisk covered in nesting birds. As Lord Howe Island slowly rose on the horizon, the winds increased rapidly to gale force all over again. Clouds shrouded the island just as I had pictured before. Short but violent squalls and large rolling breakers accompanied us towards the pass into the lagoon.

The mainsail was double reefed yet we still surfed down the waves at nine knots. Screaming birds wheeled above us in the gray boiling sky. Jim shouted over the din, "It seems as if Lord Howe Island doesn't want us to come."

It all was so crazy, so awful. Like the low squall clouds that scudded over us, a black storm cloud in my head blotted out any ray of hope. I dreaded Lord Howe, and again I loathed the idea of going there. I started to cry and I retreated to my bunk, my only refuge.

Alec came below, furious. "What are you doing?" he asked rhetorically. He told me I was acting as if I was crazy; that I wasn't making sense. But I couldn't stop the fear and the dread that was building inside me. I told him I wanted out. I told him I would jump overboard. In a rage, he ordered me, "You are doing no such thing. Stay there!"

He composed himself and returned to the cockpit where Jim was monitoring the sails. *Madeline* paralleled the coast and Alec called the harbor master on Lord Howe. The response was that the entrance through the reef was rough, "But it shouldn't be a problem, Cap'n."

Large swells crashed on the outer reef sending up plumes of spray. Some of the swell bounced back off the island making the seas very confused. Strange waves slapped *Madeline's* hulls and tossed her about. Alec motored in closer, looking for the pass.

He positioned me inside, next to the radio, to relay any assistance from the harbor master. I opened a hatch, needing fresh air to combat the waves of seasickness and fear washing over me. A huge wave smacked the hull broadside, cascading through the hatch, dousing our stereo and me. "You're completely useless!" Alec angrily yelled down.

Then I saw the pass. The waves weren't breaking but rolling in and crashing against a black cliff just past the reef. Alec gunned the engine and we surfed through the pass on a wave. Then he spun the wheel to starboard and *Madeline* slowly turned into the lagoon and away from the ominous rocky cliff. We motored to a mooring, and Jim and I struggled to get the stout line around our cleat.

I went back to my bunk and cried.

Alec tried to break the tension by opening some champagne, but when I looked in his eyes I could see his disappointment. A small boat appeared with the customs official, so I put on my game face and we casually went through the entrance formalities. The official insisted we carry on with our celebration, so we poured the drinks and toasted our safe arrival.

The champagne didn't taste very sweet.

In the lagoon we were fully exposed to the wind, and the surf poured over the reef at high tide. *Madeline* tugged at her mooring as she was tossed violently by the turbulent chop. We stayed near the reef, ready to leave as soon as the weather was right.

Two spectacular mountains sprang out of the ocean, adjoined by a semicircle of land with a powder-blue lagoon filling in the other half. The flat-topped mountains dominated the skyline like a medieval fortress. Vegetation clung to the dark cliffs and black specs of seabirds perpetually swirled around. On the ocean side, long unspoiled beaches filled the bays that had been carved out of the rock. The topography and beauty challenged that of Bora Bora, but without the warm tropical languor. Lord Howe was rugged and menacing.

Immediately we went ashore for hot showers. We explored the small resort island by foot and soon had surveyed the menus at the half-dozen restaurants. Lush, green vegetation hugged the quaint streets, and unique varieties of birds flitted past us as we strolled the myriad of trails.

Alec and I went for a walk, and took advantage of our time alone to talk. My mood was sour.

"I'm not enjoying this journey at all," I said.

"Alayne, we're in a small boat in the middle of the Tasman Sea. What did you fucking expect?!" He struggled to hold back his anger and quickly switched his tone. "Look, I'm sorry. I'm finding it tough too. I wish I could help you through this, but with the navigation, the sail changes, my dad and the cooking – I just can't do it all."

I sensed he was just trying to control the damage and get us to Sydney successfully, rather than argue about the past.

"You'd better get going and book that flight to Sydney," he joked.

I knew he didn't want that, but I could now see how my behavior was affecting him.

Jim treated us to gourmet meals. We had long hot showers, and loaded up on extra diesel. Anything to get off the rocking boat in the choppy lagoon. Alec and I went for a jog one morning, and the three of us hiked many of the trails and beaches.

We discovered that Lord Howe and its surrounding islands were named a World Heritage Site in 1982. Certain varieties of flora and fauna were only found here, and the island lay on the most southerly

Madeline beached in Hill Inlet, Australia

Friday Island rendezvous with *Rode Beer*

Family in Lombok, Indonesia

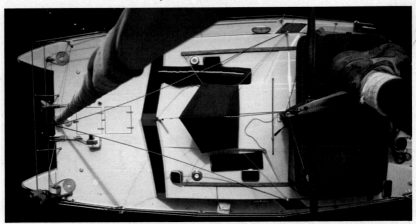
View from the masthead

Nathalie and Alayne looking at slides in Kota Kinabalu, Malaysia

Stilt houses in Borneo

Passage shower en route to Djibouti from the Maldives

Sunset in the anchorage at Isla Graciosa, Canary Islands

Homeward bound in the Caribbean

Celebrating in the Turks and Caicos Islands

coral reef in the world. The soft corals were reportedly excellent, but the water was too cold for me. The island survived on tourism, but the 280 permanent residents limited guests to 400 at a time.

Alec and I continued to talk when we could. He continued to hold back. He was angry that I had failed him, turning from an asset to a liability. I was just as angry that he hadn't considered me when I had needed him most.

While Alec and I walked several miles to the Lord Howe Bureau of Meteorology at the airstrip, I realized that Lord Howe was a welcome break after all. We had been through the worst of the Tasman, and there wasn't far to go. I stubbornly vowed to myself to continue and to carry my weight. Armed with a decent forecast of light southerly winds, we left only two days after arriving.

Forty-eight hours later I wrote in my journal: *"We're within 100 miles of Sydney facing headwinds and the East Australian Current. Our progress is painfully slow. The tenacious Tasman is not giving up, but I'm staying tough. In spite of the positive thinking aboard our ship, the Tasman refuses to cut us any breaks. The weatherman at Lord Howe didn't give us an accurate forecast. We had a night of unpredicted and unpredictable rain squalls and just one day of reasonable sailing. Our high-pressure system only lasted for ten peaceful hours and now I'm once again battling with the Tasman and my fear. But land is so close and the trip is almost over."*

Alec's call interrupted my writing. "Alayne, we need more boat speed to drive *Madeline* through these waves." I put on my salt-encrusted foul-weather gear, and went out to help him shake out a reef.

Madeline bashed through the annoyingly gusty headwinds. We monitored the wind shifts, making slight adjustments to the autopilot to keep up our progress. When the East Australian Current reached three knots and was pushing us towards Antarctica, we motor sailed through the worst of it.

Then, at long last, came the point where we were affected more by coastal conditions than by the sea. During the final 30 miles, both wind and waves gradually calmed. The sky became an unbelievably brilliant blue and I felt impossibly happy.

Classic sailor's short-term-memory syndrome took hold, and I began to forget how awful the passage was. My wounds were already beginning to heal, but I was concerned that I had done some irreparable damage to my relationship with Alec, and with Jim. There was almost a week before Jim flew home and I intended to fix everything before then. I was so happy to be finished that I wanted to cry, yet again.

We called Alec's sister, Gillian, and her husband, Dugald, ship-to-shore using the VHF radio. Symbolically, the trip was now finished.

Night had fallen and I felt it unwise to enter a strange harbor, but the sea was flat calm, so we decided to anchor just inside the Sydney Harbour entrance. I was exhausted and elated, yet tense. But we peacefully motored in, dodged a few high-speed ferries, and finally anchored in Hunter's Bay.

We opened a celebratory bottle of wine and made an easy pasta dinner. I marveled that after two weeks and 1,300 bumpy, noisy nautical miles aboard *Madeline*, we had finally found peace and quiet in the largest city in Australia.

Jim helped put things into perspective for me. "Everyone says how brave Alec is to undertake this trip around the world," he said. "But really, it's you who is sacrificing more and it's you who is doing something against your character. You show the most courage." I thought he said this to boost my morale, but also for Alec to hear. He repeated it later to others. Both Alec and Jim had been hard on me during my bouts of fear, but Jim's consolation couldn't have been better timed.

Jim declared he was off to bed, and I could no longer contain my tears. I had been pushed past my limits, to the edge of my envelope, and I'd hated it. In my darkest moments I'd been contemplating all sorts of crazy thoughts – from leaving Alec and *Madeline* and joining another boat, to flying from Lord Howe to Sydney, to flying home to my family. I even had thoughts of ending my life. Now, I couldn't believe that these feelings had been so strong. I couldn't believe they had belonged to me. I couldn't believe they had made me act the way I did.

I went outside to the cockpit and bawled like never before. I had to release it all. It was over. I felt sorry for myself. I had failed to contribute. I had failed to live up to my own expectations.

Alec put aside his frustration and comforted me while I let go of it all. He held me gently. I was absolutely emotionally drained and defeated, and I had dangerously overdrawn our emotional bank account.

Just as we were casting off from the Australian customs dock, we heard someone call, "Ahoy, *Madeline*!" I could see a Canadian flag waving, and by the time we spun around and redocked, Alec's sister was running down the pier with a bottle of champagne outstretched.

My eyes were still puffy from crying the night before, and I was hoping Gillian wouldn't ask too many questions. She was beaming with pride over our safe arrival, and we were all busy catching up on the news. I told her that it had been a rough trip, and Jim immediately agreed, but always adding the positive, that *Madeline* and crew handled it so well. Alec was quiet.

We motored through busy Sydney Harbour, past the Opera House and under the Harbour Bridge, to a bay near Gillian's home in Balmain. Jim moved up to Gillian's, just a ten-minute walk from our mooring. We celebrated that day, drinking champagne, eating tasty tidbits, reading mail and phoning home. We continued to eat our meals and spend our days at Gillian's, but each night Alec and I slept on *Madeline*.

Alec turned a stoic face to the world, not wanting to share our problem with his family. He retreated inward, saying he needed some time to think about *his* options. With the busy socializing, he was reluctant to talk about his feelings, preferring to control them. There was little time in our mornings together, but I knew we had to sort out what had happened in the Tasman.

He had been caught between entertaining his fearless father and pacifying his panicked wife, while dealing with the task of getting us all safely to Sydney. The pressures on him had been immense, but I had been so self-involved that I didn't fully acknowledge how emotionally strong he'd been during this stressful time.

Alec withdrew from me. My sadness and worries of only a few days earlier seemed trivial to what I felt now. The Tasman was the culmination of all my fears and how we dealt with them as a couple. The subject depressed Alec. I delicately dragged him into discussion after discussion, hoping to mend the rift between us.

Alec antagonistically asked, "What the hell are you doing here if you hate it so much?"

I felt as if he was driving a spike into my heart. "I don't hate cruising. I love what we're doing, and even though I haven't been happy the entire time, I don't regret being on this trip at all."

"I can't believe you," he said crossly.

I vehemently denied his accusation. "I enjoy almost everything about cruising, and I certainly don't want to leave." But his taunts made me question my real reason for continuing, the essence of the goals and morals that motivated me.

"If we're going to continue," he said, "then you have to be able to rationalize your discomfort with the satisfaction of sailing around the world. Accept your situation by understanding the gains and the losses; short-term pain for a long-term goal."

"That's sounds simple in theory, but there's more to it than just goals. During that short-term pain, I have a problem with how we interact."

"True, but the first question you have to ask yourself is: Why are you here?"

Why was I sailing around the world? Was it purely my competitive nature, or was it my refusal to fail? I had accepted the conditions of the marriage proposal, but was I determined to fulfill them at all cost? Even at the cost of a failed marriage? Or did I feel compelled to religiously stand by my husband and never leave him?

When I examined my reasons for continuing, I felt confused and uneasy.

DIFFERENT TROUBLES

WE WERE DETERMINED to keep our personal troubles from Jim. Although Jim knew I didn't enjoy the Tasman, I don't think he realized the magnitude of the problems Alec and I were having. As much as having Jim aboard interfered with Alec's and my ability to communicate effectively with each other, it was perhaps a blessing that he was with us for the Tasman. His presence stifled any serious arguments, that if let fly, might have caused the destruction of our marriage.

Things kept moving despite our emotional standstill. Having family and friends nearby probably continued to keep our life in check. Alec's father left, and we combined provisioning and boat chores with more socializing in Sydney.

A week later, Jim faxed us from Canada to tell us what a wonderful time he'd had. "The Tasman must be a high point in your sail around the world." He was so damned positive!

I wrote back, telling him the truth: *"I'm glad your memories of the*

Tasman are good ones, but the fact is that the Tasman was the lowest point in our trip so far. I was overcome with fear for most of the crossing, and wasn't pleased with how I reacted. I feel more like I failed than achieved anything by making it across the way I did."

We left Sydney on June 4th for a short sail north to Broken Bay, another large inland harbor with numerous branches and coves, similar to Sydney Harbour but mostly unpopulated. After six weeks of being with family, and keeping our personal lives relatively bottled up, we were finally alone again.

I wanted to resolve how we interacted during the Tasman crossing, but again Alec steered the conversation back to me and my personal goals. Perhaps we still grasped at the hope that if I could change how I acted, our problems would be solved. Deeper down, I sensed Alec couldn't let go of his anger and wanted to see me give first.

I reread my journal from the crossing. At one point, when I was being negative, Alec had said to me, "Go ahead, Alayne, and live your life that way if you want. Only you can decide what kind of person you want to be." This hit me, because I had never before given thought to *whom* I wanted to be. I had always just been a happy, pleasant person. People enjoyed me and my friendship. I was confident, outgoing and independent. In the past, I had just lived my life, without much contemplation.

At times of stress in our cruising, and especially during the Tasman, I had just reacted in the way that felt most comfortable. Now in retrospect, I was not proud of how I had behaved. Perhaps from a different perspective, I would have reacted differently. I had to give some serious thought to who I was, and what I wanted. Questions I had never asked before.

As we continued north we took it easy, for my sake, and twice when the wind rose to gale force, we ducked into quiet fishing towns for the night. Nearing Brisbane we left the ocean and entered an inland waterway. We followed the twisting, swampy channels past low, bushy islands speckled with white egrets, and anchored behind a mangrove island. As the sun was setting, hundreds of large, bat-like birds flew overhead, returning to their roost.

We caught the rising tide up the Brisbane River the next morning and found a slip in a row of docks outside the hotel complex where Gillian and Dugald were vacationing. The marina manager was away, and the security guard assigned us an alternate slip on the inside of two piers. There was very little maneuvering room in between the rows of boats and we knew that we had to wait for slack tide.

We checked the tide tables for the Brisbane River with the guard to figure out when the river current stopped. An hour later he informed us it was slack tide and ordered us to move. With Gillian and Dugald due to arrive, we were keen to get settled. We looked out to a buoy in the river and saw that the current had significantly decreased. I untied *Madeline* and Alec motored around and into the narrow channel between the piers.

Immediately someone's head popped up from inside his boat. "No!" he bellowed with a terrified look on his face. "It's not slack yet!"

The current grabbed *Madeline*, sweeping her sideways. Other sailors piled out of their boats, screaming instructions. Alec tried to react to the current, but it was too late. *Madeline* was pushed broadside towards a row of boats. Sailors ran to their sterns, preparing for impact.

There was a resounding CRACK as *Madeline* collided, pinned against the docked yachts by the current. In a perversely fortunate manner, all the owners and crew had been aboard their boats enjoying cocktails, awaiting slack tide. Everyone helped fend us off. They got lines to the other side of the dock and pulled *Madeline* off. Embarrassed, we went back to our original slip, which we learned was available after all.

The security guard was keeping a low profile, but Alec knew he could only blame himself. "I can't believe I listened to that guy, without using my own eyes and head."

Luckily for us, we did more damage to our pride than to *Madeline*. Our beautiful New Zealand paint job was only slightly scratched. Alec checked the inside and there was no damage, but an interior fiberglass liner had popped loose and needed gluing back in place. I prescribed two stiff rum and cokes to help get over our humiliation.

Gillian and Dugald arrived in a snazzy little sports car they had rented. We roared off on a tour of Brisbane. I felt so happy and carefree. Ironically, damaging the boat didn't bother me. We could fix *Madeline* easily. Money could fix a boat, but only time and love could mend a relationship.

Our passage north to the Whitsunday Islands alternated between calm nights and windy days, and we primarily used the second-hand multipurpose spinnaker, or MPS, that we'd traded for in Sydney. The asymmetrical MPS was much bigger than our previous spinnaker and we tacked it down to the windward bow of *Madeline*. When sailing downwind the whole sail stretched across the bows, greatly improving our speed, but without the complication of a pole.

Four days later we arrived at Scawfell Island, only to discover our propane tank was empty. Undaunted, Alec declared that dinner was ashore and he placed a screwdriver, hammer, knife and bottle of lemon juice in a knapsack. It was low tide and we found a rock covered in oysters. Alec opened them and we ate them right off the rock.

The next day we sailed to the resort at Brampton and Carlisle Islands where cruisers were welcome free of charge. As an alternative to cold food or more raw oysters, we took a bottle of wine to the B.Y.O. café ashore. Under the full moon, we ate a romantic candlelight dinner, talking about our relationship.

"I'm still working at defining my goals, but I can now better see the trade-offs I'm making by undertaking this sailing adventure. Certain goals are on hold while I work on others. We talked a lot last night – about everything I'm putting off. Having children is one of my life goals, but that's definitely on hold right now."

Two days later we made it to Hamilton Island where we could fill up our propane tank. A strong current pushed us down the channel between the luxury resort island and its neighbor. We rounded the airport and turned towards the small-boat harbor. A large boat was hesitating in the harbor entrance and I pulled back the throttle.

"What are you doing?" Alec asked as a small plane buzzed over our mast and landed on the runway. "You're in mid-channel. The current is pushing us away."

"You take the wheel," I said impulsively. Alec took over and motored for the entrance. "That boat is stalled," I yelled. "We'll hit it!"

"It's far away!" Alec retorted. "By the time we get to the entrance, we'll know what it's doing."

"No! No! You're moving too quickly," I cried. I imagined the sound of cracking fiberglass, and I got extremely nervous and upset. "The current, the boat – it's going to be a disaster."

"Shut up!" Alec yelled. "It's an enclosed harbor. There won't be any current once we get in." But then he abruptly turned the boat away, stomping his feet. He sat down, trying to calm himself. "What do you propose we do?"

Taking slow deep breaths, I tried to stop my reaction. I knew I wasn't making sense and I knew we needed propane and some fresh food. "I'm okay now," I said, after apologizing. "Let's go in."

"You can take the helm again, if that would make you feel more in control," Alec offered. I declined and he motored through the entrance

152

channel, effortlessly parking at the fuel dock. The first fifteen minutes at the dock were free of charge, so I sprinted off to get the propane while Alec fueled and watered *Madeline.*

Just before dark, we anchored far up Gulnare Inlet, both of us in a huff, not yet having discussed the incident.

"So what was that all about?" Alec asked.

"I felt out of control." I could feel Alec glare at me. "Okay, I realize I was being silly. I know that boat was far away from us, and you weren't going to smash into it, but I got scared." A large flock of white cockatoos noisily squawked in the tall trees surrounding us. "I said I'm sorry," I added.

"I don't like how I reacted to you either, but I must point out that *I* reacted to *you*." He paused, and then said, "If you could be 100% perfect in these situations, then I guarantee I would be perfect too!"

We both laughed and the tension was cut. Looking at this mini-crisis we could easily see how classically we had behaved – me getting scared, then panicky and Alec getting angry and then losing his temper. "Obviously we have to be able to communicate better when it comes to boat handling," I said, "whether it's reefing a sail, picking an anchoring spot or even reviewing a chart together. We have to work as a team."

"We know what our weaknesses are, but while we work on them we're still going to have arguments. We just can't let them bug us."

"Let's chalk it up as another learning experience."

Alec nodded, "I'll fix us a drink. Let's enjoy this magical place."

There were always small jobs that came and went, but in the last few days the to-do list had rapidly lengthened:

1. The engine tachometer was broken.
2. The wind generator output was low.
3. The engine oil needed changing, and we needed oil.
4. The main cabin light was broken.
5. We needed more fuses.
6. The navigation light swivel was broken.
7. The engine stop cable was corroded and was sticking.
8. The CD player wouldn't play all our CDs.
9. The engine was emitting blackish-blue smoke.
10. The new spinnaker needed repair.
11. The second propane tank was too corroded to refill.
12. The spare outdrive steering arm needed welding.
13. The rigging needed a thorough check.
14. The house battery was faulty and needed replacing.
15. The rudder bearings needed replacing.
16. The outdrive's engine-room oil seal needed replacing.

Beaching the boat would allow us to work on the last two problems. Our guidebook recommended Hill Inlet only for very small boats, but for beaching *Madeline* it would be perfect. The entrance changes because of the shifting sand, so we reconnoitered it by foot and then by dinghy to view the channel before attempting it with *Madeline*. We went in at high tide and dropped our hook in three feet.

Two hours later we were aground, as planned, and for half the day we were high and dry surrounded by miles of pristine white sand beach. A sandspit protected us from the inlet's entrance and a narrow strip of pine trees separated us from five-mile-long Whitehaven beach and the cerulean ocean. The first night Alec wanted to take a picture of the boat as the sun was setting. We were aground but there was still some water around us. I began to untie the dinghy when Alec said, "We don't need the dinghy. Let's walk!" We climbed down the swim ladder and walked to the fine sand beach. There was not a soul in sight.

Over the next two days Alec completed his work, racing to finish during the six hours of low water between tides. The height of the tides varies on a monthly cycle, so despite the alluring surroundings, we left Hill Inlet before getting trapped inside.

The weather turned nasty and we stopped at Border Island to wait out the high winds and lashing rain. We broke up the wasted day with a walk to the top of a hill where we sipped red wine in the lee of a big rock. The air was too cold and the water too murky to snorkel the fringing reef despite its good reputation for sea life.

On the dinghy ride home, two large manta rays were feeding at the surface right near *Madeline*, but we couldn't bring ourselves to jump in with them. From the cabin top we watched them crisscross the bay, feeding on the plankton. Gusts tore down the hills, whipping the water surface. Without thinking, I commented, "I hate the noise the wind is making in the rigging."

"Really," Alec said, immediately annoyed. "What is it this time? Fear? Lack of control?"

"I don't know – it's just such an eerie sound. I guess it scares me," I responded.

"Well, thanks for brightening my day by sharing that little tidbit," Alec said sarcastically.

My complaining was still driving him nuts. So I stopped, and we carried on with our day.

Near Townsville our engine died. We had been concerned about the engine for a while, but were shocked when it began stalling. Both Alec and I were getting worried about the equipment problems on *Madeline*. The list was growing too fast; it seemed everything was falling apart. I prayed that *Madeline* was not a metaphor for our relationship, as she was clearly deteriorating.

Townsville was the second largest city in Queensland after Brisbane, with about 120,000 people, and we stayed at the marina for over a week. There was a large live-aboard sailing community and we were immediately included in their social plans. They were an interesting crowd, living on boats as cheap, alternative housing, similar to living in a trailer park. Many of the boats had tropical plants growing above decks and thick algae growing below the waterline. They obviously hadn't been to sea recently and wouldn't last long if they tried.

We arranged for a mechanic to come to the boat Monday morning. On Sunday Alec removed the engine stop cable, deciding we'd buy a new one from the mechanic. Then he climbed the mast for a routine check of the stainless-steel wire, toggles and terminals that held up the mast.

Because I always worried about the mast falling down, I decided to also climb it to better understand the rigging. I pulled myself up as Alec tensioned the halyards. Climbing right to the top, I rested in the bosun's chair, my legs straddling the aluminum spar. I surveyed the rows of boats tucked behind the stone breakwall of the marina, and peered down at *Madeline's* deck. I could see Magnetic Island in the distance, named for when Captain Cook's compass gave strange readings. I turned my attention to the assorted fittings and pulleys.

I felt something bump sharply against my head. Dumbfounded, I thought my head had hit the mast, but then I realized that I was above the top. I looked up to see a large sea eagle gliding overhead. The bird swooshed down at me and I frantically waved my arms screaming, "Alec, let me down!"

He was talking to our neighbors and they all looked up, puzzled. "There's a bird pecking my head!" I yelled. Five eagles soared on the wind above the marina, with two watching me closely. Alec slowly let me down, laughing.

The next day the mechanic came and it was my turn to laugh. Alec explained the problem in detail and then fired up the engine. It roared to life and sounded perfect. He revved the engine and it purred away. Embarrassed, it dawned on Alec that he had removed the stop cable. It must have been partially closed off, restricting the fuel flow and causing the engine to stall.

"What about the exhaust?" Alec asked.

The mechanic put his hand in the black exhaust and asked, "Burning much oil?"

"Yeah, some," Alec responded.

The mechanic shut off the engine and pulled the dipstick. "You're going to keep losing power, unless you replace the rings. You need an overhaul."

"How much?" I asked.

"At least $3,000."

We were sure it couldn't be that bad. We never got full power out of the engine and it had always blown black smoke out the exhaust, but this had been eating away at Alec for months. Even though *Madeline* was a sailboat, we were quite dependent on the engine. Indonesia and Malaysia had reputations of light winds and strong currents, and there would be a lot of motoring up the Red Sea. Australia was the last place before Singapore to do any repairs. Over hours of discussion, we weighed the pros and cons of an overhaul.

We decided to have the mechanic do a compression test. This would quantify the problem and we could compare it with the test we did in New Zealand when the engine was healthier. The mechanic returned and the new test results were worse, but didn't indicate a desperate situation either. Watching the mechanic work, however, tipped the balance for Alec: the guy was sloppy.

Alec began studying Nigel Calder's *Marine Diesel Engines*. He wanted to better understand what exactly an overhaul involved. As he read through page after page, I could see him getting itchy. Finally, he came out and said it. "Alayne, I think I can do this myself! It makes more sense for me to make mistakes and learn from them, than to pay a mechanic to make mistakes on our precious engine."

If a mechanic did the job, we'd never be sure what was done to the engine. "I'll only go so far," Alec said, "and I'll stop if I feel I'm in over my head." There was one catch. "We'll have to buy a torque wrench."

I couldn't believe how expensive a wrench could be, but Alec assured me, "It's a tool for life, an heirloom! We'll pass it on to our children and grandchildren – a souvenir from our engine ordeal."

Townsville was a productive stop for us in the end, as we got engine oil, purchased anti-malarial medication, did our laundry, cleaned out multiple lockers, welded the broken outdrive piece and got duty-free liquor placed in bond on *Madeline*.

We sailed overnight to Cairns and anchored outside the town. For three solid days Alec slaved away, not leaving the boat, covered in sweat and grease, hanging upside down in our engine room. I kept busy running errands: gathering fresh groceries, developing film, buying a new propane tank, picking out a new deep-cycle battery, buying a cabin light and getting the odds and ends that Alec needed.

We sacrificed an old bedsheet for his work area and things moved along in an orderly, methodical way. The first day I returned to find the

engine disassembled. Each piece was labeled with masking tape and a number, all neatly stacked in the cockpit. The next day, Alec was stumped and couldn't get at the pistons, but he got the valves out and decided to lap them. Away I went to an automotive store, impressing the guy there by asking for grinding paste.

"What type would you like?" he tested me.

"I'll take some medium and some fine, please." That was fun.

When I returned to *Mad*, Alec was holding a piston in his oily hand and the mystery was over. To our relief everything looked fine, just as the book said. It was as if Alec, the surgeon, was removing an appendix by reading a manual, and learning the anatomy as he went along! The nice thing about this surgery was that he could stop for coffee breaks, and if the patient died, money could replace it.

He changed the piston rings and installed a new head gasket. Then came the special task of tightening the head into place with the amazing new torque wrench. On the third day it was all back together, not a screw short or extra. On the first try it started like a charm.

Alec had broken the spell of the mysterious diesel engine that so many other cruisers were still living with. Honestly though, the engine wasn't perceptibly better!

In Cairns we met a couple who had recently allowed a mechanic to take apart their engine. They paid for the mechanic's mistakes with not only a lot of money but with six weeks of their time. In the end, they were unsure if their engine was any better, and their experience was a nightmare. It certainly didn't help their peace of mind. The three days Alec spent gave him exactly that – peace of mind. He was intimate with our engine, comfortable with trying to fix it, and better able to judge any problems. It was no longer a black box.

I spent a lot of time photocopying charts in Cairns, because I decided to change our sailing route. At this time of year the trade winds "accelerated" as you sailed north and we'd already experienced strong winds on the way to Cairns. This hadn't bothered me since the wind was on the beam and the seas were minimal because we were behind the Great Barrier Reef.

But Alec's plan was to sail offshore, heading outside the Great Barrier Reef and sailing directly to the Torres Strait. This meant sailing a further distance without the chance to anchor, and dealing with the ocean swell. This was too soon after the Tasman, and it worried me until I saw the opportunity to change my situation.

"Why can't we sail the entire way north inside the reef?" I asked Alec.

"We can, but there are two drawbacks. We're running out of time and would need to sail overnight. This could be tricky and nerve-racking inside the reef. The other big drawback is that your plan requires a lot of charts, and I don't think we can afford them at $40 a pop." We hadn't met any other cruisers who had the charts needed to follow the winding channel up the Great Barrier Reef. "If you can produce the charts," he added, "I'm keen to take the inside route."

I dinghied to the Cairns Yacht Club and quickly found some Australian cruisers who happily loaned me the required charts. They poured over the chart list, kindly explaining which ones I needed. Their faces dropped in disappointment when I mentioned I had a husband.

Alec came with me to the yacht club the night I returned the charts and we bought a few rounds as thanks. They were wonderful people and shared with us their exotic Southeast Asia sailing experiences.

Just before we left, we received a fax from Alec's father. He had received my letter saying that the Tasman was the low point of the trip for me. Jim remained as supportive as ever: "Alayne, you must remember that the Tasman was only a micro part of a macro adventure. You shouldn't get down on yourself for being afraid during the Tasman crossing. More important is the macro courage you have shown by doing the whole trip."

Off we went up the coast, sailing overnight in the shipping lanes and stopping at some of the islands along the way. The accelerated trades were in full force and we had over 30 knots of wind for a number of days. I was pleased we decided to stay inside the reef. We just unfurled a bit of genoa and *Madeline* took off downwind in the relatively flat water. I didn't mind sailing at night, as the channel was well marked. "*The freighters we've passed are friendly and helpful on the radio and I'm completely happy during this leg. I've taken control of my situation – I've made a major decision about our sailing. And it's working."* I was feeling more confident.

Our fourth wedding anniversary was celebrated at the Flinders Group of islands, where we were the only yacht anchored among the prawn trawlers and pearl oyster farms. This year was Alec's turn to surprise me, and he knew that we would likely be in the middle of nowhere. For five months he had a large parcel hidden under our bunk, marked "DO NOT OPEN". Inside were the makings for a perfect evening: a bottle of champagne, some olives as hors d'oeuvres, tricolored pasta, pesto, parmesan cheese and a bottle of red Italian wine, followed by chocolate-covered almonds and sexy lingerie for dessert. We showered, put on nice clothes and played great music.

Alec was a romantic and he made the evening special. We danced in the cockpit and he held me in his arms. "I love you," he whispered, and I felt the frustrations of the last year melt away.

Thursday Island is balanced on the tip of the long finger of the Cape York Peninsula on the northeastern coast of Australia. North of Thursday Island, to the shores of Papua New Guinea 60 miles away, stretches the reef-speckled Torres Strait. All freighters and yachts moving between the Pacific Ocean and Indian Ocean pass through this strange little crossroad. It is one of the circumnavigating bottlenecks, which brings sailors together, but without the fame of such places as Gibraltar or the Panama Canal.

Between Cairns and Thursday Island we found ourselves once again entwined in the cruising community. Everyone sailing up the coast was bound for Indonesia. At Lizard Island we met three Dutch boats and I could not resist asking if they knew *Rode Beer*.

"Of course. In fact, we'll be speaking to them on the radio tonight," said Klaas, from the ferrocement sloop named *Brick*.

What luck! Robert and Nathalie were on a two-week passage from Vanuatu to the Torres Strait. They didn't plan on stopping, but would continue on to Indonesia. We talked to them on *Brick's* radio, and calculated that we might both be in the Torres Strait at the same time. Nathalie and I agreed to monitor the VHF radio at that time, in hopes of having a longer chat.

After two more days of fast sailing in heavy wind, our autopilot stopped working at Tuesday Island. I hand-steered past Wednesday and on to Thursday Island while Alec diagnosed the failure as a problem with the autopilot's electric motor, the first problem in 12,000 ocean miles of faithful service.

After getting advice from a drunken sailor in the local bar that night, we went off to the only service station the next morning and bought some used brushes from an old car alternator. Alec filed them to the right size and they worked. It seemed he had spent all his free time sailing up this coast with his head either in a manual or in our equipment.

We took the dinghy for a ride near the mangroves looking for crocodiles. Not that I wanted to see one, but the locals told us they were common in these waters and Alec had to have a look. We were unsuccessful, but on our way back we noticed yet another Dutch boat, *Klepel*. Just as I wondered aloud if they knew *Rode Beer*, a man waved for us to come over. Nico told us *Rode Beer* had been calling us on the VHF radio that afternoon. He'd answered the call and found out that they had sailed through the shipping channel north of us.

"They had a six-knot current with them," Nico said between puffs on his pipe. "They were moving so fast that they'll be out of radio range by now."

Repairs

I WAS SO FRUSTRATED. We raced back to *Madeline* and called on the VHF anyway.

"*Madeline*! This is *Rooooode Beer*!" Robert answered clearly.

They must be close! We switched to a talking channel. "Robert, where are you?"

"We decided to take a break. We're anchored at Friday Island."

Alec and I cheered and we could hear Nathalie hooting in the background as well. Excitedly we talked non-stop for over an hour – alternating between Robert and Alec, but mostly Nathalie and myself. Stories flew back and forth as we caught up with the cruising gossip.

They wanted to leave the next day, at noon with the favorable current, so we planned to connect with them in the morning for coffee. Technically we were not allowed to board their boat, or they ours, but how could we resist?

We rounded olive-green Friday Island flying our new MPS in red, white and royal blue. It was a beautiful day and *Madeline* looked great. *Rode Beer* was glowing brilliant red in the sunshine. It was so good to be anchored side by side again. After a bottle of champagne and two hours of gabbing, we easily persuaded them to stay for dinner on *Madeline*. We were anxious to get moving as well, but this was a wonderful coincidence I wanted to make the most of.

After coffee together the next morning, we upped anchors and *Madeline* and *Rode Beer* sailed away in tandem. It was another gorgeous day and we took pictures of each other under sail. It was downwind, so *Madeline* flew her MPS, and they had double headsails poled out. Our speeds were almost identical on slightly divergent courses. We were heading south of west to Gove, and they were heading north of west to Indonesia. For the rest of the day we continued with periodic radio conversations until we said good night and goodbye.

We discussed meeting again in Indonesia. We knew we would find them somewhere, but we were never sure where.

I hadn't told Nathalie about the Tasman, and neither did I know what I would tell her. Seeing her thrilled me, but the farewell left me depressed.

It was a three-day trip to Gove, a small mining town at the top of Australia. It had all the facilities that we needed – laundry, fresh water,

diesel, propane, telephone, post office, grocery store, bank, and we anchored outside a pleasant yacht club filled with live-aboard locals. This was our departure point for Indonesia.

In Gove, Alec and I reflected on our brief visit with *Rode Beer*, and how wonderful yet difficult I found it. Clearly it was satisfying for me to talk to Nathalie and tough when this outlet was taken away.

I had tried to control my emotions and my complaining through the entire South Pacific with little success. I was caught in a circle of failure. I would try to stifle each potential outburst until it became too much to hold inside, and then I would break down. This self-perpetuating cycle was repeated many times over.

The fears were here to stay. Ignoring them didn't work. I had become more confident with the boat and knew the things I could do to make me feel more in control. Some fears had subsided with time and others evolved, but Alec's thrill-seeking and the very nature of our sailing meant new uncertain situations almost every day.

I had always been an emotionally-expressive person, and Alec liked that about me. I made up for his abnormal control of emotions, and together we made a balanced pair. In our life before cruising, I expressed all that I was feeling. I had been a positive person and wasn't characterized as fearful or a complainer. In the South Pacific, I had argued that expressing my emotions – which was complaining in many cases – was a healthy, rational and important mechanism that helped maintain my sanity and reduce my fear. Suppressing my feelings, depressing or otherwise, was impossible. But Alec disagreed and couldn't understand this. I even explained it as a gender difference and that this was a completely socially acceptable female activity.

While much of this reasoning was true, the verdict was now out. My way of coping with stress was interfering with the success of our venture, and maybe our marriage. Our trip across the Tasman had proven that expressing my fears and frustrations helped me to the detriment of others.

I hated to think I had to control how I expressed myself. I liked who I was. I just wished all my emotions were happy and positive.

Seeing *Rode Beer* allowed me to share with Nathalie, making both Alec and me happier. We realized I just had to control to whom I expressed my emotions! And when. And how much. And where.

I could still share my feelings with Alec, but we both knew he was limited in his ability to be a girlfriend to me. He knew he needed to be more supportive and accepting.

"I'm doing better, aren't I?" he asked smiling. "I can talk with you much longer now, but I just don't have your endurance."

Nathalie filled that gap for me. *"Another reason I enjoy Nathalie's company is because we chat for hours together. It isn't that I complain to Nathalie, but we talk about all of our thoughts, our worries and everything. Alec is too caught up in analyzing exactly what I say and he always wants to help me, rather than just listen. Nathalie and I simply listen and agree with each other. Even when we don't agree, we feel we are completely understood and that our feelings are valid simply because they are ours. She's a wonderful support."*

When Nathalie wasn't around, there were outlets other than Alec. Anchoring when we had guests on board was a perfect example of using another person. I could chat with someone in the cockpit, explain what we were doing and express my concerns. This talking relieved me of my worries and left Alec free from feeling he must listen to me at times when he needed to concentrate on the foredeck. I had to actively direct my emotions down suitable avenues.

My journal had already proven an excellent place to vent my fears and frustrations. It had saved me during the Tasman and many other times, and I enjoyed recording the daily events, just as I had recited them to my mother each day after school when I was a little girl.

My visit home to Canada had shown me that contact with my friends and family was also important. Writing frequent letters made me feel closer to everyone at home, and with support from home, I felt stronger in dealing with all the challenges.

I was amazed it took me so long to figure all of this out.

As we were sailing up the east coast of Australia, Alec was making plans for us to explore the uninhabited and apparently lobster-filled

Wessel Islands just north of Gove. At the same time crocodiles were entering the conversations of cruisers, with none of us knowing much about them, except that they lived along the north coast of Australia and were "dangerous". Alec remained determined in his plan to dive for lobsters, saying, "Of course, I'll be careful." This bothered me because I didn't feel we knew enough about crocodiles to know what being careful entailed. With all our engine troubles, I never got the chance to go to a library and read about these man-eating creatures.

We started hearing tales of Australians and tourists being eaten by crocs. Day after day, Alec's increasing enthusiasm for lobster hunting escalated my anxiety about the Wessel Islands.

In Gove, we met "Crocodile Bob" on his trimaran, *Tao*. Bob was an Aussie cruiser who had actually worked as a crocodile hunter for seventeen years until 1972, when it was outlawed. He had hunted mostly freshwater crocs, and showed us an old photo of him with an enormous 25-foot one that he'd killed for a farmer. This croc had been eating livestock on one farm for three generations, and Bob got the contract for the entire river after he caught the big one. We looked up crocodiles in our Guinness Book of Records and the largest one in captivity was only nineteen feet.

Bob knew crocs. He said *he* wouldn't swim in the Wessels. Our initial thought was that crocs were found only on the mainland, but Bob

confirmed that saltwater crocodiles had been sighted many miles out at sea. "The Wessels are croc country," said Bob.

"There you go," I said to Alec. "If Crocodile Bob says he wouldn't swim for lobster, do you still plan on going?"

But before Alec could answer, Bob took it upon himself to educate us. "Go ashore at low tide and look for tracks," he suggested with a thick Aussie twang. "If there's a salty in the bay, you'll see him, or signs of him. Also check the water visibility, 'cause crocs like it cloudy. If there aren't tracks and the water's clear, then it's likely safe to swim." Alec liked this approach. I had to admit, using this reasoning, he was only being adventurous rather than foolhardy.

Around Gove there were signs posted warning of crocs. Bob assured us that the big crocs preferred a quieter environment than busy Gove Harbour and Alec used this as an excuse to dash off at low tide to the exposed rocks just outside the harbor. After five minutes of hammering while keeping one eye on the water around him, he returned with twenty large oysters. We fried them in batter for a delicious meal.

The next day at the yacht club we heard that a local sailor had been bitten by a crocodile while cleaning his boat at the careening grid on the beach. Apparently while walking in the shallow, murky water he stepped on the tail of a two-foot baby.

Alec disassembled the wind generator in Gove – our third motor failure that month. This was the fourth time he had taken it apart. He borrowed a blow torch to get the hub off the motor, and again he lost a day to the job, but it cost us no money, and for motor repairs he was batting a hundred.

I thought back to the start of our voyage and to the experienced cruisers who had warned us that our biggest challenge wouldn't be the sailing, but our ability to repair things. I wondered now if they meant more than they had said.

Alec and I had never had to fix our relationship before. In our nine years together before *Madeline*, we always got along, always agreed. With thousands of miles still ahead of us, we were sure to have more problems with the boat. Now I had the confidence we could repair any breakdown and I had reason to hope we could mend our relationship too.

But ahead lay our most adventurous cruising yet. I thought that sailing to remote islands and a foreign culture fit my goals, but how would I deal with crocodiles and pirates?

DIFFERENT ADVENTURES

THE WESSEL ISLANDS WERE OUR NEXT STOP on the way to Indonesia and the first night we stopped at a peninsula attached to the mainland.

Alec was set to start the investigation. At my request, he wore his dive knife strapped to his leg and carried his fishing spear, poised to attack anything that should threaten us. The mainland coast was also home to the wild buffalo and the cassowary. Both were potentially dangerous, but neither had the reputation of the salties. As we rode to the beach in the dinghy, Alec was beaming.

"We're going to look for crocs! Isn't this great?"

All I could say was, "Isn't this nuts?" We were miles from any civilization, the only boat on the coast, and we were going ashore prepared to attack potential predators with a blunt knife and a small spear. "Why are we doing this? We're enjoying our cruising life. Why should we end it all by getting eaten by some crocs on a deserted beach?"

"Really Alayne, I doubt if we'll see anything!" Alec responded. "Any wild animal will be afraid of us, and will run away. It's very unlikely," he reasoned, "that anything would run clear across an open beach and pounce on us."

Alec's approach to any potentially dangerous situation was to use logic, and there was no place for fear in his equation. He carefully calculated the risks, educated himself, avoided unnecessary risk, and chalked up the remaining risk to adventure. I appreciated his common-sense approach, but there was always a certain amount of worry accompanying me through life.

"Can my first aid kit cope if one of our legs gets bitten off? What if only one of us gets eaten? What if it's you who gets seriously injured? Then I'd have to sail *Madeline* back to Gove by myself. I guess I could do it."

Alec had learned to stop listening by this point.

We arrived at the beach. He suggested I wait in the dinghy if I was too afraid. The worry of adventuring seemed less than the worry of staying alone, so off we went. The first thing we came across was tracks. Not croc tracks but buffalo tracks, with huge mounds of dung piled everywhere.

We followed those for a while and then came across more tracks. Cassowary tracks this time – a large ostrich-like bird with a fierce temperament. The place was teeming with signs of wildlife and, despite my worry, I was getting curious too. We climbed through the dry dusty shrubs and up a large chocolate-brown outcrop. From our vantage point, we surveyed the land. The sun was getting high and Alec stripped off his shirt. "It's getting hot," he said. "I think any sensible creature is probably hiding in the shade."

We "captured" two dozen oysters. The water wasn't clear, so we left for the Wessels.

At the Gove Yacht Club there had been the usual group of fear mongers making sure we knew what to worry about next. After the popular discussions of Australia's saltwater crocodiles and Indonesia's pirates, the next biggest topic of conversation was the "Hole in the Wall". Everywhere we went, someone was always trying to instill some fear. Maybe to justify why they themselves weren't out there.

The Hole in the Wall is a very narrow strait, over a mile long, between the cliff faces of two islands in the Wessels. The brisk tidal flow was best negotiated at slack tide, and even then, with the greatest of care. There was no consensus in the yacht club as to when slack tide actually occurred, so it seemed you had to estimate it as best you could and then just go for it.

I adopted Alec's approach and ignored their stories, researching it myself in our guidebook *Circumnavigating Australia*. To explore the Wessels, we had to go through this pass, and I was keen to visit these seldom frequented islands. I was less keen when I read, "...the adrenaline-pumping feeling of navigating the Hole in the Wall is akin to riding a paper boat down a stormwater channel... this is for the intrepid." Translation: "Not for me, but perfect for Alec."

It was a gray, gloomy day, and as we approached what appeared to be solid rock, I could feel that familiar sense of panic beginning to surface. The opening was so small it wasn't until we were practically on top of it that we knew we were in the right spot.

Alec remained calm, and we slowly motored into the channel between the two islands. My nervous tension was prolonged as we faced a strong current. Moving at only one nautical mile per hour, we inched our way through the 40-foot-wide, rock-lined pass. Alec casually read off the boat names scrawled on the rock walls, while steering through whirlpools and eddies. Without incident the channel opened and exhilaration rushed through me as we motored out the other side.

We dropped anchor at the Wessels late in the afternoon. They were low rocky islands with large irregular bays and white sand beaches. It was uninhabited, aboriginal land covered with low trees and bush.

"Let's take a preliminary look ashore."

167

"Why?" I asked.

"To look for tracks, of course," Alec replied.

These adventures Alec created fulfilled his needs. Although anxiety-provoking, they were ultimately fun for me too. Alec teased that he often dragged me complaining through one of his expeditions, only to find me excitedly recounting the adventure to cruisers a few days later. He pointed out that I loved adventuring almost as much as he did.

We set out in the dinghy, and there it was! A croc in the water, about 200 feet away. Its eyes and the ridge on its back were protruding from the water. It was maybe ten feet long. It silently submerged.

"There. We've seen a croc," I fretted out loud. "Why are we still going towards the shore?"

"To look for signs of lobster, of course," Alec stated.

I took control of my fear and accompanied him on a short trip down the beach, where we saw tracks. Human tracks this time, and evidence of a small boat having been beached. Crocodiles stalk their prey. I imagined that the croc had seen these people on a previous day, and had watched them, ready to attack the next time they came ashore.

"These tracks are old," Alec assured me. "Crocodiles can't remember from one week to the next."

I was still worried. That croc was watching us.

"Look at this!" Alec cried with glee.

Two large lobster exoskeletons were washed up on the beach. "Oh no," I moaned. Just the evidence I was hoping we wouldn't find.

Back on *Madeline* that night we were a bit inhibited taking our evening skinny dip. Normally we lathered up and rinsed in the salt water before a final rinse in warm fresh water from our solar shower. It was an evening ritual to cool and cleanse ourselves after the hot, sweaty, tropical day. Now, I had thoughts of the croc waiting in ambush under *Madeline*, hidden between her two hulls.

A completely freshwater shower was out of the question, even though we had filled our tanks in Gove. We wanted to minimize the need to get water in Indonesia where the quality might be questionable. Did splashing attract the croc, or scare it away? I wasn't going to risk jumping in, so I got a bucket and poured the sea water over me.

Instead of risking ourselves snorkeling, Alec suggested we hunt for lobster on foot, on the ledges at low tide. We'd caught a lobster without getting wet at Minerva Reef, so it wasn't a far-fetched idea in a place like this. I actually enjoyed the trip ashore the next morning. The bay was lovely, lined with black and rust-colored rocks, and we walked the entire perimeter, from rocks to beach to lobster ledges.

As we were intently scouring the submerged crevices for waving antennae, I happened to see our croc surface about 100 feet from the ledge we were standing on. This was definitely his bay. I was alarmed when Alec took the camera and moved towards it, but the croc submerged like a submarine, resurfacing further away. He seemed wary and was keeping his distance, but swimming was certainly out.

I knew the lobster hunt would crop up elsewhere, but we weren't likely to share a bay again with a salty.

Like Australia, cruising in Indonesia involved risks. Some real, some imagined, and some that still managed to keep yachts away. Pirates were a theme in every bar between Cairns and Darwin, and while in Australia, we actively questioned cruisers who had already sailed these waters. The occasional strange yarn surfaced, but later it was always discovered to be a friend of a friend of a friend. We didn't allow anyone to influence our decisions, unless the story teller had had a direct personal experience.

All our discussions with experienced cruisers and all the magazine articles we read revealed no evidence of anything resembling pirates or danger from locals. You had to bargain well with the merchants in the market, but true robbery was unheard of. In New Zealand we changed our route to include Southeast Asia, since the infamous Indonesian bureaucracy towards sailors had reportedly improved due to a new policy promoting tourism.

Even armed with all this first-hand information, we still knew very little about Indonesia. We were sailing for the first time into the waters of an Asian culture. Besides the obvious language problem, the huge cultural differences would make all interactions rather confusing. We followed Alec's logical approach to risk-taking, but again I wasn't certain if we knew all we needed.

Alone, we left Australia for the seldom visited islands of Aru. After three days of sailing we neared the islands and I sensed we were both feeling a little apprehensive. As Alec cut a

square from our white bedsheet to sew the Indonesian flag, I said, "I can't believe we'll be there tomorrow."

He responded, "If we don't like Aru, we can leave."

Aru wasn't popular with tourists; there were no hotels. There was no *Yachtsman's Guide* for Indonesia and we'd never heard of a yacht going to Aru. The archipelago was large but low-lying and most of the islands were joined by dense swamp with narrow saltwater channels between. Perhaps that was one reason they were bypassed by the cruising fleet. Sailing up the coast, we examined our ancient Dutch chart originally surveyed in 1910 and corrected up until 1934. We scanned the flat, homogenous coastline with our binoculars searching for a landmark to confirm our position.

As we cautiously sailed into a little bay, we could make out a cluster of huts. The rest of the shoreline was jungle. Seeing the modest and primitive dwellings made me feel that we'd just landed our space ship in an alien world. I wondered how the locals would perceive our craft. Alec asked if I wanted to anchor in front of the village. Feeling both excited yet wary, we agreed to take it slow. For our first night we would anchor a few miles away, and go by the village once we were rested.

Within an hour I heard the unmistakable putt-putt of a boat's engine approaching. "Here we go, Alayne," Alec called into the cabin. "Our first visitors."

The greeting party consisted of four small men. They were polite and friendly. One indicated he was the *polisi*, and we invited them aboard. The policeman took a seat in the cockpit, while the others squatted timidly on the transom.

We started the preliminary small talk, guided by our Indonesian phrase book. We asked questions and he asked questions in return. The policeman's name was Mad, and he smiled, pointing to our boat name. One standard question was "What is your occupation?" and naturally he turned the question on us. Like people around the world, when Mad found out I was a doctor, he began to tell me of his ailments. He was suffering from headaches and occasionally he felt dizzy. I got confused translating, mixing up "*kelapa*", coconut, with "*kepala*", head, and we all had a laugh over the pain in his coconut. I questioned if he drank and he joked that maybe it was too much whisky.

After a lot of sign language, we finally deciphered that Mad wanted me to take his blood pressure. I carried a BP cuff and a stethoscope in my medical kit, so I unpacked them and slipped the cuff on his arm. His pressure was normal and I wrote it down for him.

He asked if I could take the pressure of his friend. The other two guys then felt left out, so everyone got a turn. I breathed a sigh of relief that their readings were normal. Mad invited us to come to the village the next day. He wanted to give us some *kelapas* and offered to show us around.

We felt a little more relaxed after this pleasant encounter, but took all precautions for our first night at anchor in Indonesia. One very real risk was malaria, and we spent the rest of the afternoon hanging white cheesecloth over our bed to keep the mosquitoes out.

Since we were concerned about potential intruders, we decided that this would be the perfect night to set up our burglar alarm. We had received a small motion detector for Christmas but had yet to use it. Alec mounted it inside facing aft so that the alarm would sound if anyone climbed into the cockpit. We snuggled into bed, roasting in the heat of the tropics, and fell into a post-passage slumber.

At midnight the siren blared.

Impulsively I clasped Alec, startling him out of a deep sleep. "Ah! Oh! Ah!" we shouted frantically, scaring each other with flailing arms in a tangle of bedsheets. If the alarm didn't scare off a burglar, I thought to myself, our confused shouting had.

Alec got a grip on himself, put on his glasses, and started into action. He turned on the light, blinding himself with the reflection off the mosquito net. I turned off the light and handed him the mace. "Get out there," I whispered, pushing him to the door.

"Give me a second, I can't see anything," he whispered, adrenaline in his voice.

He quietly crept out to the cockpit.

All was completely still. The water was flat calm, and there wasn't a breath of wind. There was no sign of movement: no water rippling, no bubbles, no other boats. As I joined Alec, he dodged a creature that flew into the cockpit. "Did you see that?" he asked. "It must be a small bat."

Immediately we had the answer to what had set off the alarm. We sat outside a long time, waiting for the pounding of our hearts to slow down.

We arrived at Mad's village the next morning with a gift of fresh dorado we had caught on the passage. Mad was pleased, since they didn't catch pelagic fish, only small reef fish. We had coffee together and he took us for a walk in the village.

After greetings from about thirty villagers during our tour, we were escorted into someone's home. All thirty followed, and we crammed into one tiny dark room. Mad asked if I could take the blood pressure of his friend. I'd thought this might happen, and in no time, it became an assembly line.

I asked Mad if there was a doctor for the village. "*Tidak,*" he said, "*hanya tua!*" No, only you!

One by one, each villager came and sat with me, and Alec wrote down the details: name, age, and blood pressure. What a great way to meet everyone and practice their language. Fortunately, all the readings were normal, except for one obese woman, whom I expected would be high.

Everyone laughed when she sat down. Her teeth were rotten and stained red from chewing betel nut, a mild narcotic common in the area. The group knew the range of numbers that were acceptable; it was the first thing they had asked. I fudged the fat woman's numbers slightly to be just at the high end of the range. There wasn't much I could do in this single encounter, and I didn't bother telling her to lose weight, increase her exercise and cut down her salt intake!

These villagers were healthy and in good spirits. Just the simple act of touching them with my magic instruments made them feel renewed.

Mad then took us to see some other villagers. Now it was time for the sick ones, those who really needed help. Several people were suffering with malaria. Some had been sick for years, and had never received any medication. They told me their diagnosis, and their symptoms fit the bill. I didn't have anti-malarial medication to spare, but wished there was a way I could assist them. Mad asked me to examine them, and I did.

Finally, Mad took us to see his 60-year-old father who had been feeling weak and short of breath for a year. He showed me a tumor the size of an orange, under the skin on his chest. It had also been there for a year. His medical condition was clearly beyond the scope of my medical kit. He needed to be investigated, but I wasn't sure if this was practical. I left them with the advice that if he was feeling worse, or losing weight, that he should be taken to a hospital. I got the impression that this would be a great expense, and that no one felt he'd reached

172

that stage.

They were very thankful for my visit – and we were given gifts of coconuts and bananas. Despite their poverty, our first contact in Indonesia had been a good one.

The capital of Aru was further up the coast. It was Mad's hometown, and he said we would like Dobo. "They have cars," he said proudly.

Over the next few days, we had several friendly meetings with locals. In Aru, we put away the burglar alarm for the rest of the trip. The Indonesians we met were well mannered and came aboard only when invited. At night, we had dugout canoes circling our boat, with shy locals giggling and peering from afar into our illuminated cabin, but this seemed to be simple curiosity.

It was a rainy overcast day, and we donned our foul-weather gear before going ashore in Dobo.

The fishermen gestured for us to tie our dinghy to one of the large wooden fishing boats crowding the pier. I reached to grab the dark gunnel. I gasped when a carpet of charcoal-gray insects parted from under my approaching hand. We clambered aboard and walked towards the pier: through the kitchen, past a man having his hair cut, bugs scurrying from our every step.

All eyes were on us as we wandered down the dirty, puddled streets, sticking out like bright-yellow sore thumbs. The buildings were dilapidated and the drizzle added to the gungy, slummy look of the place.

Groups of children marched in military style, preparing for the upcoming Independence Day celebrations. Many lost their step as they passed, and occasionally one stopped in his tracks, staring at us, mouth hanging open.

Word must have spread of foreigners, because after about ten minutes, a gentleman introduced himself as the only person on the island who spoke some English. "What are you doing here?" he asked. "Nobody comes to Dobo."

He couldn't understand our attraction to remote destinations, and he seemed especially puzzled that we chose Dobo. We were pleased to have it confirmed that we were in a land seldom traveled.

Word also reached the harbor master, and although our documents didn't require we check in, we were ushered into his office. We had rehearsed this already and Alec played the polite captain role while I pretended to be a subservient wife. Alec slipped the harbor master a small, department-store perfume sample I'd brought from Canada and after reading our papers, he sent us on our way.

After five quiet days in Aru, we sailed west to the Banda Islands. Unlike Aru, this small cluster of islands was mountainous. The highest island was an active volcano, having erupted as recently as 1988. Everything was so lush and green that our landfall reminded me of the Marquesas Islands in the South Pacific – except that our relationship was definitely improving.

Banda was an enchanting area and full of history. For hundreds of years it was the only place in the world that grew the once extremely-valued spices of nutmeg and mace. The Bandanese had traded with China, India and other parts of Asia as early as 100 AD. The spice trade eventually involved the Europeans directly, and these islands were fought over by many: the British, the Portuguese and the Dutch. Evidence of past battles remained in tumbled down forts and ancient cannons. In the 1600's the Dutch won, and eventually took control of Indonesia. But the importance of these spices as meat preservers diminished with refrigeration, and plantations were secretly established in the Caribbean destroying the island's monopoly. Nutmeg, mace, cinnamon and cloves still grew in abundance.

We motored quietly towards a few cruising yachts tied along a wall, pleased to see the old familiar red hull and wooden mast. It was still early morning and no one was about. I called, "Nathalie. Wake up, we're here! It's *Madeline!*"

Nathalie rolled over in her sleep, and said to Robert, "I hear Alayne."

"You're dreaming," Robert muttered, but she insisted, and jumped up on deck.

"I knew it was you!" she said. "It's fantastic that you're here!" We

tossed her our lines and rafted up beside them.

With Nathalie and Robert, we explored old Dutch forts, visited tidy little villages, watched the Independence Day parade, climbed the smoking volcano, swam above new coral growing over a recent lava flow and bathed in hot saltwater springs. Our weather was perfect, with a little rain falling only at night. We ate out for lunch everyday and the bill was 50 cents per person! For a small fee the locals did our laundry.

One afternoon we had some quiet time, in between adventures. Alec relaxed in his hammock tied between the masts of our boats, while Robert worked on his foredeck. We had Eric Clapton on loud. Nathalie sat in her cockpit writing a letter to her parents, and I updated my journal.

"I feel wonderful. The Banda Islands are paradise. It's so inexpensive here and there are so many fun things to do – it's great to see Alec so excited. Rode Beer is icing on the cake. As a foursome, we have a great time together, and I'm thrilled to be with Nathalie again. We're doing it – we're cruising successfully. I don't feel it's all because of Rode Beer. Things were going well before we met up with them, but I'm glad they'll be with us when we face the pirates... Alec and I have been talking well together and last night we had another long discussion. I've finally sorted out my list of goals and I shared them with him..."

Ever since the Tasman I had been laboriously working out what I wanted from my life. I needed to see if cruising satisfied enough of my goals. If it did, then I should be happy, despite what Mother Nature threw at me. I would have the right attitude if I could see what was in it for me.

Alec had suggested I write my goals down. The whole process was much slower than I would've thought, and there were many nights when I anguished over the details long after Alec had given up and gone to bed.

"You want to be fit? Are you just saying that? What are

you doing to achieve that goal right now?" Alec would challenge me. "Children? Have you really thought that through, or is that just how you were brought up?"

In the past, I had always arranged for my goals and decisions to jive with the wishes of whoever mattered most in my life. Living out other people's script had worked well up until now. Going to medical school gave me a great career, even though it was my parents' idea.

Eventually I finalized a list of *my* goals, and found I was striving for many of them already. But writing them down, discussing them and adopting them as my own, made me feel much stronger about attaining them.

1. Have financial security
2. Develop a rewarding medical career
3. Have children and raise a family
4. Expand my knowledge through travel
5. Live a unique and interesting life
6. Positively impact my community and the people around me
7. Stay fit and live healthy
8. Have a happy marriage
9. Keep in touch with family and friends

These were my long-term goals – not listed in priority. Priorities would change over my lifetime, some getting more attention at times than others, but in the long term there would be balance.

Sailing around the world was a short-term goal and now it was clear how it fit in. Money, medicine and motherhood were on hold, and I could accept that. Cruising amply fulfilled the next four goals. The latter two goals, staying happily married and keeping in touch, still remained a challenge, but I'd been successfully working on these.

"Figuring out my goals is only part of a long-term solution to our problems, but I'm excited to have overcome this hurdle and to actively choose my own path at last."

Our cruising permit was valid for three months and we stopped at the city of Ambon to officially check into the country. A bustling city of over 200,000, Ambon was a fascinating place for people watching. But back on *Madeline* we were disgusted everyday when the tide switched and the city's garbage floated by our boat and out to the ocean. Along with the waste and sewage, the water was filled with millions of little, wiggling, maggot-like worms. Alec and I canceled our daily swims, although a braver cruiser said, "You just have to time it with the tides."

One afternoon, Alec relaxed under a palm tree painting a watercolor of a local boat. Within minutes he had gathered a crowd of curious Indonesian onlookers. One of the men watched for a while, and then

sauntered down to the water's edge. Then, without warning, he squatted beside our dinghy, slid down his pants and defecated! Everyone with Alec laughed at this, but the man gave no notice, examining our dinghy as if reading a magazine while on the toilet. When he was finished, he cleaned himself with a few quick splashes, pulled up his pants and trotted off down the beach.

We sailed south from Ambon to the island of Flores. At the town of Maumere, we brought our garbage ashore to dispose of it. We talked with a local and asked him where we could take it. He said, "Just leave it on the beach. When the tide comes in, the ocean will take it away."

We took the time to educate our new friend about world pollution, but he was so far removed from the problem on his little island, that it seemed to land on deaf ears. It wasn't long ago that islands like this had minimal contact with the modern world. Everything they once had used in their daily life was biodegradable, and they tossed it aside when they were finished. Cups made from coconuts, platters from woven palm fronds, banana peels, bones – all their waste was natural. Unfortunately, when inexpensive plastic bags were introduced, they too got tossed aside. The streets and local waters were littered with white plastic grocery bags. It was sad they couldn't see that this litter was different.

Leaving the shore, we lifted the dinghy into the water. As quickly as it was afloat, I jumped to the bow, while Alec tiptoed delicately through the filthy harbor water and gave us an extra push. He jumped in and we were off. After a minute or so, he said, "Human blood is so much redder than tuna blood."

I didn't know what he was talking about. I turned around to see the dinghy floor awash in bright red. "What happened?" I gasped.

177

"I cut my foot. I must have stepped on some broken glass or on a mussel shell."

We were only a few minutes' ride to *Madeline*, and then I went right to work. It was a deep, even slice, about three inches horizontally across the plantar arch. With some pressure, the bleeding slowed and on examination I determined that none of his tendons were damaged. I irrigated the wound using a large syringe, squirting saline under pressure. Then I cleaned the whole area with an antiseptic solution.

Now came the tough question: Do I stitch him up? Under normal circumstances I would without hesitation, but this was an extremely contaminated wound, even though it looked pretty good after my thorough cleaning. One of the rules of medicine rang out in my mind: "never sew in the contaminants". But without stitches to hold it together, a cut on the underside of the foot would be slow to heal. I applied a pressure dressing and prescribed no walking.

The next morning I called *Rode Beer* and we agreed to meet up in a week. I set sail, while Alec kept his foot elevated and cracked open a beer. "Trim that sail!" he joked. I had made the right decision as within twelve hours the cut was looking infected. I started him on antibiotics and kept sailing down the coast, making sure he stayed off his feet.

Thankfully my skills were needed much less than Alec's. I had correctly anticipated our needs when I stocked our medical kit; I only wished I had extra to give away. We used antibacterial ointment as often as our toothpaste. Any break in the skin could get easily infected in the tropics, and rather than "wait and see", we treated all our wounds prophylactically. We were always getting cuts, and our favorite saying was, "It's not a job well done unless you draw some blood." Alec's hands were continuously injured by his jobs in the engine room, and his skin was generally more sensitive.

During our first weeks in the South Pacific, his skin got very dry and he developed what appeared to be a recurrence of his childhood eczema. I treated the rash on his wrists and hands with topical steroid creams in increasing strengths but the rash continued to grumble along. Then it escalated out of control. The rash spread to his chest, abdomen, ears, thighs, and behind his knees. He was going out of his mind with itching. After what he'd already used up, I didn't have enough cream to handle that much body surface area.

I told him to use it sparingly, but his patience wore thin. "Alayne, I can't stand this any more. There's got to be something more you can do."

This was the point when I would normally refer my patient to a dermatologist, but we were far from any civilized medicine. I reasoned that the eczema, being an allergic type of condition like asthma, would possibly respond to oral steroids.

His pleas continued. "I'll try anything. Just stop the itching. Dooo something!" Within 24 hours of taking prednisone tablets, he was miraculously better. I tapered his dose down over ten days, and we were able to break the cycle. Any further outbreaks we nipped in the bud with the creams, and he never had another problem.

The wildlife in Indonesia was as fascinating as its people. We loved the locals and their curiosity, but we often aimed for deserted, quiet, uninhabited anchorages, away from the wailing mosques and crowing roosters.

One evening as I sat in the cockpit admiring the amazing globe of sun descending in a brilliant array of orange, pink and red, my eye caught something moving on the shore. At first I thought it was locals, but I got out the binoculars and took a better look. There were eight monkeys cavorting on the rocks by the shore! With beige fur and long tails held upright, they chased each other, effortlessly hopping from boulder to boulder. I was tempted to get closer, but it was getting dark, and we let them also enjoy the peace of the evening.

"We've just sailed for four days, with me doing most of the work. Alec's foot is healing well – limiting his activity has certainly helped. I'm glad I handled this last sail, but I still worry about how I'll cope with rough weather again. The weather has been good for months now. It's hard not to be happy. I was okay in Australia in 30 knots of wind, but that was all downwind and along a coast – psychologically easier. The Indian Ocean crossing is coming up, but there are still a few months before I need to worry about that..."

My sail along the coast of Flores ended when we entered the Rinca and Komodo Island area, home to the famous giant monitor lizard, the Komodo Dragon. This is the only place in the world where these carnivorous animals are found in the wild. The islands are a national park and were sparsely inhabited, which, considering the number of people in Indonesia, must have been for good reason. What do these lizards eat? Anything that moves. Now, instead of watching for crocodiles, I had to keep my eyes open for dragons!

As we approached Rinca, the landscape unfolded unlike anything we had seen. It was the dry season, and the rolling hills of tall yellow grass spotted with isolated trees resembled the African savanna. The islands were home to water buffalo, deer and monkeys, which seemed even more fitting. The sea, however, bubbled and boiled as it raced through the narrow reef-strewn straits, and was more suited to tales of dragons and the Knights of the Round Table.

We dashed along, with currents of up to six knots propelling us. As we entered the anchorage of Lehok Gringgo on Rinca Island, big swells from the Timor Sea were crashing against the cliffs, shrouding the

island in a low mist. Komodo Island, with its distinctive serpentine ridge, was in sight only fifteen miles away.

The dragons at Rinca were apparently a mere six feet long versus the twelve-foot ones at Komodo. But again, we were in a situation where we had limited knowledge of the risks. We knew nothing about the dragons except what our *Lonely Planet* guidebook told us. It recommended only going ashore with a guide, as the dragons were "dangerous".

"They just say that so some local can earn an easy living," Alec claimed. For him, it was a perfect chance for more adventure.

Harry and Emma, a young British couple on *Ruawaka,* also joined Robert and Alec's safari. The security of a crowd made it easier for me. I had numerous sources of conversation and the talking alleviated my fears. Alec quietly grumbled that my constant chattering would likely scare away any dragons or other critters.

We stopped at the top of a hill after spotting some monkeys in the trees. Alec scampered down to get a closer look while Nathalie and I waited, chatting. Then, as Alec started back towards us, we continued on, with me leading.

There was a loud rush of hooves, and from under a rocky ledge beside my foot bolted a wild boar! It ran like hell – fortunately, away from us. We watched it run across the savanna grass; it startled a deer and both darted off in different directions.

The expedition ended without spotting a dragon and we questioned if they were really there. Later in the day, Alec took a trip to the beach to burn our garbage. Right at the spot of our beach barbecue the night before, were fresh dragon tracks. By the spacing of the footprints, Alec estimated it was six feet long.

"Oh. A small one," Robert commented.

"Yeah," said Alec, "just a small one."

The anchorage at Rinca was well protected and the lobster hunt resurfaced. Poor water visibility and a scarcity of lobster due to the local lobster fishing boats increased the challenge of the search. Alec kept at it and each day he managed to catch at least one for our supper.

A few days later we sailed over to Komodo Island and signed up for a guided hike. At the park information center, I called Alec over. "It says Komodo Dragons swim!"

Most of the dragons gathered near a "feeding station", where in the past, tourists purchased live goats and then watched the dragons rip them apart. I was just as happy this practice was stopped. The largest lizards in the world swaggered about, their forked tongues going in and out and their feet slowly tromping along. Their scaly skin was the color of dirt and I realized how well camouflaged the dragon was. Resembling a log, it strategically waits in the path of an unwary victim.

The guide told us that two villagers on Rinca Island had recently been attacked. I wondered how long our luck would hold.

The winds in Indonesia were the most pleasant of any country I had visited. The country straddles the equator, resulting in light land and sea breezes, which predictably change as the land heats up or cools down to the rhythm of the sun.

The challenging force of nature was the currents, and they were fierce. Between the chain of southern islands the currents were the strongest, and when sailing in any strait, we timed it to travel with the flow.

In the Alas Strait we had nice wind and flat water, and were making six knots under sail. Combined with the six-knot current, our speed over the bottom was twelve knots. Suddenly I spotted some white caps in the distance. "Alec, are we approaching some reef?"

"Not that I'm aware of." He quickly re-examined the chart, unable to find the squiggly lines indicating tide rips. We stood on *Madeline's* upper deck and scanned ahead with binoculars. Huge breaking waves formed at the coast and stretched out into the strait.

Frantically taking action, we changed course and steered to the middle of the strait where the waves appeared less. The current swept us uncontrollably towards the monstrous scene ahead. We trimmed our sails and started the engine, desperately pushing *Madeline* across the current and away from the worst of the steep breakers.

In no time the current brought us to the standing waves. We turned *Madeline* into them and the bow drove into eight-foot waves, washing over the decks and tossing us about. Only a quarter of a mile away the band was twice as wide and the waves were twice the size with foaming, curling crests.

It happened so fast I didn't have time to be scared. As we cleared the waves and exited the strait, we could see a large swell rolling in from the Indian Ocean. Even Alec wore a grave expression. I'd heard that swell against current could produce dangerous conditions in extreme cases, and now I knew what the warnings meant.

"That could've been the end of us," Alec said, "probably the closest we've ever come, but I must say, you reacted magnificently, Alayne." He wrapped his arm around me as we looked back on the scene.

The next day we crossed the southern Lombok Strait towards Bali. We anticipated some turbulence, and it was pandemonium. The waves were different from our last experience, a wide swath of choppy water. *Madeline* was bounced around as sea water chaotically slammed the boat from every direction, often coming overboard and into the cockpit. This was a rarity on *Madeline*, and I was glad Alec had thought to close the hatches.

I felt panicky this time, but Alec grinned at me, ignoring my comments, rather than getting angry. I relaxed, and we both laughed at the ridiculous waves.

PIRATE COUNTRY

MANY OF OUR FRIENDS WERE DOUBTFUL when we told them our plan to sail around the world. It was even harder to convince them we were following a *common* route. Thousands came before us and we would be followed by thousands more. Most boats stopped at the same places, did the same things and formed a floating community, with the dynamics of a small town.

But in 1994, Indonesia was a relatively new frontier for cruisers. Certain islands had been open for years if you entered the annual Darwin to Ambon race, but only in the past couple of years had a cruising permit procedure been established to allow anyone to sail anywhere.

Because of the thousands of Indonesian islands, there were innumerable opportunities to stray to places rarely visited by yachts. Our trip to Aru was an excellent example. We had asked the Dobo harbor master if they had many yachts visit.

He eagerly answered, "Many yacht come here, many yacht."

"How many?" I asked.

"Two yacht," he answered, nodding his head vigorously.

"Two yachts? When?" I questioned, wondering if he meant yesterday, last week, or per month.

"Ummm, one year before."

The main cruising fleet lying anchored around us in Bali would be leaving soon and sailing straight for Singapore. Our plan was to head north up the Macassar Strait and around the top of the Island of Borneo, first to Indonesian Borneo and then on to Malaysian Borneo. This was the plan developed by Robert, Alec and Nathalie back in New Zealand, knowing it was avoided by cruisers. It was not a

183

matter of a small detour. This would add several hundred miles to the journey, but the real problem was piracy.

The route took us along the Malaysian coast of the Sulu Sea. The Sulu Archipelago, part of the southern Philippines, was lawless, controlled by rival warlords. Small ships traveling in this area ran severe risk of attack. We planned to hug the Malaysian shores, but the Sulu Archipelago stretched to within a few miles of the coast.

The whole Borneo idea was hatched by Alec after he read an article by an American couple who had sailed the same Borneo coast just two years earlier. They described their interesting trip and gave advice on how best to avoid an encounter with pirates. The Malaysian Marine Police had suggested they sail in the company of another yacht, only in the daytime, and to anchor at villages near the Marine Police stations at night. *Madeline* and *Rode Beer* planned to do exactly that.

We had gained only a little information since leaving New Zealand. In Australia, Alec and I had the good fortune to meet a cruiser who had recently sailed this very same route. Originally a Canadian, Jim Russell had bought his boat in Singapore and sailed it to Australia via the north coast of Borneo. He was a personal friend of the Americans who wrote the article, and followed their route, buddy-boating with a British yacht in July 1993. The two boats had no problems, saw no pirates and never felt threatened or in danger. He wondered if there was really anything to worry about. He didn't stray from the advice of the Marine Police, and gave us the confidence that if we did the same, we should have "no worries".

Bali was the last chance to abort the plan with *Rode Beer*. We could cancel the Borneo trip and make a straight run to Singapore like everyone else, but so far, our time in Indonesia had been absolutely peaceful. We quickly dismissed any rumors about pirates in Indonesian waters, as we'd never found any supporting evidence. Although no one knew much about the Sulu Sea, we had no solid reason to change the itinerary.

We left Bali ahead of *Rode Beer*, intending to meet in a few weeks, before our exit from Indonesian Borneo. Alec and I sailed five days up the Macassar Strait to Sulawesi where we met a German and his Indonesian wife at their dive resort near the small town of Donggala.

With Peter, we made two spectacular scuba dives on an unspoiled wall. He was the first person from the area to tell us, "Yes, there are pirates." Peter had never had a personal experience with pirates, but the local fishermen who ventured north had told him stories – nothing specific, only vague warnings.

Continuing up the Macassar Strait, I spotted a boat on the horizon. It wasn't the typical Indonesian fishing *perahu* that we often saw near

the coast, and I was relieved it was going the opposite way. But then it turned around and began heading straight for us. Often boats that were in our vicinity would make a detour to have a look, but we'd never seen such a dramatic course change. They were chugging away, with thick black smoke blowing from their exhaust, and slowly gaining on us. We were alone, out of sight of land, and I couldn't help feeling a bit uncomfortable. I started our engine to increase speed, and then changed course to see if they were really following us. They also altered course.

I wondered what pirates would look like. After an agonizing half-hour they finally caught up to us. "Surely pirates would have a faster boat than that," I said to Alec, but noticed he had taken out the flare gun.

"I certainly won't wave the gun around," he said, "and I don't intend to use it, but you never know." Alec turned off the autopilot and took the wheel, ready to turn away should they try to board.

As they came close, I could make out a Muslim haj cap on one man and a traditional Chinese straw hat on another. Following a firm wave from the driver and from a guy at the bow, with reciprocal waves from us, they turned back the way they were originally traveling. It was likely just the usual curiosity.

Even though I was fairly confident we weren't in pirate country yet, it still felt very eerie going north up this strait knowing we were the only cruising yacht for miles and miles. After the encounter with the curious fishermen, I let my imagination get the best of me.

Once again, I began to dread the unknown ahead. Fear gripped me for the first time in months. *"This Borneo thing wasn't my idea, and now I'm feeling scared and pressured into doing something I don't*

*want to do. I thought I was taking a more active role with the boat, but
instead I just went with the flow. I've finally sorted out my goals, but
that doesn't make this any easier. Do I have a choice?"*

I questioned Alec on why we were doing this. With what I'd
learned, I kept my panic under control, and we had a rational
discussion. Alec was very supportive and just talking about it was half
of what I needed. We'd done everything possible to cut our risks to
zero for this portion of the journey. Logic won, diminishing my fears,
but I silently ached to cruise with *Rode Beer* soon. I knew I'd feel
better if we had the company of another boat. It didn't make a lot of
sense, because we were truly on our own, but psychologically it would
feel better with them around.

Alec talked about adding another year to our sail around the world.
This topic had been coming up recently, as we'd both been thoroughly
enjoying Indonesia and wanted more time exploring this part of the
world. More importantly, our budget was doing well. Living and eating
like the locals was inexpensive.

But I had to be honest with myself. I wanted to have less risk in my
life, and Alec would always want more. I didn't enjoy living with all
the unknowns, whereas Alec thrived on this. Our relationship was
improving and I definitely wanted to complete the circumnavigation,
but I was not ready to take on any more. Alec accepted this, proud of
the challenges we were taking on together.

After seventeen months in the southern hemisphere we crossed the
equator on our passage north. The last time we crossed, we forgot to
check to see exactly when the water began to go down the drain in the
opposite direction. Alec started the experiment at one degree south. As
the GPS counted down to zero, instead of celebrating, Alec was in the
head frantically flushing, trying to capture that magic moment when the
water goes straight down. Novelty quickly wore off and a few weeks
later and a few degrees of latitude further north, Alec concluded he
must have started too late. The water was still going down anti-
clockwise!

We finally arrived in Borneo and wended our way up a large
wandering river with dense jungle drooping over the banks. Alec was
thrilled silly and mumbling about *Heart of Darkness* and mounting one
of his crazy expeditions. But it wasn't Kurtz who dogged me, but the
specter of pirates.

That evening, halfway through dinner, *Madeline* was swarmed by
thousands of exotic bugs attracted to our lights. The first few were
fascinating, but when the trickle turned into a torrent, we frantically
turned off the lights, closed all the hatches and retired to our sweltering
bed. Our first night in Borneo was less than romantic.

The next day, after sweeping up the expired critters, we sensibly agreed to head to the breezy, palm-covered islands just offshore. A few days later we reached the small Indonesian island of Derawan and heard our first real pirate story.

The locals told us Derawan was robbed in 1932 and in 1968, and the neighboring island had been robbed just two years ago. The pirates came in speedboats with huge outboard engines, taking everything – even the sandals off their feet. One man who resisted was shot and killed. Since then, the Indonesian government had put Army and Navy posts on both islands to protect them.

The policeman in Derawan was named Ninang. He visited *Madeline* and immediately invited us ashore for dinner. The next day he was back for a social call, toting his camera. After taking pictures of us, he wanted pictures of himself lounging on *Madeline's* decks and we happily obliged. He felt that pirates wouldn't be a problem for us. Indonesia and Malaysia were arguing over the rights to the world-famous diving island of Sepidan on the border of the two countries, and as a result, numerous Indonesian and Malaysian Navy ships were patrolling the area. He said the pirates would be laying low. We weren't sure which was more dangerous, pirates or warring nations, but took it as a positive development.

The tiny island had many small, one-room wooden houses among sky-scraping palm trees. An upscale dive resort was half-built on the far side. The coral and sea life in the waters around Derawan were spectacular. We swam a couple of times each day to escape the fiery equatorial sun. There was little wind to cool us off, but neither did I worry about weather forecasts. Each day the cumulus clouds would build over the mainland and by late afternoon dramatic sheet lightning would flash in the distance. This worried me until I realized the clouds and lightning never moved off the land.

The water was warm, shallow and full of coral heads stuffed with lobster. With a careful approach we could swim side by side with numerous large green turtles. When calm descended at night, the silence was punctuated with gasps of the turtles coming up for air. I kept looking out into the dark to confirm it wasn't a pirate with asthma.

News of our presence must have reached the army post, because the next day a tough machine-gun-toting kid in uniform confronted us on the beach. He indicated he wanted to go to our boat. Alec refused. He didn't want an armed person searching the boat or demanding bribes. Before the confrontation got heated, Ninang showed up and assured us it would be all right. We all went out to *Madeline*, and the army guy looked at our papers. When Alec purposely handed him some upside down, we realized he couldn't read. We offered nothing and he left.

Robert and Nathalie arrived at Derawan a few days later. We had yet another wonderful reunion and everyone was excited about our upcoming adventures in Borneo. I buried my concerns, as I didn't want to be a downer.

The next night we sailed towards our last stop in Indonesia, Tarakan. The following morning Nathalie told us about her night watch. She had seen a dark blob on the moonless horizon approaching them. There were no lights on it and she feared it was a pirate ship sneaking up on them. She was thinking of calling us on the radio, but as it got closer she could see a palm tree amidst logs, and realized that it was a small "floating island" drifting by. As she told us the story, I could see I wasn't the only one worried about what lay ahead.

Tarakan was on an island in the delta of a huge Borneo river. The water was brown and murky. Immediately after anchoring, we were bombarded by a dozen local speedboats. Two or three came alongside and then more kept coming, rafting up with the rest. Normally in Indonesia, we were greeted by sailing canoes, or little putt-putt fishing boats, but these brightly-colored powerboats were filled with gawking men, aggressively calling to us, and straining their necks to peer in our windows.

We put on smiles and tried to congenially answer their questions. Alec strategically placed himself in the center of the cockpit and firmly denied their requests to come on board. If we let one on, we knew that the rest of the town would soon follow. With our meager *Bahasa Indonesia* and consulting our dictionary for new words, we discovered they were the local taxis, which ferried people up and down the river. Their boats had powerful outboard engines to make the long runs upriver. I was relieved when *Rode Beer* came in and anchored behind us. All the speedboats left to check them out.

Tarakan was filthy and smelly. There were hundreds of sloppy stilt houses on the waterfront, chaotically built out from the shore. We locked the boat and lowered our dinghy. Robert and Nathalie joined us in their dinghy and we all looked back at the speedboats as they slowly dispersed. One pier had a large building on the end with a wooden sign saying it was a shrimp factory. We tied up our dinghies and climbed the stilt poles to the factory. The river prawns were large and plentiful in these waters and Robert negotiated with the manager for a pound.

We crossed a plank bridge into the stilt village and soon were surrounded by curious dark-haired children. Cooking fires smoldered and chickens clucked about, all suspended above the filthy brown water. Groups of men sat with beautiful fighting cocks, holding the legs in one hand and lovingly stroking the bright red and gleaming black feathers with the other.

188

We reached the road that ran through town and wandered towards the immigration offices. The road crossed fetid open sewers lined with squalid houses. Garbage, plastic bags and discarded junk clogged the sewers. Little children climbed on the drainpipes and stood on the boats that had been pulled up in the muck. They flew brightly-colored paper kites, oblivious to the state of their playground. The road climbed a hill and between the buildings we looked out to *Madeline* and *Rode Beer*, swinging on their anchors undisturbed.

We found the immigration offices and began the paperwork to allow us to legally leave the country. As often happens, we were told that it was a holiday and we must come back later. Our permits were about to expire and we cursed our luck. The midday heat was building to an unbearable level and a layer of sweat coated us under our long-sleeved shirts and pants. Fortunately the chief immigration officer arrived unexpectedly and invited us into his office.

He had an affluent Javanese look to him and spoke English well. Curiously he tried to impress us with his importance and how he had held many other posts before being sent to Tarakan. He missed Jakarta and his family and hoped to be transferred soon. He said we were the first yachts in years. He stamped our papers and we left wondering whom he had insulted to be sent to such a remote outpost.

As we descended into our dinghies, the shrimp factory manager presented us with a large river fish as a gift. Back at *Madeline* we all quickly peeled off our damp clothes and I brought refreshing drinks out to the cockpit. Suddenly there was a shout. Someone had noticed we were back. In seconds the speedboats were rafted behind *Madeline* like bees attracted to honey. Their curiosity was even greater, with all of us in our underwear! We quickly pulled our clothes back on, out of cultural respect.

One speedboat kept reappearing with different passengers. We eventually figured out he was running tours from the shore, which included brief stops at both *Rode Beer* and *Madeline*.

The taxi drivers thought we were crazy for going to Malaysia – to our next stop in Tawau. "*Tidak aman*," not safe, they kept saying, telling us that Malaysia was a bad place full of thieves.

They couldn't have been more wrong about Tawau. The difference between the two border towns was immense. At Tawau, a higher standard of living was immediately evident. There were nice cars, decent roads, stoplights, luxury homes, and high-rise buildings. Indonesia's uncontrolled population was over 200 million whereas Malaysia's was only eighteen million. Indonesia had a basically rural subsistence economy, while Malaysia was prosperous and industrialized. The people in Malaysia seemed much more educated, and the British colonial influence was evident as many spoke fluent English.

There was a section of stilt houses over the harbor near the fishing docks, but they didn't dominate the town. We anchored *Madeline* and *Rode Beer* in front of the Tawau Yacht Club. There were two or three small motorboats on moorings, but no yachts.

As we walked past the pool to the modern clubhouse, the manager greeted us. Immediately he made us honorary members and gave us a tour the facilities. It was as if we'd stepped back to the time when this was the traditional welcome accorded to all voyaging yachtsmen. It was more a social club, and he was truly pleased to have our seasoned cruising yachts give credence to the club's name.

The club manager invited us for a beer the first night and introduced us to a number of club members. Waiters constantly hovered around, topping up our glasses the moment one sip was taken. We finally realized that the only way they could tell you were finished, was to leave your glass full. I had no idea how much I'd consumed, and judging from the raucous conversation, I wasn't the only one having a good time.

We were all invited to a "Lottery Club" luncheon where Alec was asked to give a short talk and show some slides. Most of the Yacht Club members were of Chinese descent, and it wasn't until at the luncheon that we realized it was, in fact, the "Rotary Club"! Quek, our sponsor, introduced us to Bernard, a local banker, who had gone to university with him in Britain. Quek and Bernard took it upon themselves to show us a good time, including karaoke at the Tawau Golf Club, and a Borneo jungle jog with the "Hash House Harriers".

As our stay in Tawau came to an end, Quek and Bernard outdid themselves. "What time do you get up for breakfast?" Bernard asked.

190

"About seven-thirty, why?" I said, looking at Nathalie to see if she agreed.

"Okay, I'll see you then at eight o'clock in front of the yacht club," he said. "I'll take you out for breakfast!"

His hospitality was sincere, but I told him, "Don't be silly. After all, we're used to eating breakfast naked." I was running out of excuses. He persisted and we finally agreed to lunch and dinner for our last day in Tawau.

During our numerous gourmet Chinese meals we thoroughly questioned them about the history of the area and whether there really were pirates. With Bernard's help we were beginning to piece it together.

He claimed the notorious pirates were Filipinos, not Malaysians. The Sulu Archipelago in the southern Philippines was populated by the Moro people. Unlike the majority of Filipinos who were Christian, they were Muslim and had been fighting the government in Manila for their independence for many years. Piracy and smuggling were age-old traditions with these people, many of them being Sea Gypsies who lived on boats. This, combined with the availability of serious weapons in the Philippines had created quite a problem.

Bernard admitted he had called his friend, the Chief of the Marine Police and he gave us various phone numbers to use should we run into trouble. The Marine Police Chief advised us to stay close to the coast, and if we kept to our plan we should be safe. But he couldn't make any guarantees, as many of the Philippine islands of the Sulu Sea lay just off the Malaysian mainland.

We felt safe in Tawau, but ahead lay the route through pirate country. Robert had read a romanticized story about pirates attacking a town called Lahad Datu. The story said a group of Filipinos raced in on speedboats with large engines, led by a woman with flowing red hair. They had robbed a bank and a security guard was killed. Bernard knew the story well since it was a branch of his bank that had been robbed ten years ago. "Thirteen people were killed in the robbery," he said. "The government felt that the Filipino pirates had gone too far, and they retaliated by bombing and leveling two Filipino villages in the Sulu Islands." Tensions rose, and the incident had purportedly brought Malaysia and the Philippines to the brink of war.

I was unsure what I should conclude. I was still worried, but the whole situation seemed remarkably similar to the Indonesians in Tarakan warning us of Malaysia. Now the Malaysians were warning us of the Filipinos. Could it all be media propaganda or nationalistic sentiments? However, concern from a well-educated bank manager and the Marine Police Chief definitely seemed more worrisome than from a crowd of well-meaning water taxi drivers.

THE 18ᵀᴴ YACHT IN 18 YEARS

THE HEAT AND HUMIDITY WERE UNBEARABLE as we motored over the calm sea past the disputed island of Sepidan. There was no wind and we both drank large amounts of water to keep up with our steady sweaty outflow.

Jacques Cousteau first brought Sepidan to world attention when he explored it in the 1970's. It is geographically separate from the Malaysian coast, a pillar of rock that rises out of the depths. The scuba diving was world renown and a couple of scuba operators had set up hotels on the island.

We turned towards the coast and entered a labyrinth of reef and islands leading to the town of Semporna, our first destination since leaving Tawau early that morning. A large Malaysian Navy boat was anchored behind the first group of islands, reminding us of the rumors that Indonesia was making a grab for some of Sepidan's tourist revenues by claiming sovereignty.

Robert called the Malaysian Navy ship on the marine VHF radio. All ships at sea are expected to maintain a listening watch. To our surprise, there was no answer. After several attempts, we switched to our own private channel.

"It's nice to know the Navy is in the area," Robert said, "but not much good if we can't talk to them."

We followed the winding channel, marked by sticks and a couple of navigation beacons. The low shoreline sprouted grassy marsh in some areas and sandy beach in others. Fishing nets and buoys crisscrossed the waters outside the channel. Groups of stilt houses perched over the shallows and as we turned the last corner, we could see them lining the shore.

Slim dugout canoes and small fiberglass boats plied the waters. Some boats skipped over the surface with noisy, oversized engines emitting blue smoke, while some were slowly paddled, brown hands jigging fishing lines at the same time.

We motored to a stone pier that extended in front of a ramshackle town rising on the banks. Corrugated iron roofs and crumbling brick walls hid amid the greenery. Around the pier the stilt houses clustered and assorted boats bobbed at anchor. The people looked different. Their eyes peered at us; cheekbones high on flat faces, bronzed skin shining in the late afternoon sun. Perhaps they were Filipinos. They did not smile or wave. They did not approach us as was usual elsewhere.

There were a few larger boats docked with men, children and breast-feeding women aboard. The boats were black with pointed bows and small cabins. These people's hair was a peculiar reddish shade, noticeably different from everyone else's. I wondered if this was a dye, a vitamin deficiency, or if they were a different breed, perhaps Sea Gypsies.

We anchored next to the pier. Robert and Alec went ashore while Nathalie and I watched over our boats from *Madeline's* cockpit. A canoe paddled by with three men wearing balaclavas. I tried to ignore their stares and then finally waved. They awkwardly waved back. They did not smile and I got the distinct impression that yachts were uncommon. Even though I knew the fishermen prized fair skin and wore the balaclavas to protect themselves from the sun, I still found it unnerving. Often the women in Indonesia wore pasty facial masks during the day for the same reason.

Alec and Robert came back with discouraging news. They had found Bernard's friend, but he was unhelpful. The other people had been strange and unwelcoming.

Just then, a small well-equipped motorboat approached with six uniformed men on board. They identified themselves as the Malaysian Coast Guard and one of them clambered onto *Madeline*. He was polite, spoke excellent English and seemed sincerely concerned for our safety. "The Coast Guard has several ships in the vicinity and we monitor the radio constantly," he assured us. "If you have any trouble, please call."

He then told us that they were having problems with pirates coming over from the Philippines. "They could have big engines or small, depending on the boat, but will race up to you and climb right on board. They are mostly interested in motors, but will take everything, even your smallest flashlight. They might even steal your boat and make you swim ashore. If you resist, they will shoot you. So don't resist," he advised. "Give them whatever they want."

We told him we planned to sail together and only in the day.

"You should have no problems, but stay away from the Philippine islands," he warned. "I have no control over Filipinos in Philippine waters." He seemed relieved when we told him we were leaving Semporna the next day. Once we were out of his territory, he would no longer have to worry about us, I thought.

We rose early the next morning and crossed the Lahad Datu area without incident. At the end of the day, we anchored near a large modern pier at a huge palm oil plantation that had been built in the Borneo jungle. The security manager indicated we would be safe at anchor but kept repeating in Malay, *"Laut hati-hati,"* the sea is dangerous.

"Every time we hear another pirate story, Nathalie and I look at each other and say, "Oh no! Not another one." Having her around to share the worry is a great relief. We're well into the trip now and can only carry on. Besides feeling safer, having Rode Beer with us diffuses the tension. Nathalie and I make a game of our daily routine. Each day we have a pre-planned distance to cover, and begin at the crack of dawn. With very little wind most days, we've had to motor. Nathalie and I pretend we're truck drivers, donning our hats and starting our engines – another day of dodging pirates. Each evening the four of us have dinner together, making sure we can see the other boat. Overnight, we leave our radios on. There is a different feeling in the air."

Tambisan Island hugged the Borneo coast separated by a narrow channel, and it felt as if we were entering a river as we motored past the stilt houses lining each bank. We relaxed on our boats and Alec began to paint a watercolor. Jungle bush overhung the bank and tall coconut palms swayed above the rickety houses. A small boat visited us, but we were guarded and unwelcoming.

A short while later, Robert dinghied over to say they were going ashore and we decided to join them. The man from the small boat greeted us and insisted we tie our dinghies to his dock. He invited us into his house, speaking Malay peppered with a little English. The house was simple but clean. We were directed to sit at a circular, wooden dining table in the center of a large room and a woman offered us tea and cookies. Next to the table was a little baby in a small hammock suspended from the rafters. Through the cracks between the floorboards, I saw water lapping ten feet below.

The man's mother hobbled into the room and greeted each of us. She spoke in a language foreign to us, but I complimented her new grandchild and she understood what I meant and was very pleased. I felt guilty we had mistrusted these people initially, turning them away, whereas they immediately welcomed us into their home.

The man told us that it was a dangerous job to be a fisherman. Usually the pirates stole their outboard motors. He said it could be a problem day or night, but only further out to sea, not near the coast.

That night we were up a couple of times when things clunked against the boat. "It's only debris flowing by in the tidal current," Alec said, but I made him check outside anyway. At about three o'clock in the morning, schools of fish began jumping out of the water, creating a rhythmic splashing. Half-dreaming, I imagined a mob of pirates swimming towards *Madeline*. I got up and locked the cabin door.

The next afternoon we entered the brown, silty waters at the mouth of the Kinabatangan River. Further off the coast another large Navy ship steamed past, ignoring our radio call. Motoring against the current and passing monkeys on the banks, we eventually anchored where a small tributary joined the river, next to a cluster of bamboo huts. During the night, clouds rolled in as the northeast monsoon started to blow. The heavens opened and Alec quickly rigged our water-catching system in the downpour while I frantically closed all the hatches.

A few hours later rain had swollen the river. Floating vegetation and branches began pelting *Madeline* in the quickening current. Sticks hit the bows and then slowly realigned, clunking down between the two hulls and past our resting heads. Bigger branches began crashing into the bows causing *Madeline* to vibrate and then, "Clunk, bump, clink, scratch, thunk, clunk and ding!", finally hitting against the metal swim ladder at the stern.

At four in the morning we woke to a loud thud and went to the bow to have a look. A large log was jammed horizontally across both bows and beginning to collect other rubbish. An hour later it was the VHF radio that broke our slumber. "*Madeline*, wake up," Robert called. "You're dragging!"

We dashed to the bow to find a large V-shaped island of palm fronds, bushes, branches and logs caught in front of *Madeline's* two hulls, gradually forcing us downstream. In the early morning glow we slowly freed the debris, and *Madeline's* anchor took hold once again.

Suddenly we noticed that we weren't perspiring. We actually felt gloriously cool for the first time in weeks. The rain had dissipated the heat, yet we knew that within an hour the sweltering sun would begin to broil us for another day. We seized the moment, and luxuriously cuddled in our bunk.

Once the sun had fully risen we called on the radio to see if *Rode Beer* was ready. They too had slept fitfully having been bombarded by logs, but their pointy bow deflected them. Alec conceded to Robert that monohulls had this definite advantage over catamarans – one that had never occurred to any of us before.

Logging of the precious jungle hardwoods had been increasing and we often spotted logs that had escaped and were flushed out to sea. Some of these were over a yard in diameter and longer than *Madeline*. They often floated at the surface, almost entirely submerged, and were well concealed by the waves. As we sailed the coast we kept a sharp lookout, but once we left pirate country and began sailing at night again, we'd just be taking our chances. *Rode Beer*'s steel hull was better protection, although fiberglass is remarkably strong as well. If we did hole *Madeline* on one of these floating monsters, I consoled myself that at least we wouldn't sink like a fiberglass monohull. Our light weight and our flotation compartments would keep *Madeline* afloat – even filled with water.

There was a nice wind blowing and we looked forward to sailing. Motoring towards the sea, we were quickly propelled by the wide, swollen river. We retraced our path hoping to avoid any sandbanks hidden in the turbulent milk-chocolate water. At the shallow river mouth, we realized the onshore breeze had become our nemesis. The wind and waves acted against the flooded river creating large, steep, breaking waves just off the coast.

We quickly convened on the radio, knowing that if we turned around immediately, we could just overcome the current and slowly motor back to the anchorage. We decided to go for it, to ride the waves. Water poured over the decks as *Madeline* bucked like a restless bronco. I gained reassurance watching *Rode Beer* behind us having the same wild ride. If Nathalie could handle this, so could I.

The boats plowed through the eight-foot waves as I watched the depth sounder bounce between twenty and nine feet. We led the way, ready to call *Rode Beer* should the depth drop any lower. They only had a few feet to spare in the troughs and I was thankful for our shallow draft.

We cleared the turbulence and hoisted our sails, leaving the muddy river water after crossing a clear line of demarcation into the cobalt blue of the Sulu Sea. Both Alec and Robert were fine-tuning their sails, trying to get the most out of their boats. Annoyed and cursing, Alec finally quit racing, accepting that *Rode Beer* was faster in these moderate winds.

We spotted a large dirty boat overtaking us from behind. The yellow, wooden hull was streaked with dirt and oily-black exhaust. They steered close beside us.

197

Nathalie called over the VHF radio. "What is that boat doing? Are you concerned?"

"I'm not sure, yet," I replied to her.

"Someone's waving," Alec reported from the cockpit as he waved back. "It looks like a coastal freighter." I relayed the message to Nathalie and thanked her for watching.

"What am I supposed to do if you're attacked by pirates?" Nathalie and I hadn't allowed ourselves to imagine such a scenario.

"You're only a deterrent," I said, unsure myself. "I guess you could call our family and let them know what happened!"

We anchored in front of the Sandakan Yacht Club, the second biggest city in Sabah, and again enjoyed the luxuries of a pool and shower. At Palmerston Island in the South Pacific, we thought it was special to be the 14th yacht to sign their guestbook that year. At the Sandakan Yacht Club, we were the 18th yacht in 18 years!

I was happy to be finished with what we thought was the worst of pirate country. The Sulu Archipelago was now behind us. Then we met Henry, a wealthy Malaysian who spent his weekends in his powerboat, sport fishing across the border in the Philippines. He had two 200-horsepower engines that used 20 gallons of gas an hour and he was proud of both numbers.

"I understand," I said. "You *outrun* the pirates!"

"No," he replied. "They have at least four 200-horsepower engines on their boats! It's not a problem for me because I pay them off!" I prodded him for more information. "The pirates near here are the Filipino army. The government barely pays them, so I pay them $500 a month and they leave me alone. I'm treated like the king of the village when I'm there."

I was tempted to ask him to put in a good word for us.

At Sandakan, we took a day trip to the Sepilok Orang-utan Rehabilitation Center, where we saw the huge apes in the wild. The rangers didn't encourage interaction between the orang-utans and the visitors as they were trying to rehabilitate them for life back in the forest. The orange-haired apes were playful and curious and interacted anyway – especially the younger ones.

Orang utan means forest man, and like humans, young orang-utans rely more on learning than on instinct. They are most vulnerable in their first seven years. When poachers kill a mother orang-utan, their babies are sold into the exotic pet trade. The Center was teaching these orphans how to survive in the forest. The first thing the little ones had to learn was to lose their fear of the dark!

Back at the yacht club, a German ex-pat told us that pirates were not interested in the *orang putih* or white man. Harming tourists created too much trouble for them. That was why they stuck to robbing poor fishermen, because no one cared and no one complained.

"Their biggest prey is their own people," he said. "Many Filipinos are working illegally in Malaysia. The jobs pay a pittance – jobs at the palm oil plantations that Malaysians don't want. After working for a few years, they journey back to their poor Filipino villages, loaded with their relative fortune. They regularly fall prey to the pirates, but neither the Malaysian nor the Philippine governments care, because the money was made illegally."

Just when I was feeling assured that being *orang putihs* would be our saving grace, he went on to tell us about Selingan Island, just 25 miles away. Pirates had taken the whole island hostage, including 25 tourists, seven years ago. The Malaysian Marine Police surrounded the island and negotiated with the pirates successfully. The hostages went free, but so did the pirates. Selingan Island was our next stop!

A few days later when we arrived at Selingan, we could see the islands of the Philippines next door. Selingan was interesting because on one hand it had a guaranteed tourist attraction, but on the other, tourism created part of the problem it was trying to solve. The entire island is a national park and research station for sea turtle nesting. Every night of the year at least one turtle was guaranteed to come ashore to lay her eggs on the white sand beach. Usually a couple of green turtles or hawksbill turtles came, but when conditions were right, they had up to thirty turtles in the same night.

Accommodations were in bungalows near the center of the small island, and at nightfall they cleared the beaches. The shoreline was unlit and only low lighting was used at the information center.

The female sea turtle prefers darkness and often waits until the moon is set before coming ashore. She digs a deep hole in the sand using a front flipper. Once she positions herself over her hole and begins laying her eggs, a ranger and a small group of tourists could approach without disturbing the process.

Sea turtle nesting sights are threatened the world over due to the bright lights of tourism. The same soft sand beaches turtles favor are desired by hotels and resorts. Fortunately, Selingan has been successful in helping the turtles survive and in educating the public about conservation. For 20 years the numbers grew gradually, until 1990 when they dramatically increased as turtles hatched years earlier matured and returned to Selingan.

On our last day in pirate territory we had good wind for a change, so we decided to sail overnight to Kota Kinabalu. We remained cautious, staying within sight of *Rode Beer* and maintaining frequent radio contact.

Just before dark, a fishing boat came up alongside, very close to us. They waved and then moved just a bit further away. They continued along, paralleling our course at the same speed. It seemed as if they had come close to check us out. Like the turtles at Selingan, they were waiting for the cover of night to make their move.

CLOSE CALLS

WE WERE SOON TO DISCOVER HOW CLOSE DISASTER HAD COME. We arrived in Kota Kinabalu, or KK to the locals, and anchored among a few other cruising boats for the first time since Indonesia. In out of the way places, our neighbors were more eccentric than usual.

A long-haired young man approached *Madeline* paddling his squat wooden dinghy kayak-style. He was awkwardly leaning over the bow with each stroke, and he looked more as if he was struggling to propel a lop-sided bathtub. Alec knew him immediately, "It's Alberto!" A few years ago we had read his articles in *Cruising World* magazine with great interest.

Alberto Torroba was from Argentina, and the stories told of his crossing the Pacific Ocean in a fifteen-foot open dugout canoe using only the stars to guide him. He had carried no aids to navigation, not even a wristwatch or compass. He had only a sail, some food and water, and his floating piece of wood capsized on three occasions. The stories ended when he made it to the Philippines, and I had always wondered what happened after that.

Alberto's life philosophy was that of a minimalist, so I was amused when he asked to borrow charts. We invited him aboard. Our paths had converged, as Alberto planned to venture into the Indian Ocean for the next season. "You travel with no engine, no clock, no compass and no sextant, so what do you need charts for?" I joked.

"Once in a while I like to know where I am," he replied. "At least what country," he clarified. "One day I will go even lower and give up using charts all together. There's a certain magic to making a landfall having no idea where you are." The charts he borrowed were very small scale: one of the whole Malacca Strait, and one of the entire Indian Ocean. "It's easier to navigate when there is less land," he said. "Once in the Indian Ocean, I can use wave patterns and bird identification to show me where land is."

He told us how he had chosen one tree in the Phillipine jungle from which to construct his new boat. With some local know-how, he cut and planed the planks right there in the forest. The result was a flat-bottomed, square-sterned schooner, modeled after the tried and true methods of Magellan. *Orion* was 27 feet long with a small cabin, but the amenities were not much different from his dugout canoe.

A twist in Alberto's adventure was that he now had a wife. Rebecca's home had been a tiny Filipino fishing village. I was

surprised that a woman would want to sail under such primitive conditions, but he assured us that with him, she was far better off than in the world she had left behind. The chance to travel and escape a lifetime of poverty rarely presented itself in her village.

She came to visit us with Alberto one night and seemed awed by the comparable luxury of *Madeline*. We gave Alberto a recent copy of *Cruising World*, as he'd never seen the magazine that had published his articles. When the pages flipped open to an 80-foot luxury yacht, Rebecca's eyes nearly popped out of her head. She asked me, "What do you think of me traveling with this crazy sailing man?" I agreed that he was crazy, but everything was relative.

Ironically, we found ourselves asking Alberto the same questions that people asked us.

"Aren't you ever worried for your safety?"

"Have you been in any big storms?"

"Do you catch lots of fish?"

"What does your family think?"

His type of cruising was as foreign to us as ours was to my parents. He lived on the fringe. He carried 20 gallons of water, compared to our 60. He cooked on an open fire on the back of his boat using wood he collected from the shore. His food staples were rice and granola. His income, which was small but regular, was from some property he had in Argentina, but then he told us he had to wait for his money before he could photocopy our charts. After his Pacific crossing, he said he'd needed some cash. "I haven't written any more articles," he said, "because I don't need any more money now."

KK was a busy, urban center with an interesting blend of Asian cultures. The weekend came and our Malaysian friends arrived from Tawau. Quek, who happened to be from one of the richest families in

202

Sabah, took us all out to the Hyatt hotel for an amazing meal of Western cuisine. We reciprocated with a sail on *Madeline*. Nathalie and Robert helped make hamburgers for the barbecue and everyone enjoyed snorkeling on the reef.

During our sail, Bernard announced the most extraordinary news. The day after we had left Tawau, he'd received a call from the Marine Police Chief. "Did you hear about the piracy attack?"

"No!" Bernard had replied incredulously.

"It's okay," the Marine Police Chief reassured him. "The attack was close, but didn't involve your friends. They were anchored at Semporna, five miles away from where the incident occurred. They're okay. I just wanted to tell you before the newspapers pick up the story."

Bernard explained that two fishing boats had been attacked. The pirates were armed with M16 automatic machine guns and drove boats with 500-horsepower inboard/outboard engines. Both fishing boats were robbed and one old fisherman was shot dead – he had resisted. Bernard had been worried sick for the rest of the time, until we had finally called him from KK.

"So now we know – the piracy threat is real. Yet, with the proper precautions and a little luck, we made it! I have to admit the past few weeks were some of the most exciting and fascinating cruising yet, and I thoroughly enjoyed them. Not only did we dodge pirates, but we successfully dodged the pitfalls in our relationship. Having Rode Beer made it easy and there was such a lack of wind that even I was hoping for a good sailing breeze. But cruising changes with the landscape and I wonder how I'll fare – the Indian Ocean is just around the corner."

We took the usual grand reception in stride. We were getting used to superb hospitality and the Royal Brunei Yacht Club didn't disappoint us. Unlike the Malaysian clubs, the Royal Brunei Yacht Club was a unique fortress in this "dry" Islamic sultanate – it was the last bastion of the imbibing expatriate population. The strict liquor laws were ignored and a blind eye was turned since the laws were meant for Bruneians. British, Australian and New Zealand expatriates arrived at the club carrying their little coolers, complete with gin, tonic, limes and ice cubes. Signs were posted around the restaurant warning Muslims to follow their faith and not be led astray. This was perfect for budget-conscious cruisers like us, and we brought our duty-free booze ashore, eating superb, moderately-priced meals at the club.

We met Derrick, a disillusioned expat, who had been lured to Brunei by a lucrative three-year, tax-free contract. There was a lot of money to be made in Brunei, as there were few skilled workers in the small population of 350,000. The Sultan of Brunei took good care of his people, which acted as a disincentive to work. He hired engineers, administrators, teachers, airline pilots and others from many countries in order to keep Brunei up to modern standards.

The offshore oil fields were not as profitable as they once were, but the Sultan was the richest man in the world due to his extensive investments. He was the royal leader of the country and also the head of the government since his ascension to the throne in 1967 at the age of 21.

Derrick had been so tempted by his own financial success in Brunei that he had continued to extend his initial contract. Now fourteen years had passed. He wasn't enjoying Brunei any more, and was no more accepted in the local community than when he first came. He would never be granted Brunei citizenship, nor did he identify with his few remaining family in the United Kingdom. His children hated their boarding school education in England and ironically identified more with Southeast Asia. He had no place he could call home. He had lost his zest for life, and we found it depressing to talk with him. A poor rich man who had sold his soul for the Sultan's table scraps.

After seeing dreams broken in the pursuit of financial happiness, we toured Brunei to see the amazing things money could do. We viewed the Sultan's spectacular palaces, including the one he was building for his third wife. Brunei was already home to the biggest mosque in Southeast Asia, but the Sultan was just finishing an even bigger one, completely gold-plated on the exterior.

Since dancing and karaoke were also banned in Brunei, the Sultan pacified his subjects with other gifts. He had just given every household free satellite television including ESPN and CNN, and he also opened the Jerudong Amusement Park that year. This was a full-scale park with roller coasters, merry-go-round, dodge 'em cars, radio-controlled cars and shooting gallery. The most remarkable thing was

that it was entirely free: admission, parking, games and rides. Some expats took us there with their kids, since it was practically the only children's playground in the country. The park opened late in the day, after the worst of the heat, and we ate our dinner on a black marble picnic table.

We left Brunei, plying the indifferent South China Sea bound for Sarawak. Dodging through the Sultan's oil fields, we tried to stay clear of the numerous freighters and fishing boats, and were spotlit by several close calls. In the rain, visibility was reduced to a few hundred feet. The squalls came mostly at night, mostly on my watch, and mostly when we were in the path of an oncoming ship.

"How was your watch?" I'd ask Alec as he got ready to go to bed.

"Fine, no problem," he'd reply.

"Any boats?"

"Oh, there's something way off to port. No problem."

"Any squalls?"

"No, but there's a black cloud approaching from the starboard quarter..."

I'd start my watch and sure enough the black cloud brought wind and rain. I'd then spend the next three hours reefing, tacking, scanning the horizon and rarely getting a chance to read. It always cleared just before I woke Alec for his watch. He would grunt or maybe complain about the poor sleep he had.

"Why were you always reefing and unreefing and making so much noise?" he'd moan from the cockpit. "It's a beautiful night out here."

On one night watch I spotted strange green lights over the horizon. They didn't appear to be moving, in which case they should have been flashing lights. I altered course and passed what appeared to be three separate fixed towers. I'd read that there were abandoned structures in the oilfields.

"I have an excruciating headache today, and only now do I realize how stressful the past few days have been for me. Sailing with Rode Beer helps, though. Knowing Nathalie is dealing with this too, I can talk myself out of being afraid."

There were no serious dramas and we arrived at the Sarawak River, catching the tide 35 miles up to Kuching for a few days' break. The passage had been the first time we'd handled rough weather since the Tasman, and I felt I'd made a strong contribution to rebuilding our relationship. On the next passage, Alec did his bit.

En route from Kuching to Singapore, we experienced some horrendous weather. Instead of the seasonal northeast monsoonal wind, we had strong southwesterlies. We were beating into uncomfortable waves, smashing through sudden squalls with pelting rain and violent wind shifts. Instead of passing over us, it was getting worse, and the wind held steady at 30 knots.

I went straight to my journal and tried to calm myself. When Alec called for a change of sail plan, I was there to help, but he could see I wasn't going to be able to take much more of this. He scoured the charts, sharing his plan with me and then gave *Rode Beer* a call.

"Hey guys. This is awful. We don't want to do this any more, so I've been looking for alternatives. There's an Indonesian island about 20 miles away. We are going to head there, get some shelter, and wait out this weather."

Robert responded, "Great idea. It *is* nasty out here, and it hadn't occurred to me to take a break."

I realized how thoughtful Alec was being. He may not have considered taking a break either, but he chose to for my sake.

He called back to Robert, "There's nothing like a cold rain outside, a snug anchorage and wild sex." Alec was definitely keeping our love alive. I was so relieved to be stopping.

It blew for two more days while we rested in comfort and safety.

The horizon was a kaleidoscope of red, green and white lights from all the ships moving around. Approaching Singapore in the middle of the night was almost a benefit. As ships moved closer to us, we could clearly see their lights and then determine the direction and type of boat. We got out our reference book, identifying fishing boats, tugs in tow, pilot vessels and even a "vessel not under command" – we gave that one a wide berth!

We stayed out of the main shipping channels, but this took us through a group of about 40 fishing trawlers just 25 miles off Singapore. They were going every which way, and displayed every size and intensity of light, often not related to the size of boat. It was too chaotic and brought back my old fears. But instead of verbalizing my feelings and making things worse, I went below and closed my eyes hoping the boats would soon go away.

Madeline was close-hauled and I left Alec to tack our way through the fleet for the next 45 minutes. When I reappeared in the cockpit, I was shocked to see him heading straight for a group of trawlers.

"Don't worry," he said. "I've got it figured out. I aim for the boats. By the time we get to that original spot they will have moved to a different spot. Before I was steering for the open areas, and then when we got there, all the fishing boats had converged there as well." The Rules of the Road dictated that we give way to fishing boats, which made for crazy sailing. I bit my tongue and the trawlers gradually moved away. His method was also working.

After picking up three month's of mail and shopping for presents, we left *Rode Beer* at the Changi Sailing Club, and wound our way around the bottom of Singapore. Sailing *Madeline* in these waters felt like riding a bicycle across a freeway. Huge car carriers, super tankers and small tramp freighters crisscrossed the channels and hundreds swung to anchors in the large anchoring zones. We examined our photocopies of out-dated charts to plot the safest route through the maze of channels and beacons.

I focused on the fearsome task of navigation as ships raced past. I constantly scanned the horizon to keep track of which ships were anchored and which were moving. I tried to take my mind off what lay ahead: the perilous trip up the Malacca Strait.

Most yachts stayed right, east of the main shipping channels. The problem was that if you strayed too far east and too close to the coast, you'd be navigating through wooden fishing structures and nets strung from buoys, often tended by poorly-lit fishing boats. Yachts had to sail the fine line between running down a fishing boat or being run down by a freighter. To complicate the matter, the Malacca Strait was a confirmed piracy area. Ninety percent of all reported cases of piracy in the world occurred there.

As consolation to the yachts paralyzed with fear of pirates, it was well recognized that these pirates were uninterested in small boats. They were professionals. They stole from the commercial cargo vessels, all of which carry large sums of money for port fees and payroll. No incident involving a cruising yacht had been reported for many years, although it was recommended to keep a good watch and to run a low-level light along with the usual masthead running lights. You'd hate to collide with an undercover pirate who didn't see you coming.

Once, a group of pirates allegedly tied up an entire crew while they robbed their freighter. The ship had continued to motor on autopilot up the Malacca Strait, the busiest shipping lanes in the world, for three hours until the crew finally got loose!

Alec's favorite story was about a band of pirates who sneaked up in the dark of night and boarded a large ship. To their astonishment, it turned out to be a Russian war ship. It was a fatal mistake.

As dusk approached we passed mammoth Persian Gulf crude carriers unloading their oil, and we turned north into the Malacca Strait. Other cruisers were surprised to hear that we were sailing overnight on our own. By now I had learned that this was classic fear-mongering, however I couldn't help but watch closely as each freighter went by, wondering if the crew was tied up.

That night we kept a careful watch, staying just east of the steady stream of northbound traffic. Some freighters had fire hoses blasting water from the stern with their lights shining backward, like a water fountain at a park. We'd heard that the ships did this to discourage pirates from hooking the back of the boat and climbing aboard.

Suddenly, a dark shape motored quickly past us, not a light to be seen. Fisherman or pirate?

I jumped as the engine-temperature alarm pierced the night air. I quickly turned off the motor and trimmed the sails for the light wind. It was 3 AM, but Alec wasted no time. He confidently changed the impeller, but soon the engine overheated again. As frustrating as this was, I was glad it hadn't happened traversing Singapore's harbor. Two days later he still hadn't sorted it out, but we found that if we motored at low speed, the engine stayed cool. We limped into Port Kelang, the harbor for Kuala Lumpur, the capital of Malaysia.

The next day we met Bernard's brother-in-law, Terry, at the Hard Rock Cafe in Kuala Lumpur. We had taken Terry out sailing in Kota Kinabalu, and now he returned the pleasure in his brand new Alfa Romeo, speeding on the highways back to his home. The cellphone rang. It was Bernard calling from Tawau, and we updated him on our adventures. Terry's apartment was gorgeous with hundreds of compact discs and videodiscs. He and his girlfriend took us for a sumptuous meal and then to a nightclub for dancing. The next morning we caught a bus back to Port Kelang, back to *Madeline* and our seemingly simple life.

"We are sailing north in light winds and oppressive heat, and I dream of an air-conditioned bedroom, an air-conditioned sports cars, anything with cool air. I'm concerned about our engine, but we still have a month before we cross the Indian Ocean, and Alec is confident he can fix it. He still has no idea what the problem is and it puzzles him because everything looked fine in Cairns. I wonder how much money it'll cost, and how much cruising time we'll lose... It'll be close as to whether we'll make it to Langkawi in time to meet Rode Beer for Christmas."

I was surprisingly happy when 25 knots of headwinds sprang up just two days before Christmas. Racing over the choppy waters, I was thrilled to get to Langkawi as planned.

Along with *Rode Beer*, we celebrated Christmas Eve with two French boats, *Papillon* and *Hippocampe*. It was a gorgeous anchorage, nestled between two towering cliffs covered in lush tropical greenery. Strong gusts created eerie, green phosphorescent-tipped waves lighting up the scene like lights on a Christmas tree. We celebrated late into the night on *Papillon* with their two high-spirited children.

On Christmas Day, Nathalie and Robert joined us for eggs Benedict and champagne and we exchanged gifts. Being far away from family,

we reveled in our friendship. I couldn't help but reflect. *"Life's good. I've had good telephone calls with home lately, and they sent a lot of mail to Singapore... Alec and I are connecting too, despite all our engine woes. It's amazing how our moods are affected: equipment failure with Alec and weather with me. Still, we're working well together, and I've worried less about the sailing recently."* Following a swim in the nearby freshwater lake, we said farewell to *Rode Beer*, *Papillon* and *Hippocampe*. They set sail on an overnight to Thailand, and we agreed to meet up for New Year's Eve.

After a few days of socializing and buying more duty-free beer at the town in Langkawi, we sailed to Phuket in a brisk breeze. It was a rough overnight sail, but I was surprisingly calm. When I woke Alec late for his watch, I confessed I had fallen asleep for half an hour. Obviously there wasn't enough adrenaline flowing. We were only seven miles from our waypoint when I woke, and I felt terribly guilty. If I'd slept another hour we would've been in serious trouble.

When we reunited with *Rode Beer* and *Papillon*, *Hippocampe* was missing. Nathalie told me that Claude had been single-handing the boat while his new girlfriend slept. He was unable to stay awake the whole night, and when he fell asleep, *Hippocampe* had sailed onto rocks outside the anchorage. Pierre on *Papillon* heard their radio call for help and went to assist, but *Hippocampe* bounced on the rocks in strong wind for hours, until dawn, when Pierre managed to tow them off and to an anchorage nearby. The boat was steel and hadn't been holed, but the side was severely bashed in and the interior cabinetry destroyed. Claude still had his boat, but his plans were shattered.

I grimly vowed never to fall asleep again, for I knew *Madeline* would not have fared so well. Our trip would be over.

There was always the temptation to travel inland to see the sights and many cruisers did this at each port. They would dock their boat at a marina, take a bus or hire a car and tour around, staying in hotels. Alec and I mostly avoided this, for a number of reasons. Our budget couldn't bear the added costs of a marina, a hotel, and meals out, whereas staying on *Madeline* cost us nothing. When we did travel to the "must see" places we often found them expensive, tacky, touristy, crowded, overdeveloped and overrated. Traveling with *Madeline* was the antithesis of this.

We wanted to make the most of our time with *Madeline* and concentrated on seeing places that were best seen, or those that could only be seen, by boat. Why endure the discomfort of sailing huge distances and not reap the rewards of leisurely cruising once you arrived?

We'd spent three enjoyable days traveling through the Balinese countryside with Robert and Nathalie, but told them we didn't intend to do that in Thailand. They teamed up with *Papillon's* crew and flew from Phuket to Chang Mai. I was a bit perturbed, but only because Nathalie hadn't told me of their plans until the last minute.

After beaching *Madeline* and slapping on a few coats of antifouling paint between the tides, we sailed into beautiful Phang Nga Bay. Huge pillars of limestone studded our path through the myriad of islands. The water was calm and peaceful. Surprisingly there were only one or two cruising boats, in contrast to the hundreds we had just left in Phuket. The first night we traded with local fishermen for prawns, and the next night Alec jigged for squid.

In contrast to the South Pacific, the waters of Southeast Asia never gave us any big fish. Squid was tender and tasty if cooked properly, but the real challenge lay in the catching. After being shown the ease of capture and cleaning by another catamaran owner, Alec had bought a small squid jig.

When he saw squid hovering in the water by our boat, he'd toss in the lure. Immediately they would all come over for a look, and eventually one squid would grab the lure with its tentacles. The tentacles would catch the hooks, and the squid would try swimming away while squirting its ink. The trick was to pull the lure fast enough so that the squid could not get off, while still leaving it in the water as it squirted ink. Then there was about 30 seconds to get it in a bucket before the squid built up more squirts! It was complicated by the squid being just five feet off the back of the boat, not leaving much water between Alec and the squid's ink. It was often a messy ordeal.

Our ten-day cruise was filled with great exploring, bizarre caving, and delicious Thai food, but was also studded with continual equipment problems aboard *Madeline*. We were barely keeping ahead of the chores, as it seemed something broke everyday. We finally claimed victory over the engine's overheating problem. Scale had built up in the water cooling passages. Together we flushed muriatic acid through the engine, and then, after cleaning out the exhaust manifold, Alec declared the engine fixed. That day the head broke.

Every year or two, it's common for the exhaust hose of a head to get plugged. Calcium from human excrement builds up in the hose, like cholesterol in an artery, until one day it's clogged. We took the fat, black hose to shore and Alec swung it over his head, smashing it violently onto the deserted beach. I ducked away from flying crud, as we cleared it.

There were other little things, like a loose alternator belt and faulty wiring in a solar panel. *"It's simply the best person for each job, and I play an essential role in many of them. But when Alec is working away,*

211

I end up doing more of the cleaning and cooking. I remember how I used to hate that role, but now I realize how important it is for us to work as a team, and that all these jobs must be done."

We were definitely working much better together, and our infrequent disagreements were short-lived. I had learned to keep my outward worrying to a minimum and Alec had learned to no longer express his irritation when I did verbalize. He now realized that his anger over an argument, which often lasted a couple of days in the South Pacific, benefited neither of us. He also allowed me to talk about what was bothering me, which was often all I needed, but it took an effort on both our parts not to lapse into our old ways.

Although everything was going well between us in Phang Nga Bay, I was feeling unhappy. This perturbed Alec just as much as me. He found it difficult not to take it personally, as everything else seemed perfect. After another round of talking in circles, I finally figured out the cause.

Soon, we'd say goodbye to *Rode Beer*.

GOODBYE

RODE BEER AND *PAPILLON* SHARED the common interest of traveling inland and both boats were planning to travel to the Andeman Islands of India, and then on to Sri Lanka together. Due to the civil war in northern Sri Lanka, only the southern port of Galle was open to cruising boats. An inland tour was the only way to see the country. Alec and I had decided months previous to bypass Sri Lanka and go straight to the Maldives – to scuba dive.

I was feeling a little jealous that Nathalie and Robert had found new friends, but I was sadder at the prospect of not seeing them again. After Thailand, there was the entire Indian Ocean to cross, and then a grueling slog up the Red Sea. That would be our last chance to see *Rode Beer* because once in the Mediterranean they would be racing back to Holland. I was missing Nathalie even before we said goodbye.

With the sadness came apprehension as well. I would be leaving more than Nathalie. *"We've spent much of the last four months coastal sailing with Rode Beer, but also with many other boats. Can I successfully cross the Indian Ocean alone with Alec and my journal? Will my goals help me through the daily hardship of an ocean passage? Cruisers come and go, their personalities vary, and we enjoy them for who they are: tough, independent individuals. For me, the eternal extrovert, I hope to draw enough strength from within, for it's only a week from now that I say goodbye to them all."*

We sailed back to Nai Harn and found *Rode Beer* and *Papillon* anchored in front of our favorite little beach restaurant. We invited Nathalie and Robert for dinner, eager to hear about their trip to Chang Mai. We cooked a simple meal and swapped stories from the past weeks.

They shared the news that they wanted to be pregnant for their arrival home, and we congratulated them, toasting their decision. I took on the role of family doctor, gladly answering their questions and assisting their planning. I was so happy for them, but also sad that in seven months their circumnavigation would be over.

Alec felt duty-bound to share his newly acquired skill of attaining food cheaply with his good friend, so he and Robert retired to the back transom with the squid lures. I was delighted to talk alone with Nathalie.

"You were very secretive about your trip to Chang Mai," I told her honestly, "which is unusual for us."

"I'm sorry, I really feel bad about it." Even though she knew we weren't interested in going, she confessed, "I couldn't tell you that *Papillon* didn't invite you." Sylvie, of *Papillon*, found it difficult in the cruising community because she didn't speak English well and she had no friends amongst the French boats at the moment. She had wanted French-speaking Nathalie all to herself. Whenever I was with the two women, I often switched to English, and Nathalie followed as I couldn't converse comfortably in French. Understandably, this frustrated Sylvie – I felt the same way when all the Dutch boats got together.

Even though I appreciated Sylvie's dilemma, Pierre annoyed me. He had persuaded Nathalie to keep quiet, not wanting to spoil this escape for his wife.

"His intentions may have been noble," I said, "but I don't like his approach."

"It was wrong not to tell you," she admitted, tears glistening in the corners of her eyes. "I'm so glad we've talked about it now." We both cried a little, out of relief that our friendship was once again fully intact.

Meanwhile, the men were still outside while Robert enjoyed a smoke. After Alec had explained the intricacies of squid jigging, they had fallen into a philosophical conversation. They were sitting on the edge, each with a lure, legs dangling only two or three feet from the squid.

The squid were looking at the lures, but for some reason not grabbing. Unfortunately, as Robert was discussing a particularly important point, he gestured with his jigging hand in just the right fashion. A squid grabbed the lure.

Robert gave a mighty pull.

The squid flew out of the water, hitting him squarely in the chest. Jet-black ink blasted his face and clothes. Then the squid got free of the lure, bounced off his leg and plopped back into the water!

Alec could not control his mirth. Nathalie and I rushed out of the cabin to see Robert cursing squid jigging. We all laughed and laughed.

A special night with special friends.

The days before leaving *Rode Beer* were ticking away. We ate many meals ashore, having become addicted to the green curry and the low prices. The flavor created by the spices combined with coconut cream was none other than orgasmic. For our last night together, we agreed to meet Robert and Nathalie at the little shoreside restaurant. The dining was casual on the beach and we invited others to join us.

Before we left *Madeline*, I heard talking on the VHF radio. My curiosity piqued when Pierre told *Rode Beer* he wanted to pick them up

214

and take them ashore in his dinghy. Robert declined the offer. After dinner, when we were alone, Robert mentioned how strange Pierre's offer was. "I can't see any reason why I wouldn't take my own dinghy ashore," he said.

But I knew there was only one reason: Pierre wanted to control the situation and control *Rode Beer*. He should've known it wouldn't work, especially when most cruisers were fiercely independent.

We'd never had problems like this in the past. We could spend the day with *Rode Beer* and then have a different couple over for dinner the same night. Our friendships had never been complicated before, but now I was feeling all the emotions of a little girl at a schoolyard recess: awkward, confused and fighting to keep my friends.

The next afternoon I ran into Pierre and his daughter at the beach. They had just come from town and Pierre was carefully holding a cake box. I helped them lift their dinghy into the water and gave them back their guestbook. Most sailors would trade guestbooks to put in pictures, drawings and stories recounting their shared misadventures. It made a great souvenir and it was just as fun reading the books as it was signing them. I said, "We're leaving tomorrow, so I'll come and get our book in the morning, since you're having dinner on *Rode Beer* tonight."

"Oh, I am? I've been out all day," he replied.

"Well," I said, "Nathalie told me she's having you at seven."

"Oh, I didn't know," Pierre said avoiding eye contact.

"I'm invited for dinner at *Rode Beer* too!" his ten-year-old daughter chirped.

"Great," I said to her, "and it looks like you've bought a cake to bring." The young girl nodded. I couldn't believe that Pierre was lying to me so blatantly. Even his kid knew he was lying.

When I returned to *Madeline*, I shared my frustrations with Alec. He was his usual logical, cynical self. "What do you expect? If you get enough people together in a community – even a liberal-minded and laid-back community such as this – then you're going to have all sorts of personalities, politics and personal dynamics. We've been exceptionally fortunate so far, don't you think?"

He was sensible, but that didn't help my farewell with Nathalie. I just didn't feel right leaving Thailand.

In centuries past, Arab traders sailed each summer across the Indian Ocean to the Orient in small dhows. Each winter they returned, with winds that reverse direction like nowhere else in the world. For a couple of months during the transitionary periods the wind slowly dies and then gradually picks up from the other direction.

We'd been waiting for the northeast monsoon to kick in with its gentle wind, and by the end of January 1995, reports were filtering back to the cruising community in Thailand from the boats that had already set out. The northeast monsoon was well established and good steady winds were being experienced. Unhurriedly we did our final provisioning, made our last phone calls and trudged through the exit formalities.

We motored out of Nai Harn Bay after spending our last baht at our favorite little restaurant. We cleared the effect of the land and hoisted the spinnaker as the wind picked up creating perfect downwind sailing conditions.

"Thailand to the Maldives will be our second longest passage, our first major offshore passage since the Tasman eight months ago. Normally, a long break from ocean sailing makes me feel nervous and out of practice, but the dread and fear I experienced before the Tasman are not here. I feel relaxed and mentally prepared. This is a tropical trade-wind passage and I know what to expect. Even though our next destinations are some of the most remote in the world, there will be no low-pressure systems to worry about – there isn't even a weather radio station to monitor!"

But my confidence came more from the hard work Alec and I had done on our relationship, and also from my new understanding of myself. Still I was apprehensive, as this passage might be the ultimate test of whether our efforts had been fruitful.

Over the next few days, the clouds thickened and were accompanied by increasingly gusty wind squalls. Watching the spinnaker strain was starting to wear on me, but I did my best to contain my fears. As we tried to douse the spinnaker in a particularly vicious squall, it jammed. I panicked and couldn't hold back my screams and whimpers.

Instinctively Alec shouted, "Don't cry!" Then he unexpectedly said, "Okay, go ahead and cry. Sure, why not?"

It was funny, how he had so quickly changed his tone. We both laughed and laughed.

He repacked the spinnaker on our large foredeck and then returned to the cockpit. "It must be difficult living like you do – afraid of everything," he said smiling. "I'm glad it's you and not me."

We were getting along well, doing our best not to get angry over each other's weaknesses and stifling potential arguments with humor. I was proud of how we were trying to make life more pleasant for each other, but I couldn't help feeling stressed out sometimes.

One day I was feeling particularly challenged by our conditions. The muscles in my head and neck stiffened. I didn't feel well, and psychologically, I was beginning to feel uncomfortable with it all.

Alec was great. He traded watches, and came into the bunk to rub my head, helping me to relax and fall asleep. That was all I needed: for him to understand and support me when I was having a tough time.

I regularly wrote in my journal and reflected on how much we'd changed. I thought back to the South Pacific, and of our longest crossing to the Marquesas. Sailing and cruising were new to us then, but I continued to harbor many of the same fears, however, they had evolved over time. In the South Pacific I had written, "*Will we bump into whales?...a collision with a whale is not always fatal. These things happen, but not usually to you.*"

We were now seven days into our voyage, and just 150 miles southeast of Sri Lanka. It was ugly, blowing 25 knots, downwind, and pouring rain. For the second day running we had tied our record of 160 miles in 24 hours. *Madeline* was handling it well, and even I was not too bothered by the gloom.

We were snug inside with the door closed, our morning coffees sitting on the table. In rough conditions like these, the boat normally bounced around a fair bit, and the water sloshed up under the hulls making quite a racket. In the past, we proudly regaled monohull owners how we put down our drinks without fear of spilling. We were careful with full wineglasses, but otherwise did not rely on fiddles, funny-shaped glasses or non-skid bottoms, so you can imagine our surprise when our coffees spilled.

There was a distinctive, "Thunk!" It took a moment to register that this thunk was different from the usual thunks.

Then there was a second, even more definite, "THUNK!"

Madeline jolted and the java jumped. As I was wondering what could be happening, Alec's eyes popped out of his head.

"We've hit a whale!" he shouted.

"No!" I begged.

"Yes!" he yelled.

"No!" I yelled back. "Not a whale!"

Looking past me through our port window, Alec saw a huge whale head, as the mass of mammal rose out of the water trying to get out from under our boat. The blowhole opened and the spray shot against *Madeline*. Alec ran outside to get a better look, and I hesitatingly followed him. Would there be more? Had we run into a sleeping pod? Had we wounded the whale? Would it try to attack us?

Madeline sailed on. The whale surfaced erratically behind us blowing several times, looking a little flustered, although I'd never seen a flustered whale before. It was easily the size of our boat, probably larger, but we only saw its back, never the tail. It had a blunt head, or melon, like that of a sperm whale. After a moment or two the whale disappeared behind the wind-whipped waves. As before, we were alone with the ocean.

"Wow! Unbelievable!" My hands were shaking as we sorted out what had happened. Our "hit and run" victim was probably blissfully asleep when we surfed right over. The first knock was the bow riding up and the second heavier, coffee-spilling blow must have been when the keels hit. After we'd overcome our shock, we called on the radio to another boat, *Pandarosa*, that we knew was in our vicinity.

"Are you in your life raft?" Craig asked, questions pouring out. "Is there any damage? How big was it? Did you get a picture? Are you all right?"

"Oh, yeah," Alec responded, "we're fine." But then he added to me, "Alayne, maybe you should check the bilges!"

I knew that the impact was too light to damage *Madeline*. The underside of our boat was strong, and even if she'd been hit in the stern, her rudders were protected by skegs. In this instance we were very glad of our boat choice: a shallow-draft, well-built catamaran. Other catamaran designs may have had problems, and certainly a deep-keeled monohull would have stopped abruptly, instead of skipping over the whale as we did.

Shortly after, Alec read an article about a racing catamaran that hit a whale and ended up in their life raft. I thought of the other catamarans that we'd met along the way and specifically of a very fast cat with centerboards and spade-hung rudders that we parted company with in Thailand. I wondered how they would have fared. I wondered what would've happened if the whale's head had surfaced between our hulls. We were fortunate.

The passage to the Maldives continued to be a rough and wild ride. It remained the fastest long passage in our circumnavigation. Of course we had a series of mishaps: we lost a line overboard, the alternator bearings went, causing the belt to smoke and melt to bits, and we found maggots in the potatoes. There was no doubt that my positive mind-set helped me to cope with the conditions, and in one journal entry I wrote, *"I'm enjoying my night watch so much, that I don't want it to end."*

I even managed to make it through a watch of 30-knot winds and pouring rain in the pitch black without waking Alec. I spotted *Pandarosa's* light, and later told him that when I saw it, I immediately felt better to have their company. Alec responded, "That's stupid. Another boat does not change anything about the conditions."

"I think most people would feel the same way I do."

"Does that mean if most people are overweight," he countered, "that overeating is justified?" He hated it when I compared us to the average. "Alayne, you're crossing oceans in a small catamaran," he added. "You're definitely not normal. I don't care what *most* people would feel. I don't live with *most* people. I live with you!"

"How do you explain all those organized rallies, like the Atlantic Rally for Cruisers, that have developed in the past few years? Obviously many sailors enjoy the camaraderie and sense of security that sailing in company provides."

Alec argued that these rallies only gave a false sense of security and created peer pressure.  "Ultimately, each boat must face the conditions alone. Thirty knots is always thirty knots. The only thing that changes it is whether you're sailing into the wind or away from the wind, not whether there's another boat near you."

"Well, I feel what's more important is the perception of the situation, and I gain support from *Pandarosa's* light."

"Good. I'm happy for you then," he said, shrugging his shoulders.

It was okay that we didn't agree. The key was that we hadn't upset each other.

When I read over my journal entries from the

Pacific crossing, I was proud that I'd evolved into a stronger person. Sure, I still felt occasional gloom and doom, but only bits were emerging versus the scoops and scoops I inundated Alec with during those first long passages. I now understood my limitations and I didn't expect to enjoy bad weather. I could see each day from a broader perspective.

After 11 days and 1,500 miles we arrived at Male in the Maldives. Alec dove into the crystal-clear water in the small-boat harbor and checked the hulls. He couldn't see any damage from the whale. We went over to another boat and exchanged passage stories.

They told us the story of a monohull, *Finnigan*, who a few days earlier had diverted to Sri Lanka after bending their rudder when they hit a whale. They'd been taking on water and were unable to steer. Mid-story I slipped in that we had also hit a whale. The woman carried on and then suddenly stopped. She said incredulously, "Did you say *you* hit a whale?"

We were now elevated to seasoned-sailor status.

Back at *Madeline*, we chuckled at their response. "They seemed disappointed when the story didn't end in tragedy," Alec said, touching my hand. "In actual fact, it was the opposite, wasn't it?"

Yes, I thought. We had triumphed.

BOOK THREE

ALL SAILS SET

THE MALDIVES ARE A GROUP OF FLAT SAND ISLANDS, much like the Tuamotus in the South Pacific. The highest points on each atoll are the palm trees, and the word *atoll* originates from the Maldivian language. The 240,000 Maldivians have their own culture and independent government, but have similarities to India in appearance, clothes and choice of food. They are strict Muslims, more so than the Indonesians, but less than the Arab countries that lay ahead in the Red Sea.

Having just come from the lush, jungle-lined streets of Thailand, stepping onto the shore in Male was like beaming down to another planet. The streets were sand or dirt and bordered by houses built from sun-bleached coral. Cobblestone sidewalks lined the dusty streets and crews with shovels were emptying the gutters of silt. Maldivians

pedaled past on bicycles – women in flowing saris and men in business suits. The busy pace and style of dress belied the underlying poverty. In the back streets women carried their jugs to the central taps to fill with desalinated water. They walked home balancing big pots on their heads. The men ran the market in Male, and amongst several hundred, I was the only woman. They wore sarongs hiked high above their knees, and many were hajis, wearing white skullcaps that showed they had made the pilgrimage to Mecca. February was Ramadan, and each evening, after the daily fast had been broken at sunset, the streets came alive with families strolling about.

Male was unexpectedly

intriguing, but we were excited to explore the reefs. For the next three weeks we were under water as much as humanly possible and smiles became ingrained on our faces. Swimming with sea turtles, eagle rays, manta rays, sharks, dolphins and schools of big fish everyday put us in such a euphoric mood that nothing else mattered.

The weather was no longer stormy and we sweltered in the heat. In the calm our boat was invaded by dozens of bothersome flies. At night the flies slept and were not a problem, but they rose with the sun early each morning.

"What is it with these flies?" one cruiser bemoaned. "I hate being rudely awakened by a big fat fly kissing my lips!"

We didn't care because we knew that we were only on board to eat or sleep before diving back in the water again. The sea life followed us as we snorkeled amidst their world. It was like taking a walk in a forest, but these woods were buzzing with such colorful activity, with animals all around us, all the time. With each swim we identified a new plant or animal. We came to recognize the bigger creatures, as they were always in the same place on the reef. Alec often dove down to 40 feet or more and would stay there for a minute while he became one of them.

The small islands of the Maldives rise out of the ocean floor and the mighty ocean currents are squeezed between the islands at an accelerated speed. Fish hang out in abundance in these passes. They are attracted by the swiftly flowing water, which means more nutrients passing by. It is nature's version of fast food, and where there are more fish, there are more sharks too.

Our budget had done well in Southeast Asia, and we signed up for some serious scuba diving. The dive boat took us out into the deep blue ocean, and lined up outside the pass between two islands. Once we were in the water, the current would push us towards the pass.

The divemaster instructed us to remove every last drop of air from our buoyancy control devices, so that we would sink straight away. Our masks had to be on perfectly because there would be no time to adjust them. We had to all stay together and we were to jump in one after the other, paratrooper style.

As we lined up at the side of the boat, nervous sweat fogged my mask. There was definitely pressure being in a group; I would have never done this on my own. I tried to remember the last time I'd been scuba diving – only three months previous in Kota Kinabalu. But those were shallow dives, and I remembered having mask problems then.

"Go! Go! Go!" We all jumped into the fathomless water and quickly swam downward. Soon I saw the bottom steeply sloping out of the depths. A big, gray shape cruised out of the blue fog, effortlessly zigzagging towards us. I saw the divemaster spin around and settle into a hollow at the bottom of the pass.

I got out of the current and Alec knelt beside me. I poked my head up, and the current ripped at my mask, almost knocking me off balance.

I glanced at my dive computer. We were at 134 feet and could only safely spend eleven minutes at this depth. I scanned the dark blue water rushing towards us. Undulating cobalt fingers of sea whips poked up uniformly across the bottom. Above this, dense schools of brilliant orange fish danced as they fed in the current. Sleek, gray sharks weaved back and forth. The little fish retreated before the sharks' path, diving into the yellow and purple coral, before returning to their dance above the bottom. The sharks came in close, deftly moving through the current with sweeps from their tails. Were we watching them, or they us?

Alec gestured to me his delight; the nitrogen narcosis enhanced the psychedelic surrealism of the scene. The beauty was stark, yet colorful; pure, yet menacing. Our visit was over, and I wondered how long these fish had been dancing. We tumbled out of the hollow, slowly rising up as the current shot us through the pass.

Alec and I were on a high.

Two cruising friends had left their boat in Thailand to take jobs as dive masters at Fesdu Island in the Maldives. Lotar was German and Ellie was Dutch, and they had previously run a dive operation in Yugoslavia before they lost it in the war. To get away from their troubles, they had taken off cruising on *Bonbini* and were with the fleet cruising from Australia to Thailand. Alec and I were keen to do more diving, so we telephoned them. Lotar encouraged us to visit, claiming he could show us the best diving in the world.

The weather was beautifully calm as we sailed with the spinnaker up to the tiny island. Conditions were perfect for diving and for leaving *Madeline* precariously anchored in 97 feet of water off the edge of the island. We lowered all 200 feet of chain and reasoned that if we couldn't raise the anchor, then Lotar would scuba dive down and help us out.

There was a German diver who, in the 1970's, put the Maldives on the map. He entertained diving tourists with his shark-feeding antics. Although shark feeding was no longer encouraged, we still saw many postcards of him holding a dead fish in his mouth with a shark biting the other end.

"We have to go to the place where they used to feed the sharks," Lotar said. "It's one of the best dives in the Maldives." Again, I went along with the crowd.

As the four of us descended, I stuck close to Ellie. Big, gray reef sharks were everywhere. These grays were thick and bulky and up to twelve feet long. They slowly swam up to us. Just behind long blunt snouts, beady white eyes stared at us. Ellie and Lotar didn't appear fazed. If they weren't scared, I told myself, then neither was I.

There were hundreds of other smaller fish swimming unconcerned around the sharks. There were also several huge and friendly Napoleon wrasse. These fish were six feet long and almost as tall. Their bodies were thin with thick lips and strange rotating eyeballs on each side. Lotar had brought a few hard-boiled eggs. They sucked the egg in, spitting out the shell a few seconds later.

Alec and Lotar both indicated that they were short on oxygen. Ellie and I each had surplus air, so we waved goodbye as the guys ascended. We stayed near a ledge of coral, and another group of divers descended, perching themselves on the same ledge in front of us.

Trancelike, I watched the sharks circle round and round. One shark cocked its head backward and began to swim in an exaggerated side to side motion. I'd read about this behavior; it was a pre-attack display and it was bad news!

The small reef fish immediately became agitated, as if some signal had been transmitted through the water. The whole marine world vibrated in anticipation – brilliant yellow, magenta, and cobalt shook in fear – as the shark contorted in its dance.

With a flash of jagged teeth, it chomped on a fish, gulped twice, and the fish was gone. The shark was swimming directly for me, but just as quickly it ceased dancing and swam nonchalantly over my head. All the small fish calmed down and resumed their activities, and I reminded myself to breathe.

I looked at Ellie and her eyes looked widely back. I motioned to ascend and she quickly nodded.

Back on the boat we all talked excitedly. "I've never seen a shark feed in the wild like that," I said. "What made him choose that fish at that time?"

"We watched it from the surface," Lotar said.

"One of the divers in that group was waving a dead fish around," Alec explained. "He kept tucking it into his vest and bringing it out again."

"And when the shark was ready to strike, he swam backward into his group." Lotar shook his head. "He was inexperienced, and threw the fish at the shark bringing it dangerously close to the group."

"Dangerously close to Ellie and me!" I added.

"The danger with shark feeding is that they get very excited," Ellie added. "With their poor eyesight, they aren't always accurate."

"Once we had our divers at a feeding – not organized by us – and it turned into an unorthodox feeding frenzy. A shark came up to one of our divers and bit her leg. The shark realized its mistake and quickly retreated, but our diver was in shock and had big tooth marks on her thigh."

I was glad they told me that *after* our dive.

During the ride back to Fesdu Island, the wind sprang up. After only a brief discussion Alec and I agreed it was time to move on. We said our thanks to Lotar and Ellie for four days of excellent diving. They wished us good fortune, as this next passage would be even longer than the last.

Ideal Indian Ocean sailing conditions settled in and soon the trip was vying for our most wonderful ever. Six days into the passage, I finally sat down to write. *"We've had pleasant winds on the beam, which makes the boat roll side to side a bit and it took me longer than usual to shake off the nausea and apathy of seasickness. But now I can finally enjoy the persistent sunshine and perfect sailing conditions. We're catching a lot of fish and I cooked banana bread when our stock of bananas suddenly ripened. Life is good."*

As we rounded the horn of Africa we spotted land, but were then warned by a passing freighter to keep offshore. When we arrived in Djibouti after fifteen easy days, we learned that a British yacht had been boarded by pirates not far from where we had sailed, off the coast of Somalia. Luckily, a Canadian frigate had responded to their radio call for help.

Stepping onto land in Djibouti was stepping onto Africa in every sense. The locals were black, as one would expect, but also very tall. It was the first time we'd ever had the locals tower over us; a real contrast to months of small Asians. We quickly called our families, guessing correctly that the frigate's rescue had made front-page news back home.

The port town was dirty, with hundreds of large black crows swooping overhead and hoards of flies buzzing about. A chic perfumery or other such extravagant French store with black iron bars across the windows occasionally interrupted the dilapidated buildings. Ceasing to be a French colony in 1977, there was nonetheless, still a strong French influence.

The French military base had been shrinking, hurting the economy. Djibouti was the poorest place we'd visited. Children were begging in the streets, hands outstretched, calling, *"Baksheesh Madame, Baksheesh Monsieur."* The term *baksheesh* is Arabic and is used when asking for extra payment, usually for a service rendered, like a tip. However these children were not performing any service. In the mornings we saw them reluctantly walking to their street corner. In the afternoons they argued with each other over the day's earnings, as they handed a portion to an adult. We preferred to give them food, as we were never sure where the money went.

The streets were filled with scarred, emaciated people and amputees hobbling on crutches, likely victims of the wars in neighboring Somalia and Eritrea. There were children without fingers and limbs, some unable to walk with spina bifida, yet others with a leg wrapped around their neck, likely to enhance their profits as professional beggars. I passed an old woman with cataract-clouded eyes, hand outstretched, sitting on corrugated cardboard that doubled as her bed each night. The hopelessness was numbing.

In contrast, the market was a kaleidoscope of color and vivacity. The healthy refugees who had fled to Djibouti tended the stalls. The women wore every color imaginable, in every conceivable pattern. It seemed the more conflicting and confusing the color schemes, the better. Their heads were wrapped in brilliant turbans, ears garnished with big gold earrings and wrists adorned with rows of bangles. All of this flowed freely on lovely black skin, and they greeted us with wide

smiles of bright white teeth.

The urge to pull out the camera was intense, but we'd been warned that people didn't like having their picture taken. Some got downright angry, yelling and shooing us away. After learning this truly offended many, we made a point of asking first. To our surprise, some were thrilled and posed readily, flattered they'd been chosen as our subject.

After a few days in port, Alec and I split up to do some last minute things before starting on our journey up the Red Sea. He went off to pick up our visas at the Egyptian embassy and I went off to the market to get some fresh fruit and vegetables.

Locals treated me differently when I was alone. People were even friendlier and often stopped to talk. My North American ways made me feel a little reserved and on guard with strangers, but each time I was treated with such genuine kindness, that I'd learned to discard any fears.

I decided to take a thorough walk through the market before making any purchases. I came to the end of the stalls, and continued to walk around the perimeter. I realized I was getting away from the center, so I turned back on one of the roads.

Even though there was a scattering of stalls at people's houses, I didn't think I was in the market any more. People were staring at me, and I became acutely aware that I was the only foreigner. I quickened my pace, sensing I should hasten my way back to the market.

I wasn't carrying any valuables or wearing any jewelry. My empty knapsack was on my back, and I had about US$4 worth of French franc coins in my clenched fist. I carried small change like this, to avoid having to dig through my wallet, and display my relative wealth, when making a purchase.

Something smashed my wrist from behind. My right arm jolted forward. Pain shot through my hand and my fist opened involuntarily. The coins spilled into a puddle on the muddy clay street.

A man brushed past me and frantically sifted through the filthy water, desperately looking for the money. I was shocked and angry, and looked around for help. Empty faces stared back at me.

"*Un homme terrible!*" was all I could muster. The man looked up at me slowly, and then went back to sifting, still without success. This gave me a sense of satisfaction, but then I realized I might be in real danger.

A lame child hobbled by on all fours, flip-flops on his hands and his feet. These people were desperate. A sense of urgency struck me, and I quickly slipped away. A local teenage girl walked briskly with me. She was muttering away in French about the thief, and from what I could tell, she was trying to console me. I started to cry. She touched my arm, and I told her I would be okay. "*Merci.*"

The contrast reinforced that there are good people and there are bad. It was a minor incident and the only one of its kind during our whole trip. Of all the people we had contact with, the good people held the overwhelming majority.

We'd heard from other cruisers that the food was quite good in Djibouti. So when *Pandarosa* told us about a restaurant that served Ethiopian cuisine, we decided to try it out. After cocktails aboard *Madeline*, the four of us enjoyed an interesting buffet. On the first pass, I happened to miss one dish that the others raved about. They insisted I try the "Ethiopian steak tartar". Even though I thought they were joking, I was relieved to discover there was no more.

The next night Alec began to feel ill. He had explosive diarrhea all night, felt awful and looked green. He was more concerned than I was, and was drilling me about what we should do for him. "In the acute stage," I explained, "I treat all diarrhea the same way." I gave him only clear fluids, controlled his fever with Tylenol and dispensed a little TLC.

Diarrhea is usually self-limited and runs its course in a matter of days. I was prepared for treating any bacterial causes, but had chosen not to stock a treatment for parasites as they tended to be a long-term, chronic problem, and not an emergency.

We discussed whether we should wait until Alec recovered, but he said he'd rather waste his time being unwell during a passage than at anchor. Early the next morning we set sail up the remote Red Sea, with Alec still sick. The wind quickly increased as we expected, while Alec exhausted his arm pumping the head. He continually questioned my medical judgement, saying, "I hope you're right!"

I was sure he would recover, but my mind was preoccupied with the sailing ahead of me. The opening at the bottom of the Red Sea is named Bab el Mandeb. I tried not to be influenced by the translation – the Gates of Sorrow.

By nightfall the wind reached 30 knots, and I turned *Madeline* into the strait.

THE RED SEA

FORTY KNOTS OF WIND BLEW us to the uninhabited, volcanic Hanish Islands of Yemen at the lower end of the Red Sea. Alec was nearly recovered and despite a nagging urge to take advantage of the southerly wind, the urge to explore was stronger.

The topography of these bleak islands was like nothing we'd seen before. Desert sand swept over volcanic rock of differing shades of brown, red and black. Tufts of wind-blown scrub were scattered around, and loose rock crumbled under our feet. We climbed to the top of one peak and with such loose footing and terribly strong winds, I was afraid I'd get blown right off the top. Alec laughed with arms outstretched like wings, leaning into the wind. Above us ospreys hovered, and we followed one to its nest of rubbish strewn haphazardly over the rocks.

In the afternoon a small, open boat approached *Madeline*. The men displayed a large snapper and we traded with two packs of cigarettes and a jar of hot sauce. We carried cigarettes, as it was the universal currency in this part of the world. Alec watched with the binoculars as they motored away, stopping at another larger boat anchored about a mile down the rugged coastline. He could just make out the interaction, which included excited pointing towards us. We wondered if we'd been too generous.

230

Just before dusk the larger boat came into our small bay and precariously anchored in front of us. We watched closely as they casually tossed over two homemade anchors. Bullets of wind tore across the ruffled water and we worried about them dragging down onto us.

The fishermen began yelling and held up a lobster for us to see. They waved frantically, with their hands pointing downward, palms facing them and their fingers waving back and forth together. The motion resembled "go away", or "shoo". But here, we were sure they wanted us to come to them.

The wind whipped "Smokes!" past our ears, and it was obvious that they'd been talking to the other fishermen. We smiled back at them, and Alec mimed that we had enough and that we didn't want to trade for the lobster.

It was getting dark now and we both wondered if we were safe. Alone in the remote southern Red Sea, our neighbors were a boatload of aggressive-sounding Yemeni fishermen anchored almost on top of us. Alec imagined them letting out their anchor line and then boarding us in the middle of the night. When he saw my alarm, he went on to rationalize that group mentality would be in play. There were at least ten men on the open deck of the brightly-painted boat and not all would be party to a robbery. There were nets on the deck, a small mast and a large outboard engine on the stern. They were clearly fishermen, not pirates. However, my imagination got the best of me and I locked our door.

In the morning we popped our heads out to see the fishermen still there. At first sight of us, they sprang to life, making signs that one of them had a stomachache followed by the universal sign for medicine – holding the baby finger so that only the tip shows, to represent a pill. The lobster appeared again and so did the shooing hand-waving. They were certainly persistent. They had no small boat to launch, but could see we had a dinghy. Alec reminded me that we'd come here for the adventure, and apprehensively I agreed to go over. Maybe I could help someone.

I put some innocuous medicines in a knapsack. I could be dealing with anything from the flu to malaria, to hepatitis, to cancer. We rowed over, and they eagerly welcomed us aboard. They ushered us to the bow of the boat, past a large open hatch where a cauldron was simmering. We were seated on the wooden deck and they held up a glass and spoke unfamiliar words. Finally I heard *"Tay?"* and we each graciously accepted a glass of tea. The crew left their net-mending and gathered around. From a small hatch, a man was led. I examined my patient. He had no signs of serious illness, but we deciphered he'd experienced vomiting and diarrhea for three days. I treated him with an antinauseant and gave him some multivitamins as well. They might help, I thought, if only by placebo effect.

The captain called for the live lobster and he re-enacted how they'd accidentally caught it in their nets the day before. He presented it as a gift. My patient went off to lie down, and the rest of the thirteen men eagerly watched as we drank our tea. They signaled, asking if we wanted more, and we politely accepted. They all sat silently watching us sip. Again they asked if we wanted more. I shook my head, "No thank you," and one man reached for our glasses. He quickly ran below, washed them, and poured tea for the next two men.

We shared no common words, but it didn't take long to figure out that they only had two glasses for all these men. More sign language explained that the rest of their glasses had accidentally broken. We briefly returned to *Madeline* to get some plastic mugs we had been carting around. Our neighbors were very pleased with our gift.

Even though Alec and I had already eaten, we felt it appropriate to accept their invitation for breakfast. Out came two huge buckets filled with mush that had the color, texture and consistency of vomit. The group divided into two, and the men squatted around the buckets, reaching in with their right hands and scooping out the grub. They encouraged us to dig in, but I could feel myself gagging inside. I took a little and pretended to enjoy it. Alec teased me saying, "Gee Alayne. You're not eating very much. What's wrong?"

Breakfast consisted of a tomato hot sauce, broad white beans and chunks of precooked bread. Alec sat on his haunches eating with the men. We were careful only to use our right hands. Toilet paper was unheard of in this area of the world, so the left hand was used with water to clean after defecating, with the right hand reserved for eating. In some Islamic countries, the punishment for a convicted thief was to chop off the right hand, leaving the criminal forever facing the embarrassment of eating with the left hand.

After the feed, we lounged with the men on their open deck, learning their Muslim names, like Ali, Abdullah and the ever-popular Mohammed. Alec gave the captain a pack of cigarettes and joined him in a smoke. Although Alec didn't smoke, he said to me, "There are times when it's better to go with the flow."

The captain reached into his pocket and pulled out a plastic bag of brown powder, and offered it towards Alec. Alec shrugged his shoulders and raised his hands, asking, "What is it?"

A slow smile came to the captain's face as he said, "Hashish!"

Here was a word we knew! We looked around at the other men, and they had furrowed brows, waving their hands to say no, and circling an index finger at their temple. When the smiling captain grabbed a pinch of the powder and tucked it in his lip, Alec was puzzled.

Alec gestured, in the form of a question, "No water pipe?" and he made the bubbling noise of a bong.

The men immediately understood the charade, and they all began to laugh and suck on imaginary water pipes. When they began assembling a real pipe, Alec stopped them, indicating, "No, thank you." Although he felt it would have made a fascinating experience, it was already too weird. "We're sitting in an open boat with thirteen Yemeni fishermen, who we can't talk to, in a remote corner of the Red Sea, in 40 knots of wind, at nine in the morning," Alec said. "I don't need drugs."

Later, after speaking with a friend who lived in the Middle East, we found that Alec had made the right decision. The powder was likely opium. Taken by mouth, it was highly potent and addictive, but very common throughout the area. They had probably said "hashish" because the Arabic word for opium would be unknown to foreigners.

As we said our goodbyes, they handed us the big lobster and we gave them three more packs of cigarettes. I left with the strong feeling that deep down, all people in this world were good. As had happened many times in our trip, the risks of adventuring had paid off and I craved more.

Cruising the tropics involves a lot of bugs. Mosquitoes in Malaysia, sandflies in Australia, swarms of houseflies in the Maldives and microscopic no-no's in the Marquesas have been a nuisance to many a world cruiser. Fortunately on the boat we were not bothered that often, as we were usually anchored far enough offshore and generally there was a breeze.

When there were mosquitoes at night, I was always the one who got bitten. Alec awoke when I was up using the toilet, not from any noise I was making, but from the mosquitoes attacking him when their favored prey was out of the room. We devised several theories on why mosquitoes preferred me.

The possibility that Alec might be getting bitten and just not reacting was disputed by the fact that he did get the odd bite. My favorite theory was that Alec was hairier, and therefore it would be more work for a mosquito to find his skin. This made sense, until our surveys of other couples gave conflicting results.

Thus, the temperature theory developed: the person who has the warmer skin temperature is the one who gets bitten. I am a furnace and Alec is a reptile. Mosquitoes are attracted by the carbon dioxide and heat emitted by their warm-blooded prey. They could easily distinguish me from Alec who has the surface temperature of a wall. We began surveying cruising couples regarding body temperatures – an interesting survey in itself – and whether one or the other was bitten more often. Invariably it was the hot one who had the bites.

Mosquitoes were a real problem in Borneo, but malaria was the greater concern. The best defense was prevention, so we had nets, coils and sprays out in full force. Many nights we couldn't avoid being anchored next to the jungle, and there was often no breeze. Despite our precautions, I was being eaten. On a regular basis, we searched and sprayed the boat to eliminate any mosquito stowaways, but I still had more bites than anyone else.

We wondered if I was getting bitten ashore. Sandflies on the beach bit during the day, but caused itching at night, and since I had many red welts on my feet, we blamed sandflies for a while. But it seemed strange that no one else was complaining.

When we left Thailand, I hoped I had left the problem behind. Strangely, my scratching in the night persisted on our passage across the Indian Ocean. How could I be getting bitten at sea? It had to be something on the boat.

We were always careful when bringing food onto *Madeline*, discarding all cardboard boxes because cockroaches laid their eggs in the packaging. We submerged in sea water all suspect produce, like pineapples or bananas. It was astounding the variety of bugs and spiders that would flee a banana stock Alec had just lugged from the market on his back.

The only bugs on board now were some fruit flies. During one of my night watches I noticed some bites on my leg and then a fruit fly flew by. Actually, the fruit flies were looking larger and larger, and were flying much faster, zipping around more like houseflies. We'd finished our last papaya, so I wondered what they were living on. One

234

landed on me and when I smashed it, there was bright red blood. I developed a new theory that the fruit flies had mutated from harmless nothings into blood-sucking beasts – Killer Fruit Flies! I began a campaign to get rid of them, but disappointingly, weeks after the last one was seen, I was still getting bitten.

Alec pulled out an old book given to us by *Rode Beer* called *Blue Water Cruising*. There was a small section on bedbugs. This seemed a possible solution to our mystery, but the book gave no description as to what they looked like, and we figured we would've seen at least a dead one by now. We read that they often came aboard in laundry that had been washed ashore.

I specifically remembered getting a big bag of laundry done at Derawan Island off Borneo. I had approached the communal wash area crowded with gabbing women and they sweetly cleared a space on a log for me to join them. It was amusing as I explained I wanted *them* to do my laundry. They stated a price of 3,000 Rupiah, about US$1.50. I remembered as I walked away, seeing our clothes and sheets being tossed into the basin with everyone else's.

The book said bedbugs could be difficult to exterminate because they get into the wood, and you may have to pick them out with a needle. *Madeline* was mostly fiberglass, but there were two wooden shelves in our bedroom, one at our feet and one next to the side that I slept on.

In the Maldives we cleared out everything in the bedroom. Every piece of clothing was shaken and aired in the brisk breeze. We inspected the wood and found nothing, but sprayed it all down with insecticide just to be safe.

In Djibouti the biting was back. Alec suggested that the next time I noticed myself scratching in the night, we should flick on the light and search the room at that instant.

Now, we were anchored outside Massawa, Eritrea. I began to scratch shortly after we'd gone to bed. I was awake enough to feel that the itch was in one spot, and then moved again and again down my leg. "Alec, I'm getting bitten right now!"

He turned on the light and began to look.

"There *must* be something here," he muttered. After searching ten frustrating minutes, he spotted a dark brown bug scurrying in the folds of the sheets. It was small, the size of a grain of rice, with a flat round body and an amazing ability to hide in the sheets. He killed it. Then he was smart enough to check along the edge of the wood. The flashlight beam revealed two more bugs, poised to go out for dinner.

Bedbugs! They had been feasting on me for months. Disgusting! With my legs alongside the wood shelf, it had been easy for the bugs to hop down, grab a quick meal and scurry back up to safety.

Alec took the shelves apart and in the crevices behind we found at least two dozen culprits – big ones, small ones, old carcasses from previous generations and microscopic babies. My blood had been feeding the whole family.

We showed no mercy. We sprayed and mashed until not a single one was left, but we still slept outside on deck that night.

Once I was living free from bites and scratching, and enjoying restful sleeps again, we both couldn't believe how long I put up with it. We learned that bedbugs often acquire a taste for certain blood, explaining why Alec wasn't bitten, even on the crossing when he was alone in the same bed.

I thought to all the times my mom had said, "Sleep tight and don't let the bedbugs bite." When the bugs were eliminated I could joke about it, but the little white scars on my legs would be a permanent souvenir.

Already we were facing the notorious headwinds that would plague us all the way to Suez. In the past, the wind had been a major problem, as the coastline was politically hostile making it unsafe to stop. But in 1995, things were relatively peaceful in the Red Sea, and when faced with headwinds we could stop anywhere along the coast of Eritrea, the Sudan or Egypt.

Alec and I had adopted a strategy for the Red Sea, one that tended to pulse the cruisers northward together. We expected a calm every few days, when all the boats would make progress north, until slowed again by the wind. Sometimes the wind could blow for weeks, so it was imperative to take advantage of the calms.

When we arrived in Massawa, I wrote in my journal. "*The Red Sea brings back that special community feeling unique to cruising in remote places. There is instant camaraderie among the cruisers. We're all on the same mission, and we've all sailed thousands of miles across the Indian Ocean to get here. In the South Pacific, many of us were new to cruising, sailing away from home to places further afield. In the Red Sea, the majority of boats are sailing closer to home, some Europeans only a few months from completing a circumnavigation. The naive enthusiasm of the South Pacific isn't here, but the desire to savor the last moments of remote cruising is.*"

We had hoped *Rode Beer* would be with us, but our Thursday Island friends, *Klepel*, told us that *Rode Beer* had safely arrived in Djibouti, 400 miles behind us. Nico told us that *Rode Beer* planned only a brief stop in Djibouti, so we let a weather window pass hoping they would catch up.

Eritrea had just fought and won a 30-year war of independence from Ethiopia and was open to cruisers for the first time. Interestingly,

the people were predominantly Christian, surrounded by Muslim countries on all sides. Land travel in and out of Eritrea was blocked, but we had been able to enter the port of Massawa without difficulty.

An Italian influence remained from the colonial days, and this was especially evident in Asmara, the capital city. We traveled on a local bus, a four-hour ride high into the mountains, for US$1. The city seemed frozen in time. Art deco diners offered cappuccinos and Italian pastries for pennies. We ate out every meal, drank local beer, stayed a night in a luxury hotel and bought souvenirs, but after a week we still hadn't come close to spending the US$100 we'd exchanged.

At a dock in Massawa, a man asked for a ride back to his boat. Within the cruising community everyone did favors, and although this man wasn't a cruiser, we unhesitatingly offered to take him. He directed us to a big wooden cargo ship, and as we approached, he invited us aboard. We discovered that our new friend, the captain, and his crew were from Pakistan; they transported goats and camels from Massawa to Saudi Arabia.

They took us to the bridge deck and into the control room. Behind the steering wheel was a raised platform covered in Persian rugs. They had radar, an autopilot and all the normal electronics. Just like fellow cruisers, the Pakistani men offered us drinks and food, and we had a pleasant visit unaffected by cultural barriers.

A voice came over the radio and the eyes of the men lit up. Even though we couldn't understand the words, their excitement was evident. The captain grabbed the microphone and made contact. One of the men explained to us in broken English that a similar cargo ship had just come into the port. They were good friends with the crew and hadn't seen them for a long time.

Later that afternoon, that same excitement struck us.

"*Madeline, Madeline*. This is *Rode Beer!*"

THE RODE SEA

"SO GOOD OF YOU GUYS TO WAIT," said Robert, climbing aboard and hugging both of us.

After two months apart, I was relieved to know we would share the Red Sea experience with our good friends. Combined with the uncertainty of this reunion and the knowledge that our cruising days with them were numbered, we were all bursting with excitement for the adventures ahead.

"We have so much to tell you," I said, "and we've already made plans to go out to a neat little restaurant tonight, if you're not too tired."

"We've had a long trip," said Nathalie, "with only short stops since we left Sri Lanka. We need to rest, but of course we can go out! How wonderful that we're together again!" She hugged me tightly. They'd spent many weeks in the eastern Indian Ocean, at the Andeman Islands and then Sri Lanka. I was relieved to hear that they'd left *Papillon* behind.

"We'd like to hear about your trip to Asmara. That's something we'd like to do," Robert said. "But you must be feeling ready to move on. The weather is good for the moment."

"You're right, but we'll stay tonight and celebrate first," Alec said, clinking beer cans with Robert. "To the *Rode* Sea!"

During our Indian Ocean crossing, Alec and I both devoured the book *Hashish*, which told the fabulous adventures of a Frenchman who sailed the Red Sea over 80 years ago. We excitedly anticipated *Madeline's* similar journey and pulled out our Red Sea charts, making notes of his stops.

Henry de Monfreid's journey was taken under completely different circumstances. Instead of cruising, he was smuggling hashish in his sailboat. He figured this would be very challenging as well as profitable. In 1917 hashish was cheap in Greece, legal in Djibouti, but illegal and expensive in Egypt. Thus, he had a large amount shipped by freighter from Greece to Djibouti, and there he loaded it aboard his local wooden boat, called a *boutre*. He battled headwinds the whole length of the Red Sea without the use of an engine. Monfreid undertook his trip in summer, so the winds were high and the days very hot. His crew of ten men consumed two and a half gallons of water per man per day. Thus, besides nasty storms and treacherous reefs, one of his main concerns was a constant need for fresh water in the barren, dry and sun-scorched Red Sea. As you can imagine, there were few places that water could be found.

He traveled to the island of Errich where his pilot book mentioned ruins and cisterns. He landed at the foot of a hillock and immediately found the remains of walls and streets from an ancient city. He eventually found huge, baked-clay amphora, ten feet in diameter, which were probably fired where they lay in the earth. But they were half-full of sand, and he returned across the barren ground to his ship and empty water barrels, while questioning what had happened to the previous inhabitants. *"The climate of this island must have changed considerably, for a city could never otherwise have been established in this desolation of burning plains, which stretched as far as the eye could reach, unbroken by a human habitation, a herd of goats or even a tree."*

The next island they visited was Badhour, where the legend of the magic water cisterns was centuries old. Alec and I were immediately intrigued reading about Monfreid's visit there. At that time the mysterious cisterns were guarded by the oldest woman in the ten-hut village, and this ancient bowed apparition led Monfreid and his parched sailors to a plateau in the middle of the island. It opened up to a hollow below, with 25-foot rock walls all around.

Down they went, and everywhere there were little piles of rocks, almost like graves. The old woman indicated that these were the cisterns and they began lengthy negotiations. The miraculous cisterns filled with water each year and the people spoke of the water as if it was a crop. The water was from the previous year, and there were differing qualities.

They agreed on a price for the best water, and the old woman selected one pile, carefully removing each stone, one by one. Beneath the stones were branches, and after she removed these they feasted their thirsty eyes on crystal-clear water. The cistern was a circular hole in the flat rock floor, about two feet in diameter and seven feet deep. The water was so clear, Monfreid dropped a small pebble into the cistern to prove his eyes did not deceive him. They took as much water as they needed, knowing that soon it would fill again.

Alec and I decided we must find Badhour and see what was there. Scanning the charts, and using Monfreid's sketchy information, we located Khor Nawarat. *Khor* means bay in Arabic, but on our chart the island inside the bay had no name.

Based on Monfreid's description, it had to be Badhour. *"The Khor Nowarat* (sic) *was a sort of large lake, connected with the sea by a very deep strait which, unfortunately, was barely eighty yards wide and strewn with rocky islets. In the middle of this stretch of water was the island of Badhour, like a fortress surrounded by moats. On the most southerly point of the island, a small village of a half score of huts could be seen."*

As excited as I was to see Nathalie, I couldn't wait to continue exploring up the Red Sea. Now I knew we'd soon sail together again, so Alec and I left Massawa, keeping to our own plan – which was what made our relationship with *Rode Beer* so special.

We hoped to arrive at Khor Nawarat 48 hours later, but the sailing was better than anticipated and we passed the bay around four in the morning. Because of all the reefs, we didn't dare enter in the dark. We were disappointed in missing Badhour, but we pressed on to take advantage of the light winds.

Three hours later, in prophesied Red Sea fashion, the wind suddenly picked up and blew strongly from the north. Our progress north became minimal and we opted to turn around. The search for the cisterns was on!

We didn't have a detailed chart for Khor Nawarat, so we sailed over to three other sailboats anchored just inside and explained our story. An Australian boat brought out a detailed chart, but the island had a different name. Their chart showed the west end to be "Village Point" and showed a plateau in the center of the island. We knew it must be Badhour. There were no hazards to navigation, so for Alec and me, this was all we needed.

The island was flat, a five-mile-long rock. The terrain was dry and desolate, brown and lifeless, like much of the Red Sea coast. Scrambling ashore, the first thing we came across were the ruins of several stone huts; only the tumbled down walls outlining the rooms. I pondered how people could have ever lived here and the loneliness gave me a sad feeling inside. There was no sign of life except for a huge osprey nest on a crumbling rock wall and goat tracks across the barren soil.

We headed inland following the tracks, and shortly after, found ourselves among dozens of piles of little rocks. "Do you think these are the cisterns, already?" I asked Alec. We found stone slabs carved with elaborate script and realized that these were graves – we were walking through a cemetery.

We walked for another ten minutes and climbed a low plateau. Past the rock walls of the plateau was a hollow just as Monfreid had described. There were dozens of circular holes in the stone basin.

We had found the cisterns! No stones or branches covered them, as they had 80 years ago, but incredibly they were all full of clear water. Some had insects and spider webs over the openings, and a few had algae growing. We didn't taste the water, being wary of fresh water in

Africa, but it must have been the source of life for the island's previous inhabitants.

The miraculous cisterns were still replenishing themselves, but where were the people? What had happened to them? Does history repeat itself?

During our reunion with Robert and Nathalie in Massawa we had exchanged adventure stories and cruising gossip. They happily reported that *Orion* had been anchored in Sri Lanka when *Rode Beer* had arrived in February. Alberto Torroba was beaming with the news that Rebecca was pregnant. *Orion* had sailed non-stop from Singapore through the Malacca Strait to Sri Lanka. They planned to travel to Madagascar for the birth, then around South Africa and across the Atlantic back to Argentina. His "Ship's Documentation Papers", created by Alec on our computer, were deceiving the officials and he'd proudly displayed them to cruisers who knew us.

Anchored in Khor Nawarat we met another extreme cruiser, Greg, on his boat *Triangle Island*. A fellow Canadian, Greg was similar to Alberto, in that he was in a small, sparsely-equipped boat. However, Greg's sixteen-foot Drascombe lugger was a popular fiberglass production boat that was more commonly used as a coastal day-sailer.

He'd sailed from Vancouver to the Red Sea. He traveled at four knots going downwind, but had a difficult time sailing upwind, and much of the Red Sea had been exactly that. His world voyage had been delayed twice because he traveled so slowly that he missed the change in seasons *Madeline* was following. In Indonesia he had no wind, and

because he had no engine, he was finally lifted onto a freighter to finish the last few hundred miles to Singapore. Crossing the Indian Ocean, he had more calms and aborted his plans of continuing because the monsoon changed. He'd left his boat in India for nine months and flew home. Now he was continuing this season with us.

"But why are you doing this?" I asked Greg.

He felt he didn't fit into the world doing a regular job. Funny enough, he was an engineer, like Alec. He answered that this was the challenge he was looking for in his life. But Greg's life on his boat seemed almost impossible. He had no cooking arrangement, so he ate dry granola, or just straight out of a can. He carried 25 gallons of water, rationing at a meager one third of a gallon per day.

That night a cold wind was howling. We pulled out long shirts and pants, and our down sleeping bags. Greg was sleeping beside us, lying outside in the bottom of his open boat, wearing wool gloves and a balaclava.

"Would you like to sleep on *Madeline*?" I offered. "We have a single bunk that is unused; it would be no trouble."

"No thanks," he said. "I wouldn't be comfortable leaving my boat by herself."

We could have just tied it on a cleat, I thought, like a dinghy when friends came to visit. We'd met many yachts with dinghies the size of his boat, but I said nothing because it wasn't his style to accept help.

When we'd first anchored next to *Triangle Island*, my reaction was one of surprise. Then I remembered the comment of an eight-year-old cruiser about *Madeline*. He was living on a 55-foot yacht and said to us, "Are you really sailing around the world too? I can't believe it – you have such a small boat!" His parents were pretty embarrassed – from the mouths of babes! But I found myself thinking the exact same thing when I saw Greg.

A few days later the wind eased and we tried beating against it, staying behind the reefs and hugging the coast. It took half a day to make it to the protection of a cape, 21 nautical miles further north. Already anchored behind the point, like a giant water spider on a leash, was a 40-foot racing trimaran named *Gitana*. The center hull and living area was long and narrow with two amas, or cigar-shaped floats, attached by long, arching beams.

Gitana regularly sailed at twelve knots and could be easily pushed over twenty. *Madeline* averaged six knots. *Gitana* was owned by an Austrian couple, Alexandra and Reinhard, and they had a crew with them, Thomas.

Reinhard was a thrill seeker – his other sports were rock climbing and hang-gliding. Alex found the sailing miserable as they had compromised comfort for speed. They were wet with waves and spray the whole time they were sailing. In order to go fast, the boat was light, with very little living space. They lived like sardines inside, had no toilet, and couldn't afford the weight of all the amenities that I took for granted.

The extremes of cruising aboard *Orion*, *Triangle Island* and *Gitana* inspired these cruisers to accept similarly bare and simple conditions. *"The way these guys live reminds me that I'm not roughing it all. I may not have a washing machine or a freezer or a king-sized bed, but compared to them we're living in luxury. Life is really great aboard Madeline, and although I've always known this, it's taken me a long time to appreciate it. I realize that once back on land I'll be wishing I'm out cruising."* I decided to savor every moment of our journey up the Red Sea.

By the time we reunited with *Rode Beer* midway up the Red Sea, we had become comfortable with the weather patterns and the geography. With *Rode Beer* as our racing competition, we sailed out in the mornings and beat up the coast, often in the shelter of the off-lying reefs.

From past experience, *Madeline* performed poorly in headwinds compared to *Rode Beer*, however with 20 knots of wind we could hold our own. When *Rode Beer* required reefing down, *Madeline* really started to hum under full sails. When the wind increased more, we pulled away.

Alec and I worked at honing our upwind performance and I fared well in these playful circumstances, even though it was the most we'd ever pushed our boat. Each time *Madeline's* tack and *Rode Beer's* tack crossed, we could judge how much further we had increased our lead. Alec smugly watched Robert through the binoculars, as he fine-tuned his sails, trying to improve *Rode Beer's* performance. I took great satisfaction from working together so smoothly.

When we pulled into a *marsa* one afternoon, Robert got on the radio and confessed he was amazed. "I had always believed catamarans couldn't beat upwind," he said. "But you proved me wrong today."

The coastline in the Sudan and southern Egypt was studded with indentations called *marsas*. Literally translated as bay, each *marsa* appeared to be the mouth of an ancient river that once poured into the Red Sea from the hazy hills in the distance. The rivers had long ago dried up leaving a narrow bay that wound tortuously for up to ten miles into the desert beyond. The *marsas* were good for anchoring and were conveniently spaced every ten to fifteen miles, so we could have a Plan A, B and C in mind, depending on our progress and how we were feeling.

One day we lifted anchor early, and started racing with *Rode Beer*, fast tacking and avoiding the scattered reefs offshore. By mid-afternoon we were exhausted and it was time to find the next *marsa*. The *marsas* extended due west from the Red Sea and as the sun began its gradual descent to the western horizon, the visibility at the entrance was slowly reduced by glare. The longer we sailed the greater the challenge to enter the scantily-charted *marsa*.

Alec stood on the bow, one hand shielding his eyes and wearing his polarized sunglasses. The wind blew uninterrupted, across the *marsa* like a hot hair dryer, baking the brown earth. After searching for a shallow place, we dropped the anchor almost on the beach and let the wind blow us off. Alec and I sprawled out on the salon benches for a little snooze. The sun beat through the windows as we napped in our usual attire of underpants.

A crackle from the radio woke us from our slumber. "Look out your front window," Nathalie said.

My sleepy mind thought to the coastline we'd just sailed: barren desert, devoid of all human and animal life. We hadn't even seen a freighter or yacht all day. Often though, even in the most remote of places, locals would find us. I automatically reached for a shirt, knowing I should cover up in these strict Muslim countries.

I popped my head up and peered through our forward windows, unable to believe my eyes. There stood a man, clothed in flowing robes, dagger around his waist, his head wrapped in a thick turban. He waded into the water towards our boat, waving and shouting.

"Robert is going to go and see what he wants," Nathalie relayed to us. Glad that Robert had so nobly volunteered, we watched him dive in and stroke smoothly to the shore. He animatedly conversed in sign language with the turban-clad man. Robert swam back to *Rode Beer*, and called us.

"I think he would like to make a trade. He wants a diving mask and will trade his dagger for one. He didn't like my swim

goggles, but I know you have an extra mask. What do you think?"

"Yeah, we've got one," Alec replied. "This could be interesting."

Robert told us that the man came from a village further up the coast. "If we want, we could all go and see his village with him, and you could make the trade."

The four of us donned our Muslim outfits of long pants and long shirts. The flat, rocky desert stretched for miles in every direction, with hardly a tree or bush in sight. How could there be a village here? Further inland we could just distinguish the outline of the Red Sea Mountains, with their crimson hue, from which the Red Sea gets its name.

After fifteen minutes of walking we approached a hut. It was about four feet high and crudely made from sticks covered in burlap and cardboard. I looked around, and could see in the distance that there were a few more huts widely spaced, maybe ten in total. But nothing else. The landscape was so bleak. An empty feeling overwhelmed me. Why were these people here?

The man offered us pieces of cardboard to sit on. A few more people appeared, and the women's robes were refreshingly bright. One wore orange; one bright green. The wind blew strongly and they

245

clasped their flapping robes, unconcerned about their exposed breasts. Their faces were like leather, weathered by the sun and wind in this harsh landscape.

Alec and the dagger trader each inspected the items, and agreed on the deal, both pleased. Just then we heard a rumbling, and saw billows of sand rising from the desert as a huge truck came out of the nothingness. There were no roads – it blasted straight across the desert, right at us, and stopped at the very hut where we squatted. It all seemed so bizarre.

Alec warned that these might be officials. We were without identification, and had stepped onto Sudanese territory without checking into the country.

Three robust African men jumped out of the truck and approached our group. To our astonishment, they began to furiously shake hands with everyone. They were in great spirits, producing a huge hose from the back of the truck and filling two rusted steel barrels beside the hut with water.

We kept wondering when they were going to start questioning us, but we stayed quiet and watched. Alec noticed that one of the men wearing army fatigues had a crest on his arm, "Sudanese Navy".

"I guess that explains the water," Alec whispered, smirking.

An officer sauntered up to Alec and asked, "How you go?"

Unsure if he was inquiring into his health or his travel plans, Alec pointed north and said "To Egypt." The man smiled and nodded, and they shook hands.

As dramatically as before, there was more happy handshaking. They all jumped back in the truck, and a few of the villagers jumped onto the roof, including the man with his new diving mask. Away they went into the desert, as quickly and mysteriously as they had come. We were left still standing in the middle of nowhere, trying to sort out what had happened.

We later read that both Egypt and the Sudan were encouraging their people to settle near the Egyptian-Sudanese border. The two countries had been disputing the border for a long time. The Sudanese government was delivering water to the nomads in hopes that they would stay, but the two drums didn't seem much to sustain the 30 people we'd seen. A few years earlier this area had been the site of heavy fighting and off limits to cruisers, and now we had stumbled upon international politics in action.

Dolphins guided us in the early morning calm into the commercial harbor at Port Safaga. The last weather window had allowed us to motor for almost three days, but by the time we left the Egyptian customs dock and anchored with the cruising boats, a north wind was starting to blow. By early afternoon the Red Sea Mountains had disappeared in a brown haze and the skippers swam their anchors making sure they were well set for the oncoming *haboob*. Soon the resort hotels on the shore were barely visible and we closed all the hatches and doors. *Madeline* was covered in fine reddish dust. We visited with the other boats, everyone keeping a close watch on the yachts. Some crews had left their boats to travel inland, but the remaining cruisers quickly went into action when untended boats started dragging.

By the next night the sandstorm had eased and all the cruisers got together for an impromptu party at one of the local hotels. The crews of at least twenty yachts convened for cocktails and a buffet dinner. I always had a vision that at the end of our circumnavigation there would be a huge party with all the cruisers we'd met, but I knew this was as good as it would get. The nature of cruising was that everyone went their own ways, and with this crowd, it meant to all corners of the earth.

On the morning radio "talk show" one of the cruisers quipped, "Now I know why they put the gyp in Egypt." The speaker went on to relate his story, echoed by many other cruisers, of how a local had tried to cheat him. We traveled with Robert and Nathalie to Luxor, to visit the Pharaohs' temples and the Valley of the Kings and dealt with similar hassles.

Just as we concluded that all the people in the world were generally good, we'd come across a country where lying and ripping off tourists seemed part of the culture. We'd already observed elsewhere that tourism changed the attitude of the local people, and since tourists had been coming to see the pyramids for thousands of years already, it made perfect sense that the Egyptians were the most spoiled.

We parted from *Rode Beer* and crossed the Red Sea, sailing overnight to Sharm el Sheikh on the Sinai peninsula to do some world-class scuba diving. Even though this was a popular diving destination for tourists, none of the Red Sea cruisers came this way. We anchored *Madeline* amidst dozens of fishing trawlers and dive boats.

The next morning when we arrived at the dive boat, we found we were the only paying guests. The boat had a full crew, including a dive master and Wahid, the manager of the operation. The diving was superb, with every color imaginable in a kaleidoscope of sizes and shapes.

When we told Wahid we would like to go again the following day, he apologized that the boat cost him too much with only two divers. "Would you mind if we took my Jeep through the desert and drive to some dive sites instead?"

"Sounds great!" we replied in unison.

"And tonight, I will take you both out for dinner," he said. Cautiously we agreed, wondering what sort of scam we were getting ourselves into.

He took us to the main tourist area in Sharm el Sheikh, and it felt more like the French Riveria than Egypt. The architecture and landscaping were lavish and well-dressed European tourists strolled the boardwalk. He wined and dined us that night, refusing to let us to pay for anything. He showed us home videos, drove us around the desert in his Jeep and explored with us the wonders of his underwater country. He took it upon himself to be an ambassador for Egypt.

We invited Wahid for dinner on *Madeline*, and he stood at the chart table, imagining himself sailing around the world. We encouraged his fantasy, and Alec promised that if he pursued this dream, he would give him our charts. Our interactions with this good and honest Egyptian restored our faith in human nature.

The last 200 miles of the 1,300-mile-long Red Sea were the most difficult. The strong north wind that blew from the Mediterranean was funneled down the narrow, twenty-mile-wide Gulf of Suez, accelerated by the bordering mountain ridges. The calm periods got increasingly shorter, and it was difficult to recognize a true weather window.

Despite this we had a brilliant sail north, with the spinnaker flying on a bright sunny day. Our progress was so good that we passed more than one anchorage, wanting to make the most of the great conditions.

Oil rigs blocked the eastern shore so we began to cross through the shipping lanes, knowing it meant spending the night at sea. Convoys of huge oil tankers raced past, having been freed from the Suez Canal only a hundred miles further north. Not surprisingly the good wind didn't last. By midnight it had reversed direction and we were beating into strong headwinds and choppy seas.

The Suez Canal now seemed a thousand miles away. I was relieved when Alec suggested we turn back to the last anchorage. It wasn't a *marsa*, but a little bit of land that poked into the sea, Ras Ruahmi. The coast didn't offer many shelters, but it was a safe place to stop and wait for the wind to blow out. We arrived at daybreak, anchoring behind the little cape as best as our catamaran draft would allow and went to bed immediately.

When we awoke later in the morning, we had neighbors. It was *Rock 'n Roll* from Finland, with Otto and Tuula on board. We'd met them for the first time in Safaga, but Otto's drinking reputation had preceded that. He was always looking for a drinking buddy and I dreaded being stuck with them at this marginal anchorage. I was doubly troubled because *Rode Beer* had leapfrogged ahead of us and was already in Suez.

The cruising lifestyle could get anyone into the drinking habit. Cheap duty-free booze was available in every port. Often alcohol was less expensive than pop or juice. Nobody had to get up to go to work in the morning, and in every port, you could find a sodden expat or fellow cruiser to drink with. We weren't immune, but we tried to keep things balanced, and in moderation.

Once again we were angry with ourselves for prejudging. Otto and Tuula were a joy, and were great company for what otherwise would have been an extremely boring five-day wait for weather. Otto was quite a character, an entrepreneur who had created a business in Finland that provided him with income while he was cruising. He worked hard and drank hard, and was proud of both.

The Suez Canal was very straightforward and almost uninteresting. We had two separate pilots assigned to us, each named Mohammed, for each day of the two-day transit. The first Mohammed was fasting for a religious holiday, as he was making up for the few days he'd eaten during Ramadan. This made him an easy guest. It wasn't until the sun had completely set that he even took a glass of water.

The second Mohammed fitted the stereotype of the slimy Egyptian pilot always asking for *baksheesh* and more cigarettes. During lunch Alec told him, "You are a good pilot. It has been a good experience so far. If we have no problems, I have a gift of money for you. If we have problems, no gift."

At the end of the day, Mohammed asked for some presents for his wife and children. Anticipating this, I'd found some things in the boat we could give to him: some T-shirts and playing cards for his three boys, a hair ribbon for his daughter, some Canada pins, some perfume samples for his wife, as well as two more packs of cigarettes. On inspecting the gifts and his cash, Mohammed was disappointed. "Was I not a good pilot? Is this all you are giving me?"

Instead of letting this irritate me, I responded sincerely, "Mohammed, you were an excellent pilot. We are giving you these gifts as a sign of our thanks. I hope your wife and children enjoy the presents."

What could he say? He bowed his head and said, "*Shukran.*"

We left directly from Port Said for an uneventful two-day motor to Cyprus. Upon our reunion with the cruising fleet, we heard some horrendous pilot stories. One yacht had a pilot who had never been on a boat before, and he vomited all day. Another yacht had a pilot who had a bowel movement in their head and used their adjustable shower hose to rinse himself clean, spraying his shit all over the walls. My complaints about cigarette ashes in our cockpit paled in comparison.

We arrived at Cyprus just in time for one last visit with Nathalie and Robert. They were leaving to cross the Mediterranean and return to Holland before the summer ended.

This goodbye marked the end of an era. We were not only closing the long chapter of cruising with *Rode Beer*, but also finishing the chapter on remote destinations. The Mediterranean and the Caribbean were ahead of us, and although there was much to look forward to, they were not the exotic places we'd been cruising the past two years.

"I know I'll enjoy having access to phones, faxes, post offices, grocery stores and laundry machines, as well as knowing diesel, water, and spare parts are always convenient and available. But there's something magical about the cruising we've done. We've been so far removed from everything familiar, and that's forced us to be self-sufficient. Having come through it successfully, I'm feeling a sense of pride and accomplishment." Our cruising had been a true test of our capabilities and of our character.

There were still many challenges to overcome before our cruising ended, but I could already sense that my perspective had changed forever.

With Nathalie and Robert, we spent a lovely afternoon aboard *Madeline*, drinking red wine and snacking on a tasty picnic lunch of salads, paté, bread, cheese, coffee cake and fruit. We indulged for hours, laughing and reminiscing about our two years of cruising since first meeting in the Galapagos.

We all knew the bond we shared would never be broken by distance, but that day we didn't talk about the next anchorage, our next meeting, or our imminent parting. When the moment arrived, we hugged each other tightly, fighting to hold back the tears. "Robert, hurry up," Nathalie said, wiping away a tear. "We must go now, before I get too sad."

Arm in arm, Alec and I watched Nathalie and Robert row back to *Rode Beer*, hoist her anchor and sail away for the last time.

THE BEST OF TOURISTS

WE FIRST NOTICED THE CHANGES IN CYPRUS, when we tied up in Larnaca marina. Many of the same cruisers who had complained about giving the Suez Canal pilot five dollars *baksheesh*, now paid eight dollars a day in the marina without batting an eye.

Only a month earlier in the Red Sea we'd felt conspicuously well dressed in our sloppy shirts and had made a conscious effort to not wear jewelry or our good clothes. Now, walking in the town wearing our neatest shorts and shirts, we still appeared as grotty yachties. After months of Muslim countries and wearing long sleeves and skirts below the knees, I felt naked wearing a halter top and mini skirt. Yet on the beach next to us, fat European tourists frolicked topless.

The greatest change was the observable history. It was fascinating to be in the places we had studied as school children. I discovered that Lazarus had come to Cyprus after Jesus resurrected him in Israel. He became the island's first bishop, and lived another 30 years before dying again. Cyprus was the birthplace of Aphrodite, goddess of love. She, however, is immortal.

I was surprised to learn that St. Nicholas was a fourth century Byzantine bishop, whose home was in Turkey. Not only was he mortal, but he had lived far from the North Pole.

I read Homer's *The Odyssey* and with the help of our guidebooks, identified on our charts the places Odysseus traveled to thousands of years ago. At the Greek island of Kos, home of the father of Medicine, Hippocrates, I reread with renewed interest the 2,400-year-old oath I took when I became a doctor.

The early Christian church blossomed in the Eastern Mediterranean, as St. Paul traveled extensively throughout the area. We climbed through the ruins of the great town of Knidos, peering into the sewage system that was working when St. Paul walked the broad streets. One of his missions took him to the town of Lindos on the island of Rhodes. There, we anchored under yet another magnificent castle built by the Knights of St. John in the 14th century.

Since many of the ancient Mediterranean people traveled by boat, they lived near the sea, which was ideal for exploring with *Madeline*. The well-preserved ruins, combined with the wonderful summer climate, were the basis for another change. The Mediterranean was overrun with tourists, and we rarely had an anchorage to ourselves. Yet, in a way, we were alone. It was similar to having many friends in a

small town, and then arriving in the big city and finding yourself lonely.

"*We've lost contact with many of the boats we'd been cruising with for thousands of miles – through Southeast Asia, across the Indian Ocean and up the Red Sea. I miss the camaraderie we had with the other yachts, all of us so far away from home and our families. We'd become that substitute for each other.*" Now our close-knit world-cruising community was dissolved amidst the hundreds of day-trip boats, charter yachts and the general mayhem of tourism.

The Europeans were racing home to their respective countries in order to arrive before summer ended. The older couples, retired and in no rush, were moving much slower as they would spend a few years in these waters. Some cruisers were having financial problems and were trying to find work. Some were just taking a break, putting the boat up on the hard and going back home. They were dropping off at an alarming rate. We knew only a handful of boats planning to cross the Atlantic in December. This handful was camouflaged and diluted in the vast Mediterranean cruising ground.

We left Cyprus and motored to Kaş on the southern coast of Turkey. Alec's cousin and his girlfriend joined us as we hopped leisurely along the coast. It was nice to spot a Canadian flag as we pulled into the anchorage at Fethiye.

Tieras was sailed by Fred and Esther, along with their two children aged 13 and 10. They had left Vancouver in 1992, following a similar route to ours. They were one of the few boats from the Red Sea fleet also planning to be in the Caribbean for Christmas 1995. We'd met them first in New Zealand, briefly in Thailand, and the last time we were together was in the lower half of the Red Sea.

Amidst the hellos and catching up on news, Esther asked a favor. She knew we were entertaining guests, so she didn't want to intrude. "If you've got a minute, Alayne, could you take a look at Fred? His asthma has been acting up since we arrived in Turkey."

Fred wasn't in distress at the time, and I resisted giving a casual diagnosis and advice on the spot.

"I'll come by later and make a proper boat call," I offered, only too glad to help.

I brought my meager medical equipment: blood pressure cuff, stethoscope and ophthalmoscope. I found Fred didn't have asthma. It was so much worse. At only 42 years old, he had severe high blood pressure, fluid in his lungs, and was clinically anemic.

I was able to get some tests done right away and had him seen by some good doctors. The results confirmed what I had suspected. Sometime during the past three years of cruising, Fred's kidneys had begun to fail. He was in chronic renal failure with severe complications.

This news was hard for the family to swallow, and playing out all the roles of a family doctor challenged me. As well as diagnostician, I acted as adviser and counselor. After a few days filled with questions and discussions, Fred and Esther began to think straight. They realized they couldn't change the facts; they could only rise to the challenge. They were able to see the positive side and were thankful that this didn't happen somewhere in the remote and desolate Red Sea. Long-distance cruisers couldn't afford to get the wrong disease at the wrong time.

"It's amazing that this is the first time Fred's been sick and we have a Canadian doctor anchored beside us," Esther said. "We're really very fortunate."

Like us and many cruisers, Fred didn't carry international health insurance, so within ten days of my first visit, he was on a plane back to Canada. It all happened so fast.

Besides being concerned for Fred, the sudden ending of their trip upset the *Tieras* family. It was difficult to discuss, as they knew we were carrying on. With the assistance of the ever-helpful cruising community, Esther took the boat to Marmaris and hauled it out. They unloaded their possessions and the family flew back to Vancouver a month later to join Fred, leaving *Tieras* for sale in Turkey.

There were many other stories of cruisers' plans changing due to things beyond their control. *Pandarosa* lost their mast in Northern Australia. *Ocean Wanderer* was struck by lightning in Malaysia and *Visitor* mysteriously sank approaching Sri Lanka. We attributed our success to common sense and good planning, but some of it definitely came down to luck. Call it fate, destiny, or the will of Allah. Whichever it was, we were happy for our good fortune, and I hoped it would continue.

Alec's cousin left us in Fethiye and we stayed an extra week helping out the *Tieras* family. After a difficult farewell, we continued to sail along the coast of Turkey.

Following the Dorian peninsula, just north of the Greek island of Rhodes, we began to feel the effects of the strong summer wind in the Aegean Sea named the *meltemi*. Most mornings were calm and the *meltemi* would build from the north until mid-afternoon when it could reach gale force or stronger. Entering harbors and getting settled for the night was often an ordeal in this weather, but the setting sun was like a signal to close the valve and a calm would descend, allowing for a worry-free sleep. We learned to rise early in the morning and motor for a few hours until the wind strengthened. Then we'd beat into the building chop, retiring to a protected anchorage by early afternoon to explore the ruins ashore.

Many Greek islands were just off the Turkish mainland and we surreptitiously crossed back and forth between the countries, depending on where the better anchorages and ruins were. We discovered how the Turks disliked the Greeks and vice versa, and nowhere was it more pronounced than on the border of the two countries. Many of the local foods and drinks were the same but each country had their own names for them, and heaven forbid you use the wrong name. Once, we were

offered what we thought was ouzo.

"Not ouzo! Raki! Ouzo taste like dishwater compared to Raki!"

Ouzo, Raki, Sambuca and Pastis are all aniseed-based, licorice-tasting liqueurs. A clear fluid, it turns a cloudy, opaque white when water is added. At the local *tavernas*, we enjoyed it as a refreshing afternoon break when topped up with a glass of ice water. We just had to remember which country we were in when ordering.

We had reached as far north as Bodrum in Turkey when I told Alec I now believed all the *meltemi* stories. Even the Greek captain of a freighter we passed in the Indian Ocean had warned us of the strong summer winds and choppy seas. After two and half years, I thought I'd seen everything and hadn't let the stories of the Mediterranean concern me. But without a doubt, sailing north in Greece's summer often became nasty. I was tired of the beating and wanted to sail downwind again.

The next day we sailed downwind to the Greek island of Niseros. We came into the harbor unaware that we were still flying the Turkish flag. Someone yelled to us to get it down, which we did instantly, shocked that we could forget something so important.

"They can throw you in jail for something like that," the sailor said.

We sailed in the afternoons with the *meltemi* propelling us to the Greek Dodecanese islands of Tilos and Symi. There were nice anchorages where we could avoid outrageous harbor charges. These islands were very dry and less frequented, but nowhere was beyond reach of the tourists.

In a small waterside *taverna*, the owner befriended us. We didn't look like typical tourists and the merchants treated us differently. We were tanned, relaxed and obviously not on a rushed, action-packed vacation from the northern climes. Our hair was long and begging for a trim, and our clothes had a faded-gray tinge from ineffectual hand-washing. After the lunch rush he sat down with us and poured ouzos.

"The food was very good," I said.

"It's not real good Greek food," he said with a thick accent. "The tourists are never happy. They want a lot of choice on the menu, but it depends on what the fishermen catch. If I run out of octopus they get upset. If it's not fresh, they get angry. One person wants more spice, but the next complains there is too much. Many restaurants buy food from companies on the mainland. It is all frozen. It is not real Greek food, but it is what the tourist wants."

"Why don't you be different?" Alec asked. "There must be a market for that."

"It is decided by the tour companies," he said. "If they don't recommend my restaurant then no one will come. That's why I must stand out front and convince people to sit down. Many tourists are too embarrassed to refuse me. I don't like doing it, but once I get enough people inside, then others will come."

We'd noticed that many of the Greeks were unhappy with the tourists and treated foreigners haughtily. It was very different from the Turks, who were so welcoming and sincere. But these Greek Isles had seen tourists a lot longer than Turkey, where tourism had just begun to develop in the last decade.

I tried not to be jealous each time a member of Alec's family came to join us. Since Florida, no one from my family had been able to visit, and my contact with them had been minimal. That was one of the reasons why I took it upon myself to visit them after the first year. They had never been long-distance travelers, so why should I expect them to be now? Although I ached for a visit from someone, I gave them the benefit of the doubt. Life was busy, air travel was expensive, and we were very far away.

After two years of sailing, everything changed during a phone call home from Malaysia. My father announced that they wanted to come see us. Their show of support meant the world to me.

My parents arrived in Rhodes on August 1st. Even though it was also full of tourists, Rhodes was an interesting and diverse island. Remnants of bygone eras were everywhere, in the form of monasteries, churches, ruins of ancient cities, medieval towns and castles.

My mother had told her friends that they would be sailing amongst the Greek Isles, but wasn't sure how it was going to work, knowing my dad would insist on staying in a first-class hotel each night.

The first day she asked, "Could we visit Santorini? I've heard it's

really nice." With whitewashed houses perched on steep cliffs, it was nice, but it was also in the middle of the Aegean Sea, a couple of days away, sailing upwind against the *meltemi*.

We compromised with some day sails on the lee side of Rhodes. The water was so very blue, the coastline picturesque and I was pleased that the strong *meltemi* abated. Seeing Alec and I sailing *Madeline* gave them confidence in our abilities and in our boat. My mother told me it helped in alleviating any anxieties she may have had, as she could now visualize our situation. I was thrilled my parents had come to visit, and the four of us had a splendid time together.

One evening, while lounging in the cockpit with our ritual sundowner cocktails, my father sighed and looked out over the water to the setting sun. It was an absolutely peaceful scene, with flecks of orange and red dancing in the sky.

Smiling and sipping his martini, he asked, "So, you do this every night?"

I hesitatingly replied, "Yes", wondering why he was asking.

He sighed again and leaned back, taking it all in. "I could get used to this."

Tears welled up in my eyes. It was the utmost of compliments, for him to imagine himself enjoying it. He finally understood.

STILL NOT THE TROPICS

AFTER MY PARENTS LEFT GREECE, we sailed down the lee side of Rhodes. The strong northwest *meltemi* gave us a fast trip to the southern tip of the island, where we anchored to wait for weather. We'd been listening to the Greek weather forecasts in anticipation of our upcoming journey, and had noted that the wind strength between Rhodes and Crete, and especially at the island of Karpathos, was notoriously fierce all summer long.

We hiked up to the lighthouse to take a look at the sea, and of course it never looks that bad from a distance. We saw three sailboats beating into it, and all seemed okay. Mind you, two of them were over 80 feet long! We opted to sail south of Crete for a better wind angle, and then west towards Malta. It wasn't going to be an easy trip and the decision of when to make the jump was a tough one.

The next day the wind dropped by ten knots and we decided to go and get it over with. By the time we were abeam of Karpathos, we were down to double-reefed main, staysail and no genoa – it was rolled up all the way. Although in the lee of the island, the wind was screaming. Water ripped from the wave crests and sprayed like foamy white hail across the sea.

The mountains of Karpathos are high and steep and instead of protecting us from the *meltemi*, the wind accelerated down the slopes

and blasted us. We couldn't imagine going on in these conditions. We decided to get a night's rest before going out and tackling it all again.

We turned upwind and sailed close-hauled towards the anchorage. Short, steep waves stopped *Madeline* every few seconds, pushing her sideways. The boat lurched and pounded, the sails stretched, the rigging banged.

Slam! Slam! Slam! Every third wave pummeled the hull, engulfing the entire boat in spray. Sea water splashed everywhere, and I was soaked.

Worse than anything we had faced, we debated aborting and sailing on to Crete. But the shoreline was so tempting and it seemed so near. Inch by inch we came closer. We had no detailed chart for the anchorage, but were relieved to find a sand bottom. Megagusts periodically whipped down on us, jerking our anchor chain taut, but we were safe.

Our journey to Malta was starting to mirror that of St. Paul's in 59 AD. He was on his way to Rome aboard a corn ship. The ship started out from the southern coast of Turkey, then past Rhodes, with the intentions of going north of Crete. Between Rhodes and Crete they met with very strong winds and were forced to head south, past Karpathos.

At night I tried to ignore the woo-woo-WOOOing of the wind. Even though I had harnessed many of my fears, I still had trouble with the howl of the wind in the rigging. But during the brutal sail to Karpathos, I was proud to have coped.

"It is Alec and I alone again, just like in the beginning. Only now we are experienced – with sailing, with Madeline and with each other. And I know exactly which conditions will freak me out, even before we set sail... My latest solution to rough weather is to hide in the cabin. For some reason I wasn't able to do this much before, fearing I had to always be on the alert or else something would go wrong, or that Alec might need my help or input. But now I realize that panicking is not

useful to any situation, and once I feel it starting, I remove myself from the trigger by going inside.

I'm sure Alec would prefer an equal partner out there, but I know he appreciates my composure. For most of the sailing I've pulled my weight, and it's important I've developed this strategy for rough conditions. I'm still available if he needs me – I took the helm for the last agonizing bash to this anchorage – but there's no point in both of us being consumed with the tough sailing. We have a good understanding, a trust, we can read each other's minds – we're a team."

In the morning the wind strength was a little less, so we decided to leave Karpathos and its windy reputation behind us. Poseidon wasn't very kind to us that day. Downwind from the anchorage we were greeted by the same horrendous wind and rough seas we had coming in. Suddenly it shifted and caught the wrong side of our mainsail.

BANG! Accidental gybe!

The wind had pushed the mainsail violently from one side of the boat to the other, bending the traveler track out of shape, and ripping out three of the sail slugs holding the sail to the mast. Alec climbed onto the cabin top with the spares to fix the sail, while I continued sailing under our staysail alone. With winds this strong, I expected things would start to break.

We arrived at the southeast tip of Crete late in the afternoon and suddenly were becalmed. It was a short break, though, and within an hour we were again battling with the *meltemi*. It seemed that some of the Cretean mountains blocked the wind, whereas others behaved as in Karpathos, accelerating it violently.

A pattern developed after nightfall. We'd be blasted by a sudden gust and would painfully reef down to just a scrap of sail. *Madeline* would fly along at eight knots for an hour, and then just as suddenly, the wind would die completely. We'd motor for an hour and then, whoosh! When morning came we noticed our wind direction indicator had blown away from the top of the mast.

St. Paul's ship had stopped at Kali Limens on the south coast of Crete, and intended to winter at Loutro, a little further west, which was where we stopped. They were sailing late in the season, and could not trust the upcoming winter weather, but with the arrival of some good weather, the captain decided to continue on, against St. Paul's advice. Alec and I were sailing in the best season, and we had the advantage of weather forecasts to help us decide when we too would carry on.

Loutro was a charming bay surrounded by high cliffs rimmed with little white inns and houses on the shore. The water was still and the sky azure, revealing no evidence of the vicious night we'd endured fighting the elements. We absorbed the relative silence: children splashing at the beach, couples giggling, some kayakers paddling smoothly by, and a big sigh from the crew of *Madeline*.

Much of our time was taken up with jobs on the boat and the sailing, but we still had many hours for reading, writing and reflecting. I valued our time together as a couple, especially moments like this, talking over a well-deserved cocktail.

"I have a new theory about time," I said. "The more time you have the less money you need."

"I guess the opposite works too," Alec added. "The less time you have the more money you need – especially to enjoy yourself."

"That's true, you know. Just think of how much money we were spending in the working world, compared to the little money we need to cruise. Take clothes for example," I said.

"And cars, and insurances, and vacations, and entertainment."

I was happy that we had taken this time in our lives exploring our world by sea, and removing ourselves from the time-consuming trivialities that had gripped us. Now we were able to take a step back and re-evaluate ourselves, our goals and our lives, free from outside influences – other than each other – and decide what was really important.

"But time is not the answer," I continued. "If there's something that needs doing, but you don't really want to do it, no amount of time will bring you to do it. I *have* time now, and these things still don't get done."

"On *Madeline* you can't procrastinate by saying, 'I'll do that when I get the time'."

"No, I'd have to use a different excuse, like, 'I don't really want to do that right now'. You have to be honest with yourself."

I felt profound figuring out answers for our lives, and our philosophizing often led us to question the meaning of life, one of Alec's favorite topics. As he contemplated the sunset, his eyes started to glaze over, and I thought, "Here he goes again..."

Honking horns and blasting smoke thickly and rudely sliced our serenity as two huge, triple-decker car ferries motored straight to the shore on either side of us. I was ready to get on our way.

For the first three days to Malta we had light headwinds and calms, through which our faithful engine throbbed. We kept expecting the prevailing northwesterly wind to blow, and were confused when a light southwest wind arrived.

262

"A *sirrocco!*" exclaimed Alec.

"A *sirrocco,*" I read from one of our guides, "is a strong southerly wind from the coast of Africa bringing poor visibility with dust and rain."

Our night sky became overcast and then it drizzled. What was happening? Our Greek weather station gave us no clues, and we had yet to pick up Malta's broadcast only 40 miles away.

Then came lightning and thunder, the first signs of a storm. I'd read about terrible thunderstorms in the Western Mediterranean, but I'd seen so much innocuous lightning every night in Borneo that I was almost used to it. But in Borneo, the lightning sat over the coast, whereas this lightning was moving towards us. Even though I told myself to stay calm, I could feel my heartbeat gradually quickening. The thundershower burst, pouring rain onto us for the first time in six months. Standing outside it was difficult to breathe, but I was impressed with the magnificence of it all.

After the rain came calm, and with only 25 miles to Malta, I calculated our arrival at dawn. The wind then started to blow strongly from the northwest. As we reefed the sails, we cursed Poseidon for making us sweat it out. Our course was directly against the wind, and in a matter of hours we were pounding into big waves. Our genoa developed rips in several places; the old sail couldn't take this abuse any more. With our inhibited progress, we changed our ETA to noon, to mid-afternoon, to "will we make it in before dark?"

Even though I was angry that the wind was blowing us away from Malta, I was happy our landfall would not be like St. Paul's. After leaving Crete, his ship was swept out to sea in a storm. Lost, they were blown onto the rocky shores of Malta, and shipwrecked.

After five o'clock we finally sailed past the yellow sandstone embattlements guarding Malta's deep harbor. *Madeline* was coated in a thick snowy layer of salt. This last fight was worse than anything we'd faced in the Red Sea, but I consoled myself with the thought of ample fresh water to wash down our clothes, our bodies and *Madeline*.

"The Med gives me all the amenities I've been missing but it's combined with frustrating, unpredictable and sometimes violent weather conditions. The tropics gave us pleasant weather, but with the uncertainty and challenges of self-sufficiency in strange countries. As happy as I am now, compared to the worrisome first part of our trip, I definitely look forward to returning to the tropics."

After a week of recuperating in Malta, we sailed close to Sicily. Listening to the Italian weather forecasts, we desperately tried to learn our Italian numbers and compass points. Then we gybed towards Sardinia, always planning where we could stop should the weather turn on us. As we raced towards the southern tip of Sardinia with the spinnaker flying, we heard that the *mistral* was beginning to blow in the Gulf of Lyon.

The *mistral* is the Western Mediterranean's equivalent to the *meltemi*. Cold northern air funnels down the Rhone valley and blows at gale force into the sea between Spain and Sardinia. We stopped at the southern tip of Sardinia, rather than continue sailing into the upcoming wind. The northwest wind continued for days, gradually worsening until there was no hope of leaving.

After eight restless days in a deserted anchorage, the forecast changed – not enough to be favorable, but at least the gales had stopped. It had been our longest wait for weather, and thankfully the two-day trip to Mallorca was uneventful.

On the south coast of Mallorca, we picked an anchorage open only to the southwest, with the forecast indicating we'd be protected. I was looking forward to a solid night's sleep, but just at dusk it started to blow – directly into the anchorage. The sky looked foreboding and raindrops spattered the deck. A swell rolled into the bay, and waves began to crash onto the rocks behind us.

On this night, as with other uncertain nights in the past years, we remembered the words of many an old salt, "When in doubt, head out." We took careful note of the onshore lights and of a flashing navigation buoy. We calculated the compass course in case we needed to exit in the dark. When the wind really whipped up around ten o'clock, we decided we'd be safer outside.

Our destination was towards the capital city, Palma, so we started for there, even though we were beating into the wind and waves. After an hour or so, the wind jumped above 25 knots.

"The wind's getting worse and we're not making our course," Alec said. "We don't have to do this."

I agreed wholeheartedly. We dropped all the sails except the double-reefed main and ran downwind. This strategy worked well when there was "sea room", but we were approaching an island off the coast. The channel was only a few miles wide and we could just make out the lighthouses on each shore.

Alec followed a compass course and double-checked the lighthouse bearings with the hand-held compass. I plotted our position and monitored the course on the GPS at the chart table. Then, the rain obscured our visibility completely. As long as we had our GPS I knew exactly where we were. We'd already checked, and knew the GPS positions matched the chart.

The deluge whipped the water surface and the wind gusted over 50 knots, flattening the waves. Driving rain and sea spray combined into a white-streaked mist, like a cloud blasting over the surface, obscuring the water below.

"Wow," Alec said excitedly. Even though I knew he wasn't happy with our predicament, he got a thrill from battling the elements. "Thank goodness we dropped the sails. Alayne, you've gotta check this out."

I stuck my head out to scan the tempestuous scene, but soon retreated. No use both of us getting wet, and I knew I had to keep any panic in check.

The maelstrom raged around us. Helpless, Alec watched wide-eyed from the cockpit.

After an excruciating ten minutes, the wind dropped back to gale force and the rain poured down.

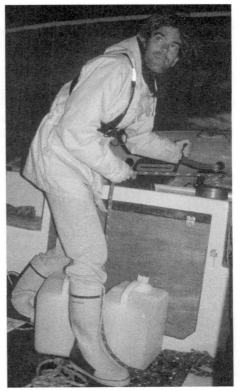

A lightning storm moved in from behind and over top of us.

CRACK! My eardrums burst and I simultaneously screamed. At that same instant I saw Alec light up like a bright spotlight. He jumped and fell down.

"Are we hit?" he yelled. I looked immediately to the electronics. The GPS and autopilot were still working.

"We're okay!" The thunder rolled around us, but the storm was quickly moving away. Had we been hit? That was as close as it could come, and I watched the GPS screen, thankful.

I plotted our position. We were into the channel now, sailing at eight knots in torrential rain. "What's happening?" I asked from inside. I didn't want to look, but I was still curious.

"Let's see. The lightning in front of us seems to be further away, the lightning on our stern is quite spectacular, and the lightning on our starboard side hasn't changed." Alec was taking it all in stride, but I wanted to know how much longer it would last. "I can see glimpses of the lighthouses now," he said. "Oh, there's another boat!"

I sprang into the cockpit to have a look, but the rain obliterated the view again. I hadn't imagined we'd have to dodge ships in this. Yet I was perversely happy that we weren't the only souls experiencing this hell.

Then everything stopped.

The lightning to starboard didn't change, but the rain ceased, the sky cleared and the wind vanished. The stars were twinkling above. We searched and spotted the other boat bobbing in the large chaotic waves. It was 4 AM, and Alec said, "Let's turn on the engine and head for Palma." We turned 180 degrees and motored through the leftover slop. Ten-foot waves knocked us around as they rolled past in multiple directions, their glassy surfaces unruffled.

Two hours later we were back to where we started the night before, and by mid-morning we were almost at our destination. The constant rumble of the engine reminded me of all the work that Alec did in Australia, and how well we dealt with the overheating problem in the Malacca Strait. What a great machine, and what a great diesel mechanic Alec had turned out to be.

Kunk, kunk, clunk, clunk. What? It seemed as if the engine was going to stop! I knew there were only three things a diesel engine needed to work: clean air, clean fuel and compression. It sounded like it needed more fuel, and the resident mechanic quickly congratulated me on my diagnosis.

Alec turned off the engine and tried a few things. Then, when he tried to turn it on again it wouldn't start. He ignored his tired eyes and started back to work. His research, using our library aboard, told him that he could start the engine using a screwdriver. He took out our extra big long one and mysteriously poked it into the cavernous engine compartment. "Start 'er up!" he said, and magically, it did. But the fuel line was sucking air badly, forcing us to bleed it continuously as we limped into the anchorage at Port Andraitx.

Alec quickly dropped the anchor and I felt my neck muscles relax. He came back to the cockpit and we both slumped down, exhausted. We sat motionless, silently watching a big German sailor fix something on the bow of his small black boat immediately behind us. He was stark naked. "Is it my imagination, or is he getting closer to us?" I asked.

"We're dragging!" Alec yelled, grabbing the screwdriver to restart the engine.

After we reanchored, Alec immediately tackled the problems and within a few hours he'd fixed the starter and the fuel line. Even though we were far from Greece, Poseidon would not leave us alone. The wind started to blow from the west, into the port. I couldn't believe our misfortune – or the Mediterranean weather!

266

The marina cost US$50 a night during the summer season, and even though the rates had just fallen, our budget wasn't calculated with such exorbitant fees in mind. Fishing boats and local sailboats on moorings had already taken the most protected places, so we made the most of our catamaran and reanchored again, deep in the harbor in a very shallow patch near other catamarans and small motorboats.

For centuries, the harbor bottom had collected nautical garbage. It was an archaeologist's dream, but an anchoring nightmare. Strong winds funneled into the harbor between the high hills on either side. Some boats were already having difficulty staying anchored, but we seemed fairly secure.

Well into a deep and deserved sleep, a banging on the hull rudely awakened us. Angrily we ran outside assuming a boat had dragged into us. We were aghast to see a small runabout hitting our stern. We'd dragged again!

We were fortunate the small boat had woken us, as 30 feet further was a rocky breakwall. In the dark we reset the anchor, and then set a second one just to be sure, but it was hard to relax. Yelling and revving engines from other dragging boats echoed across the harbor, making for fitful sleeping.

When my girlfriend flew in with her husband a few days later, the harbor had transformed – it was peaceful, sunny and warm. The cozy fishing village nestled among the soaring rugged mountains was breathtaking.

OUR LAST CHALLENGE?

THE STRAIT OF GIBRALTAR IS LIKE THE THIN OPENING at the top of a bottle of wine filled with a vintage liquid, the Mediterranean Sea. Sailing towards this bottleneck brought us back together with all sorts of familiar faces from our past travels. We were definitely back on the cruising track.

After our friends left us in Mallorca we had sailed north to Barcelona. This was the furthest north we sailed *Madeline*, at 41°22' North. Our southernmost port had been Nelson, New Zealand, at 41°16' South. I liked the symmetry.

When we'd arrived in Barcelona, *Pandarosa* heard us radio a marina and they immediately called us. Craig and Mark also missed the closeness of the cruising community and were keen to get together and share adventure stories. *Pandarosa* was the boat we had radioed when we hit the whale in the Indian Ocean. We got to know them in Djibouti and saw them again in Egypt and Turkey.

A good friend of Alec's then joined us, and we sailed down the Spanish coast. Fariborz was the perfect guest for the trip. Most friends would have been disappointed with the scenery, as they dreamed of deserted anchorages and palm trees overlooking white sand beaches and turquoise water. Fariborz, being an engineer, marveled at the busy container ports, the factories lining the shore and the oil rig and lighthouse we passed while sailing at night. He left in Valencia and we kept sailing south.

Winter wasn't far off, so we took advantage of some favorable weather and sailed non-stop three days to Gibraltar. During our sail we crossed back into the Western Hemisphere, a reminder that this was one of our last crossroads. We were almost home.

Britain's Rock of Gibraltar is attached to the Spanish mainland, and although permeated by Spaniards, it remained British after a long history of battles. There was an expectant enthusiasm in the air with the hustle and bustle of cruisers preparing for the upcoming ocean passages. The marine stores were busy with everyone getting their boats in perfect working order and buying spares for anything likely to break. These would be the last well-stocked, reasonably-priced, English-speaking marine stores for the next couple of thousand miles.

We were very surprised to see two boats amongst the traditional fleet: *Gitana* and *Triangle Island*. Alexandra and Reinhard were not aboard their sleek trimaran, but I learned they'd arrived in Gibraltar well ahead of the other boats and had gone back to Austria to fill the cruising kitty.

Greg and his small Drascombe lugger arrived shortly after us. When he'd reached Port Sudan in the Red Sea, it was getting late in the season and he knew he wouldn't survive in the strong headwinds and searing heat of summer. He put his boat on a freighter traveling to Italy, and then sailed from Genoa to Gibraltar to rejoin the cruising fleet.

Our social life improved dramatically that week. With Craig and Mark, of *Pandarosa*, we arranged a fun night out with a bunch of cruisers at the English pubs crowding the backstreets. Although Craig and Mark were a same-sex couple, their situation had many parallels to ours. Their relationship had spanned fourteen years, compared to our twelve. Craig had initiated the plan of sailing around the world, and had pretty much taken over as captain when they'd left San Diego four years previous. Mark was somewhat reluctant, and completely related to my fear. They'd dealt with the same relationship issues.

Craig and Mark initially found the cruising community difficult. Sailing down the coast of Mexico, they had felt a bit excluded. Similarly, we had sensed resistance from some older cruisers when they learned that we were still in our twenties. Once out into the Pacific though, we all experienced the same magic that every long-distance cruiser knows. Age, sex, religion, language, race, nationality – the barriers melted away, and we were all treated as friends.

Ignoring the nasty stories of the Strait of Gibraltar, we left in good weather and arrived five days later in the Canary Islands off the west coast of Africa. Ever since Christopher Columbus sailed to the New

Tracking ships in the Strait of Gibraltar

World, sailors have stopped at these Spanish islands before jumping off across the Atlantic Ocean.

The volcanic peaks on the hazy horizon made for a dramatic landfall. Dry and desolate like neighboring Africa, the terrain belonged on a Star Trek episode. The wind had been intermittent for the last few days, and we slowly motored into the northern anchorage at Isla Graciosa.

The sight of twenty boats at anchor got me excitedly cleaning the boat in anticipation of visitors. Listening on the radio we could hear the boats talking and heard someone mention *Glissade*. Mike and Lori, a fun-loving young couple who had left Alaska in 1992, were also finishing their circumnavigation. After our first meeting in Indonesia we'd seen them many places, but it had been months since we'd been together.

We came into the anchorage and circled *Glissade* honking our horn. They yelled over that we must join them right away for a cold one. In the midday heat, this was a welcome invite.

"There are many cruisers we know here, some we haven't seen in years... Being with long-distance cruisers again brings back a wonderful feeling. After months in the Mediterranean Sea of strangers, landing in the Canaries feels like home, where we feel comfortable and understood."

One evening, we climbed to the top of a volcanic peak near the anchorage for cocktails. Ten of us scrambled up the steep slope of loose lava rock, giving our legs some much needed exercise. After about 40 minutes of switchbacks we reached the summit, and found a suitable ledge for our bar and hors d'oeuvres. Our eyes feasted on the

magnificent view of the boats in the anchorage while we watched the burning globe sink slowly into the sea.

We caught up with each boat's travels and spread cruising gossip. One couple filled us in on David Clark, the single-handed senior vying for a place in the record books. After we'd last seen him in Panama, he had aborted his trip across the Pacific due to engine troubles before finally making it to Australia. The latest news was that he'd been rescued in the Indian Ocean by a freighter just as his boat sank.

Not wanting the night to end, we invited Lori and Mike over to *Madeline* for more drinks. With the cheap price of wine and duty-free booze in the Mediterranean, our drinking had substantially increased. We laughed and swapped stories and played dice games for hours. Beer after beer after beer were consumed.

Hours later, Alec and I found ourselves in a bitter quarrel. I was arguing about how I felt, and he was arguing about facts. The debate was reminiscent of our early cruising days: Alec being frustrated with my lack of logic when my emotions took over, and me being equally frustrated with his temper and inability to understand how I was feeling. These fights had for the most part disappeared, but in our drunken state neither of us was making any sense, and the argument got more and more heated.

Alec slept on the foredeck, and in the morning was chasing aspirin with orange juice when I crawled out of bed severely hungover. He handed me a glass of juice and slumped onto a cockpit cushion. Gingerly I sat across from him, the thought of ingesting anything revolting my stomach. We were both silent for what seemed like an eternity, until Alec spoke. "I'd like to blame the alcohol. That wasn't us last night."

"The booze is cheap, but we're paying in other ways." I cringed, as talking made my head pound.

"Sleeping in late and feeling hungover all afternoon just isn't enjoyable. It's not how I want to spend my last few months of cruising."

"I've been thinking of cutting down anyway, since I've gone off the pill," I said, speaking quietly.

"Well, I'm game, even if I sound like every other drunk who has woken up with a brutal headache. But I'm really willing to cut back," he said.

"If I get pregnant, I want to stop – so now is as good a time as any to taper off." The five years I'd promised to wait were up. Once the Atlantic was crossed, I was ready to risk pregnancy. I'd kept my sailing promise, and Alec was ready to keep his, despite his fear of parenthood.

He finished his orange juice and was looking less green and more awake.

"There's something else I've come up with," he said. "Something I wish I'd thought of much earlier in our trip."

"What?"

"You know how frustrated we get with each other at times. We get into these arguments that just build on themselves – and we get caught in a vicious circle. It typically starts with something trivial but always follows the same pattern."

"We know how to push each other's buttons."

"Exactly."

"But we don't have those very often any more, because now we know the minute it's happening." My brow furrowed as I thought of the previous night, and I conceded, "Still that doesn't always help."

"Right. If we could nip it in the bud, then life would be perfect. So, I suggest we have a code word. The first person to recognize a useless argument starting can say the word, and it means both of us have to stop the conversation – once the code word is used neither of us can say another word on that subject. We can talk about it much later when we've cooled off. It would certainly avoid arguments, especially in front of people, like last night. What do you think?"

"Sure, I'll give it a try. And I have a great code word..."

Only a dozen of the Indian Ocean and Red Sea cruisers were crossing the Atlantic Ocean, and of those, only a few had left North America in 1993 as we had. Replacing all the cruisers that had dropped off our path were a whole slew of shiny new boats with excited and anxious crews setting out for the first time.

Jimmy Cornell was a name all cruisers knew. He made a living compiling useful cruising information into books, as well as organizing rallies for cruisers. Passage-making in company gave a sense of security to many. Alec and I had first heard about the Atlantic Rally for Cruisers (ARC) in its inaugural year, 1987, and we had looked forward to the day when we too could join. Now in 1995 over 200 boats had signed up to cross the Atlantic together, and to partake in parties on both sides.

Since our early days though, we'd become much more confident and independent. We loved the social aspect of cruising, but knew we didn't have to pay for camaraderie, or for parties. The thing we had grown to love about cruising was the opportunity to get away from organized things, and to be completely self-sufficient. We felt strongly about upholding the unstructured, unrestricted freedoms cruising gives.

A group of cruisers started a mock organization called the NARC, or "Not ARC". They demonstrated their distaste for organized cruising events by giving away yellow flags for all members to fly. We sat in *Pandarosa's* cockpit, together with Mike and Lori from *Glissade*, looking out at the rows of masts crowding the marina and anchorage. Feeling that we were different from all the other groups, Mike dubbed us the BARC – Boozers And Ragged-out Cruisers.

The biggest difference between us and the others was our boats. *Pandarosa*, *Glissade* and *Madeline* had sailed solidly for the past year covering over 10,000 miles. With no long stops for maintenance or repairs, our boats were just hanging on. We were making do with questionable engines, baggy sails and tiring interiors. We were the kings of improvisation, not wanting to make any big purchases since we were at the end of our budgets and the end of our voyages.

In contrast, there was so much money being spent by the other cruisers in Las Palmas on Gran Canaria. Fear of the unknown drove most of the skippers into a shopping frenzy as they equipped themselves with all the latest gear and gizmos. We knew our shabby little dinghy wouldn't get stolen at the dock!

Alec's aunts, uncles and cousins visited from the United Kingdom and brought with them a huge bundle of mail. I struggled between wanting to chat with them and wanting to rudely immerse myself in letter-reading. Now we were beginning to receive mail from cruisers, and we held up the strangely-shaped, crumpled envelopes and examined the exotic postmarks, trying to guess who the sender was.

I especially looked forward to mail from Nathalie, and in the pack was a letter. She was a good writer, and I missed her friendship terribly. I'd last heard from her in Barcelona. They had arrived in Holland, greeted by family and friends in the same place as they'd said farewell over three years earlier. There were musicians playing and it was a wonderful party. As if out of a storybook, their arrival also marked the news that Nathalie was pregnant. They were on their way to new adventures.

When I opened her letter I immediately sensed something wrong in the greeting and the handwriting. She got right to the point. She had gone into labor at 25 weeks and their little boy had died at birth. Even more upsetting to me, it had happened over a month ago. I was devastated. Nathalie and I had sailed three quarters of the way around the world together, never far apart. We had supported each other in all sorts of circumstances for two long years. At a time that I could have helped her the most, I hadn't even known what she was going through. I felt sick. I wanted to jump on a plane to be with her.

I couldn't read any more mail that night. Alec and I talked and talked, and we both shed some tears for our friends. I had never felt such a deep sadness for someone – my heart ached for Nathalie.

The next morning I dug through our pile of unopened mail and found another letter she'd written a few weeks later. I was relieved to hear that she'd recovered from the shock of her nightmare, and even though she was still in a lot of pain over her loss, she was going to be okay.

We spoke on the telephone and cried together as she told me of the whole ordeal. I told her that I wanted to be with her, but she understood that it wasn't possible. Alec and I made a promise that we'd visit them soon after our return to Canada.

Alec's relatives were to depart the Canary Islands on November 24th, leaving only 22 days until his immediate family would arrive in Grenada on the other side of the Atlantic. We'd told his parents that it would take us at least 21 days to make the crossing, and made it very clear that we had to be choosy about weather. We would be sailing through hurricane spawning grounds and if we left too early, we might encounter a late season hurricane. We'd do our best, but they weren't to count on a pre-Christmas arrival. Even with all the forewarning, we still felt a lot of pressure. For the first time in ten years, his siblings would be together for Christmas.

We watched as the ARC fleet left on their pre-arranged date. It amazed us that a group who had banded together for safety reasons were leaving for their trans-Atlantic crossing on a date set a year in advance. Even though we got some satisfaction at hearing them beat into strong headwinds for the first day, the following days gave them a perfect weather system. We felt it was still a bit early, but more boats left during that week, including *Glissade*, and we listened to radio reports of excellent progress.

With the relatives gone, we had to decide if we should try and catch the tail end of this weather system, or wait until the next one came through. But who knew when that would be?

After a discussion of the pros and cons, and without anyone knowing, we silently pointed *Madeline* south to the trade winds. We tuned in on our little radio receiver, listening to find out who was where. *Pandarosa* had chosen to wait.

We set out like gangbusters, but the great weather lasted only 36 hours. The next week brought calms, light headwinds, torrential rain squalls and then shifty winds from every compass point and in every strength. Seven days later we'd hardly gone anywhere! I was getting concerned that we wouldn't make it to Grenada in time.

On Day 8 we found the trade winds, or so we thought. We'd come far enough south to enter the tropical weather pattern of easterly winds, but there was something wrong. We excitedly hoisted our big, brightly-colored spinnaker with the plan that it would carry us the next 2,200 miles to Grenada.

"All right! At last!" Alec said.

But we eyed the clouds suspiciously. They didn't exactly look like trade-wind skies. The big puffy clouds that paraded in line overhead were just a little too puffy. They had too much gray. Some had light rain sweeping down from their center, diffusing the bright sunlight and touching the sea. I remembered crossing the Pacific, when we had been naive to the subtle differences.

Some clouds brought rain; they all brought wind. We steered carefully, letting the cloud clusters slowly overtake us on one side or the other. Finally one caught us in the middle of its path.

"Let's drop sail," I suggested.

"No. The sail can handle this wind," was Alec's confident reply.

I could see the wind approaching on the water. It kicked up wavelets, rippling the water surface as it raced towards us. I bit my tongue when the wind hit us, staying dutifully silent as it howled in the rigging. *Madeline* took off like a horse at the races, surfing down the waves at nine knots. I watched our big beautiful sail, wondering how much it could take.

"Yee haw!" Alec yelled over the noise of the rushing water. "This is better than regular trade winds!"

I could see that he was sincerely enjoying himself, but I couldn't do this all the way to Grenada. As the clouds left us, *Madeline* quieted down to her normal, easy pace, but not much later another squall was upon us.

I looked to Alec and we locked eyes.

"We can't keep lowering and raising the sail every half-hour," Alec pre-empted me. "Let's leave it up for now, otherwise we'll never get to Grenada. You should be happy we have this wind and are finally making progress!"

Again, *Madeline* accelerated and whooshed along.

We both had our eyes glued to the spinnaker as it strained and pulled with the force of the gust. Suddenly, the sail ripped right down the middle, as if someone was undoing a huge zipper. We looked at each other and simultaneously said, "Wow!"

"That wasn't so bad," I said. Just like a kid who fears his inevitable booster shot at the doctor's, I had always feared blowing out a sail. It is something that happens to every seasoned sailor, and now that it had happened to us, it didn't seem like such a big deal. Except that it was our only spinnaker!

We rigged up our two gennies from the bow, sailing in the same way *Rode Beer* had crossed this ocean three years previous. Alec fabricated a pole to hold out the windward genny, using every possible material available for the job. *Rode Beer* had told us that they sailed peacefully in sunshine, not even trimming their sails for eighteen days, but on our crossing the wind shifts persisted, with each squall requiring

an adjustment every hour. Several pole configurations broke, putting Alec's ingenuity to the test.

It continued to rain, usually many times a day. It was the most rain that had fallen in any three-week period during our entire circumnavigation. We wondered if this strange weather had something to do with the record-setting hurricane season that was just ending in the Caribbean.

Alec did some reading on Caribbean hurricanes. They form during overcast and squally conditions west of the Cape Verde Islands, and begin as a cyclical storm over a small area of about fifteen miles. My nerves were on edge with the thought that conditions for a hurricane were ideal.

In recording the passage events in my journal, I longed for the day that I could write about trade-wind skies and gentle breezes. Instead I wrote, "... *the wind speed and direction change so often that it's difficult to decide what to record in the log book entries. The rain continues with a horizon of squalls and rainbows everywhere I look.*"

One night, with 1,200 miles to go, the wind picked up at our change of watch. We took down our pole, and I sailed with the mainsail and genny while Alec slept. I watched the sky for clues. Within half an hour I could see a dark band of overcast sky approaching. With the light from the moon, I could tell that rain was going to be part of the package. The wind dramatically increased and shifted direction – now from the north. This was very unusual.

I woke Alec and we doused the genny just in time. The wind blasted us with 45 knots as we reefed the main once, and then again. The rain pelted down as the sea heaped up. As the wind continued to change direction, the sea responded with confusion, tossing *Madeline* carelessly about. We ran with the wind as best we could. In the cockpit we sat patiently waiting, having no idea what to expect.

I was relieved when the wind stopped clocking and then died down. The whole ordeal lasted three hours and we were convinced this was no simple squall. Some boats not far from us had winds of up to 60 knots. This storm was the beginning of a hurricane. Had the conditions been right it might have gone on to be a full-fledged one.

Day 20 brought a long-awaited change in the weather, and even though it still rained frequently, the air became balmy and we stripped off our clothes in the welcome midday heat.

By Day 22 we were sailing in the trade-wind weather we had expected the whole trip. The sky cleared and the sea calmed, so much that it felt as if we were at anchor. There was nothing to do – no sails to trim, no squalls to cope with. It was a wonderful relief.

That evening, we sat in the cockpit watching one of our last sunsets at sea. When the lights of Barbados slowly became visible on the northern horizon, an overwhelming sense of pride welled up inside me. With 180 miles to Grenada, I was feeling that we'd already made it. All of a sudden I was struck with what a terribly important landfall this would be.

Tears filled my eyes as I said to Alec, "I never thought about it this way before, but I feel so proud of you. Of course I feel proud of myself, and proud of us as a couple, but right now I feel this bursting pride for you. You had a dream, and you did it!"

He said things like he couldn't have done it without me, and that we were a team. He downplayed the achievement, but agreed to chill an extra bottle of champagne. Our arrival in Grenada would be a huge celebration. At least he acknowledged that.

I felt we had been to battle and won. I was extremely pleased with myself – I felt strong, mature and exhilarated to have bravely met the challenges of this last ocean.

As we sailed into Grenada the following morning, we heard on the radio that a whole group of boats, only a few hundred miles behind us, remained becalmed. They would miss the holidays.

Alec's family greeted us with great excitement, but didn't show much surprise. They'd laid bets on our arrival date and time and two of them had guessed correctly.

Little did they know what a gamble it had been.

MELDING OF MINDS

THE HOUSE IN GRENADA WAS LOVELY. Perched on a hill overlooking beautiful Secret Harbour, we could look out through the huge living-room windows and see our beloved *Madeline* anchored below. Alec met his two little nephews for the first time, and together with his family, we spent three weeks celebrating Christmas and New Year's.

As much as we loved being with everyone again, our time with them amplified how different our life had become on *Madeline*. We were spontaneous and carefree, never having to consider anyone other than each other. Even when cruising with *Rode Beer*, we'd operated independently. The others didn't mind living in the same space, but we were happy to retreat to the peace and privacy of our own home every night. Even I, who used to thrive on external stimulation, welcomed the occasional half-day of solitude.

When everyone left, Alec's parents joined us for two weeks cruising north up the chain of Windward Islands. Compared to the time with Jim and Joan in the Turks and Caicos three years ago, Alec and I could see that we had changed. We were now reluctant to set plans. We considered the weather, before our heart's desires, and this meant waiting when the weather was bad, as well as bypassing certain places when the weather was good.

When Alec's parents asked, "What are we going to do tomorrow?" I answered guardedly.

"We'll decide tomorrow. There are a lot of possibilities, but first we'll see what the day is like." I was well aware of the obstacles that we could meet in the average day, and curbed my expectations accordingly.

Seasoned cruisers joked that you can only get one thing done each day. While partly tongue-in-cheek, it was often true. Phoning home was often a whole day affair. After sorting out time zones, currency and office hours, we would get ashore, find a safe place for the dinghy, hike into the town and find the telecom office, only to discover it was a holiday, or siesta, or the phones weren't working.

So we now let the day unfold rather than predetermine its course. This applied to meals as well. Since we stocked the boat for months at a time, by definition the majority of our food wasn't fresh. Our refrigeration depended directly on the amount of sun and wind power we generated each day. We didn't depend on it to keep food fresh, because when low on power we'd turn it off. On sunny, windy days our drinks tinkled with ice cubes, but on overcast, calm days we went without.

For us, fresh was a relative term. We'd evolved an entirely different approach from what Alec's mother was accustomed to. Rather than having a food at its maximum flavor, the key question was "is it safe?" On *Madeline* we used all of our senses rather than "best before" dates. If it looked and smelled okay, then it was good enough.

We discovered, to the surprise of many, that if produce had never been refrigerated, it could last sometimes for months in a cool, dark place on *Madeline*. This applied to certain cheeses, cured meats, eggs, fruits and vegetables. Often our tomatoes were at their best a month after buying them green. When shopping with Joan we noticed she bought the brand-name product; we based our choice on low price and environmental packaging. We had become acutely aware of our impact on the world.

After crossing the vast oceans by boat, we could appreciate the archaic saying that "the solution to pollution is dilution", but this was not the answer. The windward sides of even the most remote islands we visited were littered with man-made garbage that had washed ashore. We pumped our human waste directly overboard, but this paled in comparison to the millions of gallons of untreated sewage dumped by developed cities into their waterways each day. It was upsetting to think of the ocean as the sewer of the world.

On an ocean passage it was appropriate to dispose all paper, glass and metal tins overboard – making sure they sunk – but we were left with a quantifiable reminder of the plastic waste generated for that time period. This we had to take ashore, contributing to the garbage problem on some small island. Often it ended up in the ocean, making us wonder why we bothered.

We became super conscious of packaging, and avoided plastic and individually wrapped serving-size products. We cringed every time we reused the ubiquitous plastic shopping bag to hold our garbage. We'd caught too many bags in our propeller and had seen too many washed on the shore or entangled on the reef.

With Jim and Joan aboard, we day-hopped through the Grenadines and dropped them off in Bequia, so they could vacation a while in less cramped quarters. We planned to meet them two weeks later at the island of Dominica, which would allow Alec and me plenty of time to meander north on our own, or so we thought.

On the day Alec's parents left, we confirmed the suspected. I was pregnant! This was great news, as we were excited to start this next phase of our lives. With the ocean crossings completed, I felt comfortable with the medical risks.

We'd discussed starting a family over the past year, however I knew too much about what could go wrong to risk being pregnant in a third world country or taking a newborn across an ocean. In the Caribbean we were practically home, and with the huge numbers of Canadians and Americans around, it felt like we were.

That same night I was feeling unusually warm. When I took my temperature, my heart sank. I hadn't been sick during the entire circumnavigation, and now, just six weeks pregnant, I had a fever.

Why me? Why now? This was such a critical time in the baby's development; when everything was forming. A fever at this stage could have grave implications. The only other symptoms I had were a headache and pain when moving my eyes, and these didn't match any common illnesses. I tried not to get too upset, and methodically went through the possible diagnoses. Then I remembered reading something in Grenada about dengue fever. I looked it up in my Merck manual, and my symptoms, although not severe, seemed to fit.

Before panicking and jumping to conclusions, I decided to pay a visit to the island's only doctor.

The next day the fever had lifted. But I knew that if I'd actually contracted dengue fever, a day's respite was expected before my temperature would rise again. Still, my mood was bright and I was keen for a walk.

Madeline was anchored in lovely Friendship Bay on the south side of the island. Alec and I hiked over the hill to the main town in Admiralty Bay. It was a strenuous jaunt in the tropical sun, and several times I had to stop to catch my breath. Was this what pregnancy was going to be like? Exhausted and sweating on the other side, I suggested

Overlooking Admiralty Bay, Bequia

an ice cream stop.

A large black woman got up from her stool as we stood in the dim little shop waiting for our eyes to adjust. Her baggy dress billowed like our mainsail around her voluminous curves. It seemed that she'd been eating all of her profits.

"Honey, you ain't lookin' too good," she said with concern.

"I think I have a touch of the flu."

"Aah. Every one of my chillun had dat. First dey gets hot, den okay, den real hot again. I was even soakin' dee li'l one in a ice bat, I was. But dee best ting is ice cream. You come to dee right place!"

Her words were kind, and I felt she had taken me in, like one of her children. Her ice cream rejuvenated me for the rest of our walk.

Being ahead of schedule for my appointment, we walked to the local market, planning to buy some fruit. Brash Rastafarians with dreadlocks dominated the scene, trying to intimidate the cruisers. We'd dealt with their aggressive sales pitches on our previous visits, and had bargained with them mercilessly using our skills acquired in Southeast Asia. They now greeted us like long-lost friends, quickly surrounding us to cut out the other merchants.

Each encouraged us to buy his papaya or his mangoes. "Hey mon, good to see ya today, mon. Come to me. I give ya dee best prices here." I was not in the mood for their routine.

"Alec, can you tell them to leave us alone?" I didn't have the energy to bargain.

"Hey guys. Don't bother my wife. She's not feeling well today." They all seemed keenly interested, so Alec told them about my symptoms. Their tone changed immediately.

"Aah. She gots dee island flu. We knows all about dat. Dee best ting for dat is dee sea water. Ya gots to go right in an' swim aroun'. Like dee water ya come from, mon. It's dee best."

Another pushed in front and grabbed Alec, as if to tell him a secret, "No no, mon. I tell ya what ya gots to do. Ya gots to make her a drink. Ya put in some coconut water, and some lime..."

And yet another piped in, "Yeah, some lime and some rum..."

Abruptly, the first one shoved him away, "No, not rum, mon! She sick – she should'n be 'avin' no rum!"

As tiring as it was to listen to their banter, I did find them amusing, and I was warmed by the fact that they cared. They forgot about trying to make a sale, and called out as we parted, "Now take her home, mon, and take good care of her. Don't forget dee lime!"

I left Alec at the post office and headed off to see the doctor. Her office was located on the ground level of a local-style house. She was a tiny, attractive, Filipino and from her perfect skin it was impossible to guess her age. I was glad that the doctor was a woman, and felt comfortable with her right away.

I introduced myself as, "Dr. Main," shaking her hand.

"Dr. Sall, mon," she replied, gesturing for me to have a seat.

"How do you spell your name?" she asked.

"Like the street," I replied. "How do you spell your name?"

"Like the fish!" she said, smiling.

She confirmed that my symptoms were likely due to a mosquito-borne flavivirus, of the same family as dengue fever. Many similar cases had come through her office lately, but she had yet to diagnose a true case of dengue fever on the island. Dengue fever produced a higher fever and extreme pain. There was no treatment and no vaccine.

What I really wanted to know was, could the virus harm the baby? She couldn't relate any of the congenital abnormalities that she'd seen on the island to this local virus, but she'd only been there three years. Her experience in her homeland led her to believe that dengue fever did not cause damage, but she had no literature to confirm this.

She concluded by saying, "You know that at six weeks, you're at a very vulnerable time in your pregnancy, and any virus at this time is a serious concern." I smiled and thanked her, but felt the full brunt of her well-meaning words. As we parted, she shook my hand and said, "Be careful."

When I met with Alec, I broke down. How could I be more careful? I had waited for us to pass through all the potential physical dangers of our journey to conceive when I thought it was safe. The five years had come and gone, and we had practically sailed around the world. Now it was my turn to realize my dream.

I cried uncontrollably: for our unborn child, for me, and for us. My mind was overcome with images of terrible abnormalities the baby could have and how we were going to cope. We'd created a mess!

Alec was a great support. He listened patiently while I ranted and raved and shouted it all out. After I finished, he spoke softly.

"In life there are risks, Alayne. Nothing is guaranteed. We knew this, especially when we decided to have a baby. Nothing has changed since you became sick. And there are so many things that can harm a fetus or a child." He brushed back my hair and wiped away my tears. "Anything can happen, and there's nothing we can do about it. There's no sense in worrying about what we don't know. After all we've been through, we can deal with this too."

We talked and talked, and I knew I'd feel better if I could get more information. We expected to be in Antigua in about a month's time, and I decided to get an ultrasound then.

As expected, my fever spiked again, even higher. That night I became delirious, and was shaking with chills and sweats.

Acetaminophen provided some relief, but I fought the fever for another 36 hours. Alec made trips ashore to the ice cream lady. He would report on my progress, and then return with her life-saving scoops.

After I was through the worst, a sense of calmness settled inside me, deep down. It was as if a little voice was saying that everything would be all right. Alec applauded my positive attitude; we were united through this whole ordeal.

We decided not to tell anyone of the pregnancy, and chose not to dwell on any negative possibilities until we knew more. Instead, we remained secretly happy to be pregnant.

It took me a while to recuperate in Bequia, and before we knew it, our two weeks alone was over. We made an unusual mad dash for Dominica and encountered some unexpected heavy sailing. Nerves aside, I wasn't physically able to cope with the conditions, and Alec took full responsibility for *Madeline*, plowing through headwinds, wild seas and rain.

We ripped our tired old mainsail, and stopped for a night in St. Lucia to rest and repair it. I wasn't surprised at our bad luck. We were breaking our rule: never let a schedule dictate a passage. But the distances weren't great and we both felt keen to press on.

On reuniting with Alec's parents in Dominica, we discovered that Joan had also become ill at the same time. Our ailments were identical and we shared stories, without revealing the complicating factor of my pregnancy. It was difficult to keep our news a secret, but I felt strongly about dealing with things our own way, privately. It took another week before Joan and I were feeling normal, but we were still able to enjoy our cruising in Dominica and Guadeloupe.

Once again Alec and I were reminded of the contrast between our old selves and who we had become. Alec's parents were great conversationalists, but their interest was current affairs. We were largely out of date, and unable to share any opinions. Issues that concerned us were world pollution, consumerism, the globalization of Western culture and other things we'd observed in our travels.

We'd seen a vast spectrum of countries. We'd seen democracies, police states, colonies, kingdoms and dictatorships, as well as theocratic and secular states. We'd seen poor countries, immensely wealthy countries and we'd seen places that were economically growing, mature and even dying. But every country we visited had been permeated, by Western consumerism and materialism.

Some islands in the South Pacific were paradise in the way I pictured it in the Book of Genesis. The land and sea provided ample bounty and the people were happy, carefree, even liberated. They had clothes, shelter and, often to our dismay, television. In this land of plenty though, they had a sense that their lives weren't good enough. They needed whiter whites, Marlboro cigarettes and Nike running shoes.

"After three years we've adapted well to our circumstances, and I've long ago stopped missing the conveniences and luxuries of our previous life. I'm proud of the simple way we live – it feels superior to everyone's dependency on appliances and instant everything on land." We'd become minimalists, to a degree, and were happily living in direct contrast to the lives we had come from.

We enjoyed great cruising with Alec's parents: tacking into anchorages, hiking mountains and snorkeling effervescent reef. Not all our time was spent analyzing how different we'd become. After saying farewell, Alec and I continued on our own to the outlying islands of Guadeloupe. However, amongst the local cruisers and bareboat charterers, we even noticed our differences.

The biggest change was in our relationship. Alec and I were tighter than ever. He was doing his best to be the girlfriend I missed, and could gossip and chat almost as well as Nathalie. We would sit in our cockpit like two old geezers in a retirement home, watching everyone in our little cruising community. We couldn't resist making comments on our neighbors' boat gear, budget, age, nationality, and sex lives as this was almost as much entertainment as watching a charter boat trying to anchor.

We also noticed that long-term cruisers in the tropics, especially men, tended to be slim. Time spent away from land seemed to equal decreased weight. That held true for us, even though Alec and I ate extremely well on our trip. Meals were the highlights of the day; we always had plenty of treats and snacks as well. Although we had ample supplies, we paced ourselves, keeping track of what we consumed. With limited refrigeration, we prepared just enough food for each meal. Tropical heat played a part in decreasing our appetites, as well as seasickness for me. Maybe just wearing bathing suits everyday was enough to curb our consumption!

On our approach to Antigua, we sailed past historic English Harbour. Tacking into huge Falmouth Harbour, we slowly sailed by all the megayachts at anchor. On our first trip ashore, I managed to book an appointment with an obstetrician.

I told the doctor my story, and she didn't seem particularly concerned. "Let's do the ultrasound anyway," she responded in a pleasant island twang. "We have a brand new machine that will give us a great view of the fetus."

We moved to the next room, Alec included, where her colleague operated the equipment. I was in the hands of all the obstetricians on the island. I watched the screen as they searched, but nothing definitive appeared. There's nothing you can do now, I told myself. Just let them give you the information.

After several minutes, Dr. Kelsick spoke. "There is no fetal activity and no fetal heart rate. I only see an empty sac."

I asked hesitatingly, "You mean there is no fetus?"

"I would call this a missed abortion. The fetus likely died two or more weeks ago, and your body is slowly absorbing it. There is an area that shows some fetal remnants."

I heard it all in slow motion, as I tried to digest what she was saying and what this meant for us. Eventually I would miscarry. Oddly, a sense of relief fell over me – perhaps this was for the best. I whispered to Alec, "This is okay."

The obstetrician wasn't convinced that we could blame it on the virus. Since miscarriage is so common, up to one in four pregnancies end this way, any number of things may have caused it. But Alec and I still believed that it had to be the virus. I had been so sick; that little life never had a chance.

Now the question was what to do next. The obstetrician told me to expect a bleed within three weeks. She worried about me hemorrhaging on *Madeline* away from medical help. She wanted to book me for surgery the next day. Without calling my father for advice, I knew that he would say, "Wait and see." A skilled gynecologist, I knew he believed in as little medical intervention as possible.

My circumstances were unusual, however, and I spent hours agonizing over the pros and cons of each option. Alec went along with my decision to let nature take its course. Friends were coming to Antigua in ten days, so I had ample time to change my mind.

We'd both been looking forward to sailing north to the nearby island of Barbuda, but in light of our circumstances, this was a little risky. There were numerous unmarked reefs around Barbuda, making it impossible to leave after dark in the case of an emergency. Still, I felt that 24 hours one way or the other wouldn't make a big difference in my situation.

The trade winds blew steadily on our beam for the gorgeous six-hour sail. Barbuda is a low-lying island, and it wasn't until we were within a few miles, that we could make out some landmarks. We took advantage of the wonderful crystal water, clear skies and the noonday sun to navigate our way in under sail. I realized as we sailed *Madeline* into the anchorage, tacking between coral heads, breaking reef and other yachts that, three years ago, I couldn't have done this. And now Alec and I were doing it smoothly, and with confidence.

With smiles beaming, we dropped anchor under sail. Immediately we dove into the baby blue water to check out the new neighborhood below. Above, our neighbors consisted of a handful of yachts sprinkled in front of a long stretch of white sand beach. We swam over to a boat we knew, and they promptly invited us for dinner that night.

After a few nights, we arranged for all the boats to meet for cocktails on the beach at sunset. We gathered driftwood and made a big fire. They treated Alec and me like mini-celebrities because we were practically circumnavigators.

After returning home from the bonfire, I experienced some cramping and started to bleed. Without any detailed explanations to our neighbors, we upped anchor at dawn the next morning and sailed back to Antigua. No one would have suspected anything. People change plans all the time. That was what was so wonderful about the freedom and independence we had. We were accountable only to ourselves.

It was a lovely sail, and although I was increasingly uncomfortable with cramps, I was in good spirits. Once again we tacked into our anchorage under sail, even with me doubling over every few minutes until each contraction passed.

I took some medication, but it was a trying evening. By midnight it was over.

Having been responsible for countless miscarriages in the Emergency Room, I was confident that this one was complete. The next day I dinghied ashore and telephoned the obstetrician with the update.

She said that I wouldn't need any medical care unless I developed more bleeding.

I felt a twinge of sadness but was thinking positively. Mother Nature had taken care of the baby and of me. I was pleased with my body, and hopeful for the next time. Inspired by the fact that I got pregnant so easily, I put this incident down to plain bad luck.

Rather than feeling down about it, Alec popped a bottle of champagne. "To our first pregnancy. Although not successful, a success in many ways!" Sometimes he was just so damned romantic! I felt incredibly close to him and so happy.

Everything was going to be all right.

Cruising between the British Virgin Islands, I thought back to our romantic honeymoon six years before, when we'd chartered a boat. I remembered the first day of the honeymoon, and that first gust of wind when I yelled, "I don't remember how to sail!" I'd come a long way since then.

Our second trip to the B.V.I. had been in 1992 when we chartered with Alec's parents. Looking down on the ocean from the airplane window, I had seen a sailboat sailing away from the islands at four o'clock in the afternoon. "Where could that boat be going?" I asked Alec. "It'll be dark soon."

"They're probably doing an overnight passage," Alec answered.

I was mesmerized by the thought. A tiny white speck of sailboat on that huge deep blue ocean. Imagine that!

I had yet to connect our dream to our impending reality.

A mere four years later, we were in the B.V.I. on our own boat, after having sailed around the world. The image of *Madeline* as that boat, that speck in the ocean, still filled me with awe.

As we sailed from the British Virgin Islands to the Turks and Caicos – our last big ocean passage – I found myself wishing the cruising didn't have to end.

Me, who got unexpectedly irritable and seasick, sometimes even at anchor, who got frightened by the least gust of wind or threat of rain, who was eaten by bedbugs all the way from Indonesia to Africa, who hated washing the sheets and towels in a bucket by hand, who dreamed about having running water, a telephone and a VCR, who was homesick for friends and family. Was this the same person?

Coming home, I would have the benefits of global communication, an exciting career, my loved ones nearby, unlimited fresh water and electricity, and all the latest gizmos. Unfortunately I'd also have to face alarm clocks, traffic, snowstorms, busy schedules, and superficial, shallow people without enough time.

The cruising life was often difficult, sometimes scary, and a few times really ugly for Alec and me. It was also absolutely lovely enjoying the beauty of the outdoor world, the peaceful solitude, the self-reliance and independence we achieved, and the endless hours shared together. I was just not as ready as I thought I'd be to give up what I'd gained cruising.

TO ARRIVE WHERE WE STARTED

We shall not cease from exploration
And the end of all our exploring
Will be to arrive where we started
And know the place for the first time.

T. S. Eliot
from "Little Gidding"
Four Quartets

OUR QUICK DOWNWIND PASSAGE to the Turks and Caicos was half over when Alec showed me the T.S. Eliot quote during lunch. "It sums up our trip, don't you think?"

"You mean, exploring with *Madeline*?" I asked.

"Yeah, and when we close the loop in the Turks and Caicos, it'll be the first time in three years of exploring on *Madeline* that we'll be entering a harbor we already know," Alec said. "But there are so many interpretations besides the literal."

I read the quote again and began to see the possibilities. Our exploring had changed what we knew. We'd see each place in a different light – with a new perspective and insight.

I'd explored, and I knew myself for the first time. I could see the character traits that had driven me to keep my sailing promise and that might make me yearn to do something similar again.

I'd pushed myself to the edge of my envelope, and I'd discovered my limits. I'd learned what was important to me and identified my own goals. In this painful process, I'd even stretched my envelope, and things that once seemed impossible were overcome. This was very satisfying.

I was confident now that if I achieved my goals – short-term and long-term – in the end I'd be happy.

Our trip satisfied many of my goals, obviously to the detriment of my economic goal. The single-mindedness of the trip was rewarding, but it took until halfway around the world before I realized I needed balance. Soon I'd be able to focus on multiple goals, but that too could be challenging. A key issue would be deciding how much time I would devote to each.

I felt I now had the tools and the insight to always be happy. My goals might change with time – I wouldn't cease from exploration – but I had laid the foundation.

288

I looked at the quote again. If a person lived in the mountains and then one day went to the ocean, he would see the mountains very differently when he returned. Perhaps he would appreciate the soaring peaks for the first time, or maybe he'd feel claustrophobic and trapped. Our physical journey stirred up mixed feelings.

Our pending return to North America and an urban lifestyle magnified what I'd be shortly leaving behind. We were tuned to nature's rhythms, subconsciously aware of the tide moving in and out, the phases of the moon, and the clouds sweeping across the sky.

Nature surrounded us in all shapes and sizes, from huge whales to the tiny shrimp we once sucked into our toilet. Everywhere I was astounded by the amount of wildlife. Even the most uninteresting stretch of land or water was full of animals and plants if we looked hard enough or were quiet enough.

The few times we anchored near civilization, either the wildlife had been killed or its environment polluted.

Our life in the city had been the opposite of the cruising lifestyle. We'd worked in an incandescent glow, shuttling between concrete boxes. We'd washed our clothes and taken long hot showers without the thought of where that sudsy water went, or where it came from. Garbage was tossed in the bin, forgotten immediately; out of sight and out of mind.

We had sailed to the pristine waters of the world and had swum with the manta rays. Could I go back to where I'd started?

Returning home would be more than just a physical relocation. It meant readapting to North American culture as well. Only now did I realize we'd been on a philosophical journey too.

We'd sailed to a village in Indonesia where the people lived in thatched palm huts they built themselves. Anchored in their harbor, *Madeline* must have appeared as a floating castle. A farmer invited us to his hut where we met his wife and three children. He explained he earned 100,000 Rupiah per year, about US$50, from the vegetables he sold. I presumed this paid for his sugar, tea, and tobacco, as most of his food he grew himself.

Then he asked us how much money we made in Canada! I tried to explain that it was different in Canada, because prices were different. He became confused when I told him we didn't use Rupiah, and I managed to change the topic.

Were his countrymen who had moved to the city any better off? In Southeast Asia work was available in the cities, the economy was booming and the cities were brimming full. The people still lived in huts – of corrugated iron amid an open sewer next to thousands of others – but they had money. They could buy what they thought they needed. They could smoke Marlboros. The eggplants cost 20¢ instead of 2¢ in the village.

Now, as we returned home, I could see that the Western world was an extension of this. The cities were cleaner, but even more crowded. People made more money, but then there were even more things that they needed. Most people no longer smoked, but had health club memberships, squash racquets, sailboats, the right shoes for each sport and a house to store all their toys, because after all, they were very busy making money and didn't get out as much as they would like. The eggplants cost $2, but they were fresh, available year round and the perfect shape. But if you are making babaganough, the shape doesn't really matter, does it?

Had my philosophy changed too much?

As we sailed towards the pass in the reef in the still dark hours of the morning, we were both so excited that neither of us could sleep. We were chatting away about the trip, about our arrival, about lots of things. Suddenly, I just blurted out, "Congratulations to us. We did it. We sailed around the world!"

Alec, being the ever-prudent, not-wanting-to-count-your-chickens-before-they're-hatched kind of captain, said, "We're not there yet, Alayne. We still have fourteen miles to go to the Turks and Caicos."

But finally, I had a sense of complete relief. With this steady wind, with our autopilot steering and our sails perfectly set, there was very little that could stop us now from completing our goal.

"We still have a lot of reef to negotiate," Alec teased me, "and it could be tricky."

Surprising even myself, I responded, "I don't care if we smash right into it. It's the same reef we left from, and we can still say we completed the loop!"

Victoriously we sailed through the pass, Sellar's Cut. We safely anchored *Madeline* in the same place – completing our circumnavigation in 1125 days! As I put the champagne on ice, we couldn't stop smiling.

That speck in the ocean had circled the globe.

She was a great boat. We had blithely trusted our lives to her and *Madeline* had done it! The little boat anchored in Turtle Cove wasn't the same as the one that left. If it weren't for the colorful flags flying from her mast – flags of each country she had visited – nobody would have noticed her.

She was encrusted with the salt of the last passage, a rough four-day trip from the British Virgin Islands. Reddish dirt from the Red Sea

haboob was still ingrained in her rigging. The fiery gaze of the tropical sun had turned her decks a dull chalky white. Her beautiful paint job had gleamed in New Zealand, but was now scratched from dugout canoes and rough stone quays.

Inside, her skin sagged like an old lady's. Her vinyl headliner was drooping down in places where there were minute leaks. Leaks that only opened under the weight of green ocean water arcing over her bows and pummeling her decks. She arthritically creaked and moaned as her hulls flexed and absorbed the motion of the ocean around her and the crew moving about her. The wild sea hadn't been kind, but neither had the windless miles. Her exhausted engine was on the verge of death, but she still had her weathered sails to get us through the Bahamas.

Once back in Florida, we planned to clean her inside and out. We would fix the cosmetic damage, her travel scars, and overhaul her engine. She would look and run like new, like she had never left Florida.

We would clean ourselves up as well. We would cut our hair. We would discard our worn, faded clothes for new bright and stylish wear. Slowly our tans would fade, and we would look like everyone else. On the surface, you wouldn't know what we had been through except, perhaps, for the wrinkles around our eyes. Our exterior was adaptable, but our trip had also affected a part of us deep inside.

Our relationship had changed forever. We saw the place for the first time – together.

Alec had said at the start that the trip would be one of "high highs and low lows". This had certainly held true.

At the times when we found ourselves in the middle of nowhere and fiercely bickering with each other, there was no escape and no one else to turn to. We'd been forced to work things out.

Alec learned not to hold grudges, to change a situation with a smile or an apology and to accept my strengths and my weaknesses. He was trying to be less reticent and a better sounding board, just as I was still trying to change a few things for him. I was still reactive sometimes, but had learned to express myself clearly, to keep things in perspective and to have more confidence in myself.

Reality was that the trip had a beginning and now it was the end. I worried more for Alec than for myself. Our trip reinforced his love of adventure. He thrived on the tremendous uncertainty, the critical planning and the day-to-day buzz of exploration and discovery. Where I felt satiated by my experience, Alec felt his appetite merely whetted. But Alec and I had proven to ourselves that we could do anything we set our minds to and work through our problems together.

We were fortunate to have been born and raised in Canada. The money we made there had allowed us to travel to those few places where it still had no use. Our return wouldn't mean we'd have to get caught up in consumerism and materialism. We agreed that money was just a tool. It gave us the freedom to dream again, to set new goals and to live an adventurous life together.

Our life on *Madeline* was warped. We'd lived in each other's pocket, then skin, then heart. We could tell what the other was feeling and complete each other's sentences.

The trip wasn't easy. The most difficult part, the aspect neither of us was prepared for, was working out our relationship.

In the end, we'd become closer and even more in love.

Maybe this was our most important achievement.

EPILOGUE

FROM THE BEGINNING, I looked forward to writing this epilogue. Whenever I read other people's books, I always wanted to know what happened to them afterward. But I never imagined this would be the most difficult section to write.

There are so many things I could talk about. We visited Nathalie and Robert in Amsterdam. We became parents to a healthy baby boy. *Madeline* was sold. I am pregnant again.

When we arrived in Florida, we joined the culture. We ate fast food. We put ice cubes in our drinks. We took long hot showers. We bought a big old station wagon. But this place, which should have been so familiar to us, seemed foreign. We thought we craved TV, but after a short blitz we soon found it loud, intrusive and monotonous. We thought we craved air-conditioning, but we froze in the shops and buildings. We were initially excited at the freedom and fun of buzzing around in a car, going here and going there, but quickly became depressed by the plethora of concrete freeways and all the air pollution we were contributing to.

Several months after our return to Canada, I felt it was time to pack up and drive back down to *Madeline* to go cruising again. I still get this urge, which surprises me, because I had looked forward to coming home and living on land.

After working for a year in busy Toronto, we moved to a small house on a large lake in southern Ontario near my family. Leaving nature was too difficult after all. Watching the watery horizon reduces our land sickness. The brilliant sunrises, the migrating birds and the changing seasons have reconnected us.

We have dealt with the short-term adjustments, but the philosophical issues still trouble us. We've had difficulty fitting back into the lives we came from. Alec quit his job in Toronto, preferring to steer his own ship for a while. Everyone is working so hard, including us, and none of us have any time.

Nathalie and Robert remain our close and dear friends and we have regular reunions. Nathalie has her own successful business now, and they dream of their next cruising boat.

Writing this book has been an emotional challenge – the Tasman still stirs up a lot of feeling in both of us. We dream of cruising again, but I can't promise I'll sail those waters again.

Day-to-day I am happy, finally working towards goals I'd put aside, like practicing medicine. It's been incredibly satisfying and fulfilling giving birth, nursing and caring for our young son. Life is fun and diverse: we sail a Hobie cat, Alec windsurfs, I see my friends and family, and we've undertaken this book together.

But now I understand the difference between life here and the life we had cruising. We were really *living* on *Madeline*. We were *tasting* the food, *breathing* the air, and really *listening* to each other. We watched the sun rise and set each day and lived in harmony with the natural world. There was a certain mortal simplicity that made everything feel more real. We were on a low budget, but our lives were rich – with time and thoughts.

We want more of what we had on *Madeline* – freedom, independence, self-sufficiency, living with nature and lots of time. I'll keep you posted.

Alayne Main
December 5th, 1998